HORIZONTAL HOLD

HORIZONTAL HOLD

The Making and Breaking
of a Network Television Pilot

Daniel Paisner

A Birch Lane Press Book
Published by Carol Publishing Group

A Birch Lane Press Book
Published by Carol Publishing Group
Birch Lane Press is a registered trademark of Carol Communications, Inc.
Editorial Offices: 600 Madison Avenue, New York, N.Y. 10022
Sales & Distribution Offices: 120 Enterprise Avenue, Secaucus, N.J. 07094
In Canada: Canadian Manda Group, P.O. Box 920 Station U, Toronto, Ontario M8Z 5P9
Queries regarding rights and permissions should be addressed to Carol Publishing Group, 600 Madison Avenue, New York, N.Y. 10022

Carol Publishing Group books are available at special discounts for bulk purchases, for sales promotions, fund-raising, or educational purposes. Special editions can be created to specifications. For details contact: Special Sales Department, Carol Publishing Group, 120 Enterprise Avenue, Secaucus, N.J. 07094

Manufactured in the United States of America
10   9   8   7   6   5   4   3   2   1

Library of Congress Cataloging-in-Publication Data

Paisner, Daniel.
    Horizontal hold : the making and breaking of a network television pilot / by Daniel Paisner.
      p.   cm.
    "A Birch Lane Press book."
    ISBN 1–55972–148–0 (cloth)
    1. Television pilot programs.   2. Television broadcasting—United
States. I. Title.
PN1992.8.P54P33   1992
791.45—dc20   92–24143
                                          CIP

This book is for my parents, who restricted their children to one half hour of television each day, and then agreed not to count news, sports, and really, really special programs we really, really, wanted to watch in the tally.

CONTENTS

"All I want out of life is a 30 share and a 20 rating."

—Faye Dunaway, in the
Paddy Chayevsky movie
Network

"There is only so much you can buff a turd."

—Tom Fontana,
co-writer/co-executive
producer of the CBS
television pilot *Word
of Mouth,* formerly
known as *The War Room,*
formerly known as *E.O.B.*

ACKNOWLEDGMENTS ___

▢   I benefited from a great many good turns in the writing of this book and these, in turn and at the least, deserve this other. First, I am grateful to Gail Kinn and Steven Schragis of Carol Publishing for believing in this project, and for holding their breath (and their tongues) until its completion, and to Dan Levy for spotting the first signs of life in a years-ago notion that seemed a little too vague for almost everyone else. Also, I am grateful to Dan Strone, Robert Gottlieb, and Owen Laster of the William Morris Agency for working to keep me solvent during the researching and writing of this book, and to Bob Stein, my attorney, and Dona Chernoff, my sounding board, for keeping me out of trouble.

In New York, I was helped tremendously by Bonnie Mark, Julie Grossberg, Julie Martin, Kevin Richards, Hillary Danner, and Jim Finnerty in the Paltrow Group offices; Ed Devlin at CBS; Patrick Pleven at the Mayor's Office of Film and Television; Deborah Curtan and Arthur Silver at Columbia; and John Whitesell, Joanne Sedwick, Chuck Raymond, John Feld, Tom John, Bill Barol, Victor Paganuzzi, Ron Kelson, Jane Trapnell, Rich Reinhart, and Carl Woitach, on and around the set. Karen Chasin-Kavanagh helped to transcribe some of the hundred or so hours of interviews conducted for this book. My brother, Jonathan Paisner, read the manuscript with care and insight. Also, and significantly, the *E.O.B./War Room* cast members—Mary

Beth Hurt, Rich Hall, Geoffrey Nauffts, John Dye, Jennifer Van Dyck, and William Duff Griffin—were very gracious with their time and convictions, both during production and afterward.

In Los Angeles, invaluable assists came from Terry Hughes, Abby Singer, R. J. Visciglia, Barbara Brace, Ivan Fonseca, Tom Carpenter, and Kent Zbornak, and from most of the transplanted New Yorkers (or repatriated Los Angelenos) mentioned above. Associate director Lex Passaris and production associate Robert Spina were particularly helpful, candid, and otherwise generous. And, like their doppelganged counterparts from New York, the *Word of Mouth* cast members—Joshua Rifkind, Lewis Black, Haviland Morris, Michele Lamar Richards, Lee Tergeson, George Newbern, Gladys Knight, and William Daniels—were extremely patient and open.

Thanks to all.

Also in Los Angeles, I am at least temorarily indebted to my friends Jon and Erin Fain, Jeff and Lisa Stern, and Maureen Reagan and Dennis Revell for their unfailing hospitality and (mostly) unfailing home cooking. They offered a home away from home in my weeks of displacement without exhausting my already-tired advance for this book.

At home, I am grateful to my wife Leslie for a whole bunch of things, but specifically for not delivering our second child, Hana, until I was able to complete my fact-finding tour to the opposite coast; and to my oldest, Jacob, for looking after his mommy in my absence, and for giving me one of the sweetest, tightest, squeeziest, most extraspecialest hugs evereverever in the whold wide world upon my return.

Mostly, though, I am grateful to Bruce Paltrow, Tom Fantana, and John Tinker for opening their doors and letting me see what I could see. Their energy, creativity, and insight are everywhere in these pages. Hopefully, by the time this effort reaches bookstores, they will also be everywhere on our small screens, again.

—Daniel Paisner
June 1992

INTRO _____

◯ Strange beast, television.

As an industry, it has a greater impact on the way we live and work and think than almost any other. As a billboard, it can influence our ideals and our ideas in a way that is utterly and haltingly its own. As a medium, it informs, encroaches, entertains, denigrates, and obfuscates on the very grandest of scales. And, as an appliance, it is more like a microwave oven than any of us would care to imagine; it informs us from within, invades us, its left-behind messages seeping through our skin and out into the rest of the world as if they were always there and will always be; stand too close and you might get zapped.

There is nothing like television, in art or commerce. It is part mirror, part window, and part monitor. It has the power to move or to stifle, to transport or to root, to chill or make warm. It can do whatever it wants, and some things it could not possibly intend. It has fueled and funneled a half century of thinking on politics, family, economics, religion, community, race, justice, sexuality, and almost every other subject that has traveled its airwaves or cable lines. It has supplanted our dinner-table conversations. It tells us when to laugh and when to cry, what to believe and what not to believe, how to behave, and what clothes to wear. And we listen. It has underlined our world in such a way that the spectator at a newsworthy event—a baseball game, a protest march, a hurricane—must race home to relive that event on the small screen, to make it more real, or at least to make it seem more real. It has made our lives more valid at the same time that it has invalidated our lives.

Television is America's common denominator. Its hued cathode embers light our poorest homes and our richest and almost every home in between. According to one survey, there is at least one television set in over 97 percent of American households. According to another, there is more than one functioning television set for every two functioning Americans. Still another reveals, alarmingly, that the typical high school graduate of the 1990s will have spent nearly twice as much time in front of the television set as he will have spent in the classroom. And yet, despite its invasive reach, television is, also and primarily, the emptiest of vessels. Unplugged, it is nothing. Even plugged it is nothing but what programming executives, network and otherwise, put into it. And what they put into it, lately, is this: derivative cop shows, medical dramas, domestic situation comedies, workplace situation comedies, miniseries, soap operas, mysteries, multigenerational family sagas, courtroom dramas, home-shopping sprees, music videos, game shows, documentaries, talk shows, "reality" shows, concerts, stand-up comedy, news, sports, commercials... First run, then rerun, and then rerun again. Even burning yule logs have been known to register a blip in the overnight ratings. Blips are good things, and the more blips the better. Of course, network programming executives seek more than mere ratings blips and so go to great and expensive lengths to develop prime-time programming for the remote-controlled masses. Sometimes they succeed. Most times they do not.

Not too far along these great lengths there lies a peculiar little industry by-product known as television pilots, prototype versions of planned weekly shows (or weakly planned shows). They surface each spring, in large homogeneous groups, in the strangely resilient dance that invites independent producers and somewhat less independent production companies to audition for a slot on a network's prime-time schedule. They are the best and worst indicators of where television has been and where it is going.

Pilot season is the mating season of network television. It is when network executives, groping for a hit, respond almost lasciviously to any number of high-concept (and familiar) scents, inviting producers on what can politely be referred to as little more than a blind date. Sometimes there's a good match, sometimes not.

"A pilot is like the NFL draft," Brandon Tartikoff once told the *New York Times*, back when he used to build the prime-time schedule for NBC. "You can draft a player for what they are or for what they'll become. Sometimes you're wrong."

Hit shows are not born, fully formed, into our living rooms. There is a period of conception and gestation and another of struggling infancy before a series gets enough of its legs for a long run. And for every hit show there are a hundred misses....

Once, in a pilot, someone had the idea to cast Alan Alda as a young dad who steps onto his porch to find an invisible alien baby in place of his newspaper (*Where's Everett?*, CBS, 1966).

Once, in a pilot, someone had the idea to cast Joe Penney as a half-American/half-Asian San Francisco district attorney who moonlights as a Samurai warrior to catch bad guys (*Samurai*, ABC, 1979).

Once, in a pilot, someone had the idea to cast Mickey Rooney as an aged superhero who is coaxed out of retirement when his lifelong nemesis (the Yellow Tornado) is released from prison (*Return of the Original Yellow Tornado*, NBC, 1967).

Of course, some of television's best-loved and most enduring shows were also built on dubious foundations. A talking horse? Seven stranded castaways? A modern Stone Age family? Identical cousins? Their familiar singsong themes have long obscured their once (and still) silly conceits from easy view. And to what fortuitous lapses of reason do we owe shows like *The Beverly Hillbillies, My Favorite Martian,* or *The Six Million Dollar Man*? It stretches the synapses to imagine the sequence of events, the lemminglike groupthink, that resulted in a show like *My Mother the Car*—from inception ("Hey, what if a guy's dead mother spoke to him through his car? What about *that*?"), through development ("I think the car should be a 1928 Porter, because it just seems so much more...what's the right word?... *maternal* than a Mustang, don't you think?"), and on into postproduction. ("I'm sorry, but we'd all like it if the car could seem a little more vulnerable, a little warmer. We're not gonna hit the mainstream big unless we make that thing believable, maybe get someone like, oh, Ann Sothern to do the voice. Who handles her?") How many well-paid suits had to sign off on each aspect of production before this Jerry Van Dyke vehicle (forgive, please, the easy pun) made it onto the air?

Television pilots, at best, are only reasonable indicators of how well a creative and production team can deliver on a sound (or not so sound) idea. Shows can fall apart or improve or become unrecognizable after their initial episodes. At worst, pilots are trumped-up résumés, drawing on the talents of hired guns who help to dress sometimes sorry material in fancy clothing in the hopes of landing a network-series deal. Often the people who work behind the scenes on a pilot are committed to other, ongoing projects, so judging a show's potential on the basis of a pilot episode can be a dangerous thing. The networks know this; advertisers know this; industry watchers know this. And—get this!—the producers know that they know.

Still, things go on as before, as ever. In recent years, the four networks (ABC, CBS, NBC, and the upstart Fox Broadcasting Company) have commissioned among them approximately 120 prototype episodes each pilot season. In a typical year, by conservative estimate, the networks spend around two hundred million dollars on pilots. Two hundred million dollars! On programming that, for the most part, will never make it to air! And this figure does not even account for the tens of millions spent on scripts that never go before the cameras or the tens of millions more that make up the fat salaries of development executives. The major television studios also have their own hefty payrolls to meet and to justify. Every pitch meeting, and television is littered with them, takes place at a man-hour cost of several thousand dollars, not to mention the often considerable costs of travel and entertainment.

Even in Hollywood—the land of unreasonable excess in all things—it is rare to find so much being spent on so little. Lately, though, the winds of austerity have begun to flap through the sunroofs of the vanity-plated cars of Southern California. Indeed, top-shelf writer-producers such as Steven Bochco, James L. Brooks, Diane English, and Linda Bloodworth-Thomason have secured long-term development deals that signal an end to at least one aspect of the series audition process; the new climate in this rarefied air suggests that the industry's most prominent suppliers can, or will soon be able to, get their shows on the air without a pilot episode. Also of late, series ideas are being test-driven with an eye on the bottom line. "Presentation tapes" of potential series (which might include two or three short scenes, shot on an existing set) have emerged as a cost-effective way to demonstrate a show's viability, without the attendant start-up costs of a new set, a full script, and a complete cast. And CBS has found that it sometimes makes more sense to give a show a six-episode summer tryout than to commission a one-shot pilot at about half the cost. With six episodes, at least there is the chance that an on-the-fence series might spark with the audience and fall the right way.

Even so, television pilots remain a big part of a big business. They are an aspect of an industry and a town not known to embrace change with a wet one on the mouth. There may be fewer pilots produced in the years to come (as, indeed, there were in the season just past), particularly at the top and entry levels, but pilots will likely remain the dominant method of developing new series, at least for the next while. There is a reason for this. Pilots may cost a lot of money, but they promise even more. A single series, if it survives past its fourth full season (which means completed production of at least eighty-eight episodes, generally seen as the minimum number for long-term success in television's lucrative syndication market), can generate hundreds of millions of dollars for its creators and producers and hundreds of millions more for its sponsoring network. For every hundred failed pilots like *Return of the Original Yellow Tornado*, there are ten like *Bridget Loves Bernie* (CBS, 1972–73); shows that earn a shot on the prime-time schedule and disappear within their first year; and, for every ten new shows, there is likely just one that will survive to become a long-running, money-printing hit. The odds are long, but the payoff is rich enough to make the near-certain failure a good gamble.

Life, and death, for a network television pilot can occur in the space of several months. A great deal is squeezed into a small while. As often as not, the process plays out in this way: A writer pitches a show idea in the fall to a production company and then retreats to turn the notion into a treatment, a broad-strokes outline of the show's premise, characters, and plot possibilities. The treatment is then pitched to a network development executive. If the network likes what it sees on paper, it offers a script commitment by early winter. Story ideas for the pilot episode and a wish list of casting possibilities will be discussed by a many-headed team of producers, network executives, and writers. A finished script will be delivered to the network by winter's end.

Next, the network will commission a pilot episode, in early March perhaps, and commit approximately one million dollars to the production of that pilot, out of which the producers will build a set and hire a studio, a director, actors, and, through their license fee, themselves. Within weeks, there will be a hundred or so creative, technical, and support people in place for a first production meeting and rehearsal, their futures suddenly joined by what was once a simple notion in the mind of one writer. The episode will go before the cameras about a week later. Postproduction will take anywhere from one to several weeks before the completed pilot is delivered, usually by hand, to network programmers.

A hundred sets of fingers will be crossed.

This is the way things happen for most would-be shows. Sometimes, though, things happen like this....

HORIZONTAL HOLD

One

IDEA _____

○   No one wants credit for this one.

The idea, simply, is this: presidential speechwriters. That is all there is to this series, at first. The rest follows naturally, and soon after. The setting, of course, is Washington, D.C. Specifically, the setting is the old Executive Office Building (or E.O.B.), which sits on the White House grounds at 1600 Pennsylvania Avenue. More specifically, it is the office of the speechwriters for the president of the United States.

The premise, also simply: A young, green Middle American kid— a novelist, perhaps—is tapped by the president to join his group of passionate, articulate, harried, hurried, and somewhat jaded speech-writers, reporting to a presidentially appointed and stuffed-shirted politocrat and working out of a run-down office managed by a lifetime civil servant with a barbed tongue and a ground-floor view of government doings. It will be a smart, occasionally political, adult situation comedy, written for people who read newspapers. It will be on the air forever: *The Dick Van Dyke Show Goes to Washington,* sort of.

John Tinker, the thirty-one-year-old child of television (and, not coincidentally, of television producer and executive Grant Tinker), is the one to whom credit for this series idea is most often given; he accepts it, reluctantly; he allows, also reluctantly, that if the idea for this still-unnamed show came to him at all it did so on its own, without any help from him. It happens that way sometimes.

1

"I honest to God don't remember who had the idea first," he says in talking about his latest germ for a situation comedy; it is fall 1989, and he is thinking ahead to the 1990–91 network television season. This is something he does a lot of these days. "I really don't remember," he continues, "but it might have been me. It doesn't matter. All of us, we're always thinking of venues where we can set a show. At least I'm always thinking that way, all the time, and I'm always thinking about places that are understaffed, where people are overworked and underpaid. I'm always looking for a place to put a show."

One of the reasons Tinker is credited with the initial spark for this speechwriters idea is because he has a friend, Ed McNally, who works as a speechwriter for President George Bush. This coincidental friendship, Tinker guesses, was probably his inspiration, conscious or otherwise. After the idea had been shuttled between New York and Washington and after polling some of his speechwriter-colleagues, McNally wrote a memo to his television-producer friend suggesting possible titles for this possible show: *Typewriter One* (as in Air Force One, or Marine One), *Writers Block* (as in the block of rooms along the speechwriters' hallway in the E.O.B.), *West Exec* (as in West Executive Avenue, the street on the White House grounds that separates the E.O.B. from the west wing), *Gone to Cards* (as in, the speech has been put on cue cards, or "gone to cards"), and *Public Affairs* (as in, the Office of Public Affairs, a branch of the White House Office of Communications). One of Tinker's favorite titles is *No Known Ranking,* which McNally reports is how the current crop of speechwriters was recently described in a *Washington Post* article.

In network television, an idea for a series is only as good as its title. If you do not know what to call it, you do not know what you have. John Tinker still does not know what he has, but he is working on it. The idea, fleshed, suggests rich and endless fodder for intelligent, provocative situation comedy, peopled by likable, opinionated, and ethical characters. Even reduced to its high concept—presidential speechwriters—there is enough to get Tinker and his partners going.

Tinker is joined in his efforts and his enthusiasm by Tom Fontana, a thirty-eight-year-old would-rather-be playwright, and Bruce Paltrow, forty-six, a veteran television producer, writer, and director. Together, these three men represent one-half of the creative team behind NBC's long-running hospital drama *St. Elsewhere,* one of the most critically acclaimed programs in television history. They are themselves smart adults who read newspapers. As the Paltrow Group, based in their raw, no-frills New York offices overlooking the Hudson River, they are trying to make television shows that they themselves might want to watch. And—harder, still—they are trying to make them in New York.

"We're not always going to do *St. Elsewhere*," Tinker explains. "This show will be a little different. Its hard to say the White House is a second-rate institution with first-rate people. It's not like *WKRP in Cincinnati*, which was about a second-rate radio station with first-rate people. It's not Korea. It's not a tiny little news station in Minneapolis or a crappy little jail."

"It's a great setting," says Fontana, who instantly warmed to the speechwriters idea. "You can do the presidency and national and international issues. The reason a show like *M*A*S*H* was so funny was because what they were doing was important and it was serious. You don't find that in most comedy shows. When people can be funny in a bad situation, or in a serious situation, that's wonderful. That's funny. When people are funny and they work in a pizza parlor, I think, well, who the fuck cares? Then it's just jokes about dough and stuff."

For Paltrow, the presidential premise promises great and lasting things. "You look at the great television shows," he says, "the classic shows, and all of them are about a group of people, good people, a few of them or a lot of them, who band together to do the best they can in an honorable way, to do well against overwhelming odds. *The Honeymooners, Taxi*, the doctors at the shitty hospital in Boston. The shitty Hill Street station. They're all about people who have less and want more. This seems a natural."

This, for now, will be called *E.O.B.*, named for the Executive Office Building that will provide its setting. (The title, incidentally, is at the top of McNally's short list; it is also at the top of everyone else's.) It will also be one of the half-dozen or so series ideas the Paltrow Group will seek to put on the air during the next television season. This season's development strategy seems to be to try everything and hope for one thing. Last season's seemed to be to try for one thing and put everything into it. The Paltrow Group's sole entry in last season's prime-time sweepstakes, the hour-long comedy/drama *Tattinger's*, debuted on NBC with considerable fanfare but fizzled after only a few episodes. The company, backed by MTM Studios, lost a good deal of money on the project. Expecting a long run, they converted warehouse space on New York's Pier 62 into a full-fledged film production studio. They also lost a great deal of momentum, following hard on their *St. Elsewhere* success. And, most significantly, they lost MTM in the fallout. The relationship between the two companies soured and severed, leaving the Paltrow Group without studio backing, at least for the moment.

On of the lessons learned seems to be that if you keep as many balls in the air at one time as you possibly can, you might be able to keep at least one of them from hitting the floor. And so, this time out, the balls in the air include:

High, an hour-long high school drama set in the fictional New Jersey town of Hackneyville, a New York City suburb. The high school of the title, according to the show's working legend, was once named to honor the explorer Henry Hudson and later renamed to honor the late founder of McDonald's, Ray Kroc. No one knows why. The school newspaper is called the *Pluvianus,* named for the plover-like bird (*Pluvianus aegypticus*) that is fond of sitting on the backs of crocodiles. The pilot script, as it is being written, features a hip, young ensemble cast, given to hip, young arcana and adolescent extremes.

Modern Marriage, a half-hour domestic sitcom that seems to borrow from *Family Ties, Married...With Children,* and *Father Knows Best,* in strangely equal measure. Dad, Mom, and the two teenage kids are loosely based on Bruce Paltrow and his own family. So says nearly everyone in the Paltrow Group offices, except Bruce Paltrow. Dad wears a ponytail; Mom recycles; Junior wants to race at the Indy 500; Sis wants to sleep with her boyfriend under her parents' roof; they are all in therapy.

A period drama, *1761,* set, neatly, in 1761. A kind of play on manners, it is about an American boy sent to live with relatives in London, where he is expected to learn to become a gentleman. Prospects for this show appear hobbled by the unavoidably steep production costs for a period piece such as this, although interest in the chance to explore the mores and manners of eighteenth-century England continues to run high.

Black Tie Affair, a half-hour comedy about a Trump-like tycoon, and his wife, and his lover, and his wife's lover, and his wife's lover's lover.

An untitled hour-long international espionage drama about two brothers who find themselves, and their families, in a tangle of global intrigue and deception. The idea, in-house, is known alternatingly as *The European Show* and *The Expensive Show,* this last probably foretelling why it may never get made.

And, in its nascent stages, *New Year,* an hour-long serial set sometime in the near future, in New York, in and around the high-stakes pharmaceutical-industry. No one can remember the last time they watched a really good pharmaceutical industry drama. The lead character, Danny Hartman, a fifty-something CEO and board chairman, keeps a charred Fender Stratocaster guitar in a glass coffee table in his power office; he's got a kid named Jimi; he works out his frustrations at the virtual-reality-based A-Mazing Center Playing Area, an intra-active video-game center. He has something to hide, and to run from.

Paltrow, Tinker, and Fontana are really, really, excited about all of these shows—their babies. This is a good thing, but it is also to be expected. Series television producers become really, really, excited when these things happen, in confluence: An idea emerges that is simple, viable, and malleable (it helps if it is also new, or at least improved); characters spring, fully realized, from the imagined setting, as if they actually exist; story lines and plot twists unravel without effort; real-world events begin to mirror, shadow, or foretell their pretend ones; the entire enterprise generates a rhythm and energy all its own; casting possibilities, scheduling possibilities, and possible Emmy acceptance speeches begin to infect nearly every waking moment. When only one or two of these things happen, television producers are just plain excited. And when there is nothing to get excited about, they keep looking, or they move on to the next thing.

The idea behind *E.O.B.* has been lent serendipitous steam by a soon-to-be-published, sure-to-be-best-selling book called *What I Saw at the Revolution: A Political Life in the Reagan Era,* by former presidential speechwriter Peggy Noonan. Noonan wrote President Ronald Reagan's famous speech delivered on the night of the Challenger space-shuttle disaster. She also wrote the "kinder and gentler nation" and "thousand points of light" speeches for then-presidential-candidate George Bush. She also wrote this book, an affectionately acerbic account of a speechwriter's lot in the age of spin control. The book was excerpted in a *New York Times Magazine* cover story on October 15 and has since generated a good deal of media heat, from Washington to Hollywood.

No one at the Paltrow Group has read Noonan's book (or no one admits to it), and none plan to, at least not until after they shoot the *E.O.B.* pilot. It is far from certain they will ever get to shoot the *E.O.B.* pilot, but these are their plans. Still, they are all aware of the book and its author. These subjects are unavoidable. They come up every time someone hears the idea for the show.

Ah, the someones will say. Speechwriters? You mean like Peggy Noonan?

Well...um...er...yes. And no.

Oh.

To the Paltrow Group, Peggy Noonan and her book must appear as assets and liabilities, both. They are assets because, as a kind of cognoscente flavor of the month, they will help to push the hot buttons of the television community; they are liabilities because they leave the project smelling familiar, derivative, tired. Also, they present the very real possibility that *E.O.B.* will be beaten to the small screen by a made-for-television movie based on the book; worst of all is the unspoken fear that once Noonan and her speechwriter-colleagues are out there, and talked about, this natural, simple idea for a sitcom might occur to someone else. The possibility of this last is almost too horrifying to consider.

For now, though, *E.O.B.* is a high concept worth pursuing. Aggressively. And so, in pursuit, Paltrow, Tinker, and Fontana spend a generous amount of time thinking about politics, consulting texts on the various branches of government, scanning the newspapers for salient, speechworthy topics, visiting Washington and studying its ways and means, and creating the characters on whose shoulders their premise will live or die.

This green kid, from the Midwest, the one who may or may not be a novelist, he should be naive and idealistic, someone suggests. But it's not his show. It's not *Mary Tyler Moore.* It's not about him, it's about this place. It's an ensemble show. It's about what these people do, and who they are, and how they are together.

This civil servant, the office secretary, she should be a kind of fulcrum, a locus, Yeah, she knows everything that's going on in the whole town. Everyone can interact around her. And this chief of communications, the appointee, he should be the authority figure, the voice of unreason. And what about the president? Should he be introduced as a character? Or should he just be heard, through the speeches? Yes, yes, that's it. Keep him off-camera. Just the voice. Maybe make him a Bush soundalike? or a Reagan soundalike? or, better, just presidential-seeming? Yeah, great. And the other speech-writers, what about them?

They're making it up as they go along.

Two

BACK-STORIES, REAL

○   Bruce Paltrow, co-executive producer of *E.O.B.*, loves making television shows. It is what he does. He has made some very good ones and some not so good ones. He has made some that have never been seen, and developed others that have never been made. Right now, he is trying to make some good ones in New York, three thousand miles away from his industry's core. He likes his chances, even if the edge is against him.

"It's a little harder here," he admits one afternoon in his Pier 62 production office. He is wearing blue jeans, a turtleneck shirt, and a ponytail. He looks like New York trying to do business with California. "We're a parts manufacturer, away from the GM plants. Everything's just a little off. We miss out on a lot of the fallout, a lot of accidental stuff that you could take care of out there, socially, easily. Gaps get created where there shouldn't be gaps, or there are communications problems. It's just a little harder."

There is some David Brenner to Bruce Paltrow, in voice and manner. He even looks like the Philadelphia comedian, in the face, a little bit, particularly when he smiles. He does this often. Also, he likes to move around a lot when he talks. He fidgets, pantomimes, paces. He sound-effects his speech with relevant exclamations:

8

"Boom!" "Bravo!" "Bam!" "Bang!" He appears, on first and subsequent meetings, to be a bundle of various energies. He does not sit still. His sneakered feet are at first kicked casually onto a coffee table, then folded under him, then flitting about the room. There is so much going on—in his office, in his life—he has to keep moving to keep up with it.

There is a lot going on in Paltrow's head, too. He talks fast, but not fast enough. He solves problems before they have a chance to arise. He answers his own questions before they occur to him. Jokes alight on his face before he can tell them; sometimes he doesn't seem to bother; it is enough that he thought of them. Sometimes, when he is racing to keep up with his thoughts, he appears to be willing the right words directly from his brain and out into the room. Come on, come on, come on. He seems to want to think of something and then have it be known.

Paltrow has been working in television for nearly twenty-five years. He has been successful for about the last seventeen. Somewhere in there he was even ridiculously successful, as he hopes to be again. It was not easy for Paltrow, getting started. He sort of backwarded himself into the business. He studied fine arts in school, but it slowly dawned on him he did not have the talent to be a fine artist, so he hit on the idea of becoming an art director. For television. He had always been fascinated by the entertainment industry. He watched a lot of television as a kid, growing up in Great Neck, New York, on the north shore of Long Island. He had a good eye. He figured he could get a job as a set decorator, or a scenic designer, without too much trouble. He figured wrong. He had no contacts, no prospects. Not only could he not get a job; he could not get into the guilds. He could not even get anyone to talk to him.

Finally, in January 1966, he landed an entry-level gofer position at Screen Gems, in New York. Screen Gems was then the television branch of Columbia Pictures. "I was a lackey," he recalls, "a carrier. I took home like sixty-five dollars a week. I was just kind of around, trying to learn the business, trying to get some direction. I wasn't very happy. It was a job, but I wasn't very happy."

At the time, Screen Gems was cranking out small-screen fare like *Love on a Rooftop, Bewitched, Gidget,* and *The Monkees.* For the most part, Screen Gems was not about quality television as much as it was about quantity television. Most of the company's shows were produced in Los Angeles, but the scripts and the rough cuts of each episode regularly flowed through its New York offices. Paltrow, bored and hungry for an inside track, developed sticky fingers. He started to read every script and interoffice memo he could get his hands on. He watched everything. He found ways to attend meetings or to listen in. The assorted eavesdroppings told him something about how the business worked and how it did not. From the left-about phone messages, he tried to learn who was calling the office and what they were calling about. He monitored the evolution of each script as it passed from draft to rehearsal to shooting form. He was trying to soak up as much as he could, to gain whatever advantage he could, as quickly as he could.

"As I started to read these scripts, I realized how awful they were," he says. "They were really and truly terrible. I mean, why would anybody write this stuff? It was just terrible. And I thought, I could do that. That's exactly what I said. I could write these terrible scripts. And it was true. Anybody could do this."

To do this, Paltrow actually sat down with a ruler and measured the margins on each script. He learned to center the dialogue on the page. He learned to put the stage directions in parentheses and the character names in capital letters. He literally copied the format. That was all he needed to know. The actual scripts were so bad, he thought all he had to do was get his efforts to look professional and he would be in business. Once he got the grid down, he felt sure the rest would come. And then he sat down and started writing.

He made a conscious (although not entirely practical) decision not to write for up-and-running Screen Gems shows; instead, he started with blank pages. He had lots of ideas for series and for movies, and he wanted to put them down on paper as fast as he thought of them. Let these other hacks write for *Gidget,* he figured I've got my own stuff to do. And that's what he did. Trouble was, Paltrow could not get anyone at Screen Gems to consider his stuff. They would not even look at it to offer advice or an opinion. He knew his margins were correct, but he was unsure about what he was putting between them. He also knew he did not need any talent to succeed in this business, at least not judging from the Screen Gems productions that passed through New York, but he thought some small measure of it might one day come in handy.

Eventually, Paltrow grew so frustrated in his going-nowhere job that he quit. He had nothing else lined up, but he knew he could not get anywhere from where he was. Unemployment was not much worse than sixty-five dollars a week, he reasoned. By this time, he had found a writing partner, and the two of them had an idea for a screenplay. He also had a play he wanted to write, on his own. He started to do research for his play. He and his partner tried to sell their screenplay. No one was interested. Paltrow spent most of his days writing, or standing on line for his unemployment check, or researching his play, or kicking around some ideas, or looking for another, more creative job in television.

"When I was a kid, I didn't know that these were jobs you could have," he recalls of this stalled period, trying to find a place for himself in the entertainment business. "Once I found out these were jobs you could have, I wanted them, I really, really, wanted them, but nobody would hire me." He wanted to stay in New York, but he began to realize that most of the jobs he was looking for were in Los Angeles.

During this career downtime, Paltrow met and married Blythe Danner, the actress. She was his first big break, and she supported him while he tried to catch a second. "I had no career," he allows, "I had no money. I was dying. My wife was the queen of New York. She burst onto Broadway." He punctuates himself with applause, yells "Bravo!," and then continues: "She won a Tony Award. She was offered everything. She never wanted to go to California, but finally I just said to her, 'Look, I can't make it in New York. There is no television here. I have no shot here. We've got to go to California.' She said okay, but she wanted to come back. She made me promise we'd come back. And I did. There was no timetable, it was just, when we can come back, we will come back."

Once in Los Angeles, Paltrow hit pay dirt, or at least exploitable soil. He sold a screenplay to the independent movie producers Tony Bill and Julia Phillips. Phillips had gone to high school with Paltrow, in Great Neck, and she liked what he had done with an idea about six young professional men who settle their considerable differences on a basketball court, in a regular game at the Y. She and Bill optioned Paltrow's *Shirts/Skins* for one thousand dollars and then offered Paltrow another thousand to rewrite it. It was not a lot of money—

two thousand dollars for two years' work—but it was a lot more than he had been making, and Paltrow jumped into the rewriting with eagerness, and hope. Unfortunately, one of the other projects on the Bill-Phillips plate was a period shyster piece called *The Sting*, which at this point was just a notion, but by the time Paltrow wrapped his revisions it was a full-fledged star vehicle for Paul Newman and Robert Redford. It would soon consume all of the producers' time, money, and enthusiasm, and the option on *Shirts/Skins* was allowed to lapse.

Paltrow was back where he started. The rights to the movie reverted to him. This turned out not to be a bad thing. In Hollywood, Paltrow was soon to learn, there is nothing like a project in turnaround; if it was good enough for someone once, then it would be good enough for someone else again. And soon. M-G-M expressed sudden interest in *Shirts/Skins* on the rebound. The only hitch was they wanted Paltrow to cut the script down for television. It was too long, they felt, the language too strong. They offered him four thousand dollars to make the cuts.

"That was just to cut it," he says, smiling at the easy-money memory. "It took me four days. Out, out, get it out." He pantomimes flipping through imagined pages, discarding. "So I made in four days twice what I had made in two years. No problem. And then, boom, it jumped over to ABC, and I got I think another eleven thousand, so I was up to fifteen thousand, plus the first two. I didn't know what to do with myself. I had never seen that kind of money."

But there was more to it than the money. There was also the juice. Suddenly, Paltrow's words were coming from the mouths of actors like Bill Bixby, Doug McClure, Leonard Frey, and McLean Stevenson. He had his own made-for-television movie. An entire production, costing hundreds of thousands of dollars, was moving to Paltrow's rhythms. He had never been so excited. He was, finally and legitimately, a television writer. This was not quite everything he wanted, but it was a lot of what he wanted, and it was something. ABC aired *Shirts/Skins* in 1973, to good ratings and good reviews. "In the town, it was a big success," Paltrow enthuses. "It was innovative, it was smart, it was funny. It was terrific. It was one of the first television comedy movies. Almost right away, I got asked to write another movie-of-the-week, so I was writing, and writing, and writing. People kept giving me work."

Like every other television writer in town, Paltrow was not content just to write. He wanted to produce and direct. He wanted to create and own his shows. That was where the money was, he knew, and that was where the control was. "It's funny," he says. "I was writing pilots, writing pilots, and every time I would write a pilot the people I was working with would louse them up. Whatever these network guys wanted, the studio guys, all their changes, you know, would just louse them up. I would do all the work, they would louse it up, and then it wouldn't get made. So I said to myself, I could louse this up myself. I don't need someone else to louse this stuff up for me."

One of Paltrow's first three-hatted efforts, as writer-producer-director, was the 1974 spin-off pilot for a *Shirts/Skins* sitcom. Leonard Frey was the only member of the original cast to return for the proposed ABC series, which was produced at M-G-M. The pilot was not picked up by the network, but Paltrow kept on. In 1977, he wrote and directed a CBS pilot at Warner Bros. called *Everything Is Coming Up Roses*, which focused on an over-the-hill Broadway star, played by Ethel Merman, and her talent-agent son, played by Austin Pendleton. It also never went anywhere. In the middle of all this were assorted series ideas that were never scripted or scripts that were never made into pilots. Paltrow was busy, and making good money, but he was living from one pitch meeting to the next.

Paltrow worried he would never get out of the starting gate. He was bursting with ideas, but they were like well-blown smoke rings; for a moment they would hold their shape, and their grace, and then they would dissipate into nothing. Finally, in 1977, he conceived a series about a former basketball star, his career cut short by injury, who accepts a coaching job at an inner-city high school. He called the show *The White Shadow*. He liked the ingredients, the possibilities. He pitched it as a half-hour comedy, and CBS, sold, offered a script commitment. Trouble was, by the time he finished the pilot script, Paltrow had convinced himself the half-hour format was all wrong for the show. It was like fitting a square peg into a round hole, the way he came to see it. He went to the network and tried to beg out of the deal.

The network, according to Paltrow, was confounded. No one had ever pulled a paid-for script from pilot consideration like this before. The half-hour development executives looked at Paltrow as if he had sprouted horns. Perhaps he had. He offered to rewrite the script as an hour, at no cost to the network. "I figured, let them decide," he reflects. "I told them we'll get the half-hour comedy guys together with the one-hour drama guys and we'll just look at it and make a decision. No memos. Nothing formal. And they agreed, so I went off and wrote the hour."

CBS bought the hour, and Paltrow was in business. The only snag was that the network would not let him do the show without studio backing, so he shopped around for a financial partner to produce the pilot. His friends told him MTM Studios was the best place in town for creative work, so he went there. He could have gone anywhere. With his pilot commitment in hand, he was a hot commodity; MTM was happy to have him. Production proceeded quickly. The actor Ken Howard was signed to play the basketball coach, sets were built, locations scouted. Paltrow shot the pilot in April 1978. It felt like he was on to something.

The network screened the *White Shadow* pilot and offered a series commitment, provided Paltrow did the series as a half hour, as originally conceived. Paltrow refused. Once again, the network was stymied. No one turned down the president of a network if he wanted to order their show. It was unheard of. It was like auditioning for a prized role, and then turning it down because rehearsals conflicted with a dentist's appointment. "I wish I could say I was sticking to my guns," Paltrow says of his resolve, "but creatively, I had done the half-hour and it didn't work. I didn't want to do it to fail. What's the point of doing it? It just made no sense as a half-hour. What, a white guy goes in and makes jokes with black kids? It's not right, it didn't work, it's flawed. So I said, 'Boom, no, there's always next year, thank you very much.' And I was out the door."

Someone, somewhere, must have admired Paltrow's brash spunk. Or, maybe the pilot was so good the network could not let it go, despite Paltrow's refusal to do the show as a half-hour. By June, CBS came back with a five-episode commitment, for the hour. *The White Shadow* went into production immediately. Paltrow was making good money. He also had the juice back, the excitement. He ran a skunkworks operation, at first; he had nothing to go on, so he invented the process as he went along. "Today you have executive producers, writing producers, line producers, story editors, executive story editors, and story consultants," he says. "On this show there was me, Mark Tinker, who was associate producer, a gofer, and a secretary. That was the staff for the first five episodes. I didn't know. I just didn't know.

"I'm making money like I couldn't believe, like seventy-five hundred a show, but I'm working like a dog. I just didn't know how things were done. And after the five episodes, the network said they needed two more. And then it was one more, then two, then four, then two. It was like piecework. That was the first season. They didn't know what to do with it. They couldn't categorize it. It was a funny show, but it was a serious show. They couldn't figure it out. They never embraced what it was."

The fate of *The White Shadow* was so uncertain after that first season that Paltrow hedged his bets with another pilot. For NBC, he directed and co-wrote a show called *Doctors and Nurses* (the title was later changed to *Operating Room*), an hour-long hospital comedy/drama set in and around the surgical unit of a Los Angeles hospital. The pilot, written with Steven Bochco and produced by Mark Tinker, was shot at MTM. It never made it to series, but perhaps presaged Paltrow's greatest success, still to come with another medical show.

Paltrow took the bad news about the pilot with customary good cheer and unaccustomed good fortune. *The White Shadow* was picked up for a full season. It knocked around the CBS schedule for three seasons, and although it never became the breakaway hit producers dream about, it was a durable, respectable, money-making effort. Paltrow had security and a solid reputation. He was on his way.

Then came *St. Elsewhere*. The idea for *St. Elsewhere* did not originate with Paltrow. He is quick to point this out. Joshua Brand, one of Paltrow's story editors on *The White Shadow*, was the first to propose an ensemble medical series; he likely borrowed the idea from Bochco's *Hill Street Blues,* an ensemble police drama that debuted to considerable acclaim (and viewer disinterest) halfway through *The White Shadow*'s final season. Brand's was the "nub" of an idea, Paltrow says. Brand asked John Falsey, another *White Shadow* story editor, to work on it with him. They pitched it to NBC programming chief Brandon Tartikoff, who loved the idea. He called it "Hill Street in a Hospital," which, in a way, it was.

According to Paltrow, NBC offered to do the pilot if he would oversee the production, so he signed on. He helped his friends develop the idea and give it a title, bending the name of their fictional

Boston city hospital, St. Eligius, to reflect the dispirit of the institution and its denizens. Mark Tinker and John Masius, the other *White Shadow* writers, rounded out the creative team, and *St. Elsewhere* prepared for its October 1982 launch. "It was a very unhappy marriage, the four of them," Paltrow lets on. "Falsey and Brand thought they were these creative geniuses, and they thought they were just being saddled with Tinker and Masius, they just thought they were assholes. There was tremendous friction, and factions, before we even started. And we floundered when we started. We got bad reviews, odd reviews, people couldn't follow the show. It was vicious, but Falsey and Brand were intractable. They wanted it to be this, and Masius and Tinker wanted it to be that."

Brand and Falsey left after the initial order, thinking the show would be canceled. The show was at, or near, the bottom in the weekly ratings; some weeks, in some markets, it attracted fewer viewers than the local independent news; after its first full season, it was ranked eighty-sixth out of ninety-eight shows. But the critics loved it, and so did Brandon Tartikoff. NBC ordered another batch of shows. And then another. And another. That's the way it went for one hundred and thirty-seven episodes, over six seasons.

"We never had any security with that show," Paltrow says. "Probably the reason they kept ordering more is they didn't have anything to replace it with."

Tom Fontana, another third of the *E.O.B.* writer-producer team, never thought he would be writing for television. He never wanted to be writing for television. He does not want to be writing for television now. But he has, and he is, and he probably will be for the next while. His problem is he is good at it.

He was kind of roped into it at first. Better, he was lured, by the promise of a rich paycheck, and the freedom it would have afforded him to work on his own plays. Bruce Paltrow did the luring. Paltrow's wife, Blythe Danner, introduced the two men one summer in Williamstown, Massachusetts, where Fontana was working on a play he had written based on a Washington Irving short story. He spent a lot of his summers in Williamstown, working on plays, eking out a living. He vagabonded from theater group to theater group in those days, thirsty for the rewards of the stage, trying to make a living doing what he loved.

"I was starving to death," he says now, behind a salting beard and a white *Story Theater* T-shirt. He is folded into a comfy chair in his Paltrow Group office, opposite a signed, framed blowup of the model Carol Alt selling Amaretto. He is thinking of shaving his beard because someone recently told him he looked like Jerry Garcia of the Grateful Dead. He does, down to the shoulder-length hair.

"I was ready for a change in my life," he continues, back again at the beginning. "My playwriting was not setting the world on fire. So I kept busy doing some casting, some stage-managing, whatever I could. I was lucky in that I was always able to find a job in the theater, a paying job. I never had to be a waiter."

Paltrow invited the Buffalo-born Fontana out to Los Angeles to work on a *St. Elsewhere* script. It was summer 1981, and NBC had just ordered thirteen scripts before the pilot was even produced. Paltrow was looking to assemble a writing staff, and there was something about Fontana that he liked. He liked his play, but it was more than that. He liked his style and his sensibilities. And his sense of humor. Tom Fontana has a pretty dead-on sense of humor. He is quick and cutting. In group situations, he appears to be the guy who sets the mood of the room. When his television shows play before a studio audience, he likes to warm up the crowd. "So," he'll say in mock stand-up patter, "anyone here from out of town." That he gets a big laugh with such as this is testimony both to his hip-sarcastic delivery and to his clear (and clearly good-hearted) disdain for the conventions of show business.

Authority and Fontana do not seem to get along, although authority does not seem to know it. He is disarming, but underneath his many charms there seems to lurk a quiet disregard, and mistrust, for the people in charge. That, or he just likes to kick up some dust. Consider his thoughts on writing for the small screen: "What's frustrating about television is not writing for television, or even producing for television, per se. It is ultimately the business restrictions and the narrowness of censors and the kind of overall sense that the people in charge have that the American public really is stupid and easily offended and lazy. I think there's an overwhelming lack of respect for the audience that I find very debilitating. People are constantly saying to me, That's not gonna play in Omaha. Well, I fucking know people in Omaha, and I know they are as interesting as anybody I have ever met at a cocktail party in Los

Angeles. They may have more religious background, or there may be other reasons to take them into consideration, but they are not stupider than we are, and we should not treat them that way."

Consider, also, this: "I never wrote a show for an audience. I have only written to please myself and maybe a handful of other people that I respect. So it's not like I'm going, Oh, I've got to reach forty million people. I don't care about reaching forty million people."

And, finally, this: "Television is a stupid business. I don't know why I'm doing this. I honestly don't. I can't answer that. I ask myself that every single day. I really do. The two things I come up with are I like the people I'm working with, and I like the projects that I'm doing, and when I stop liking the people I'm working with or we're doing projects I don't want to do, I'll finally say, Yes, okay, it's time to go."

This is the acquired baggage of Tom Fontana's short course in writing for television. When he started out, in 1981, he did not know what to expect, suspect, or fear. By his own admission, he wasn't very good at it. He spent more time on his first *St. Elsewhere* script—the show's third in its inaugural season—than he did on some of his plays, and even then he was reluctant to let it go. Paltrow says Falsey and Brand wanted to fire Fontana, they thought his first effort was so terrible. Fontana does not disagree with the criticism.

"You have to understand," he explains, "I was an off-off-off-Broadway playwright, so to me a stage was this big"—he gestures to the coffee table with his dirty Etonic sneakers—"and it had three people on it. And suddenly, to be able to go from place to place, and to show things, that was very exciting to me. Exciting, but I was terrible at it. I was completely lost, didn't know what I was doing. And on top of all that, doing a medical show itself was not very appealing to me at all. At that point, I was very afraid of medicine. But the problem at first, I realized, and this is something Bruce helped me with, when I started writing *St. Elsewhere*, I was writing it proscenium, because that's where my eyes were, that's where my muscles were trained to write from. That was the picture. And what Bruce taught me to do was to use a different eyeball. The eyeball in your head sees an image before you start to write it. He got me to cut in my head. I had never allowed myself to do that before. I never had that luxury, but actually, when I thought about it, I realized that I was already doing it. I just needed to grab those images before I dismissed them."

Despite the slow start, Paltrow asked Fontana to write a second script. Fontana still isn't sure why. He also isn't sure why he accepted, except for the fact that the money was better than he could hope to make in regional theater. Mercifully, the second script came easier than the first, and it led to an offer to join the *St. Elsewhere* writing staff, as story editor. "I didn't go out there thinking, Gee, I want to make good, or anything like that. I'm somebody who never has any kind of real plan, so I never work that way. I have no clear ambition and no clear goals other than just to live a good life and to enjoy myself in that life."

Fontana stayed on for the rest of the *St. Elsewhere* run, and he is credited with helping the show to find its footing, and its course. He enjoyed parts of what he was doing and dreaded others. He liked the money, for one thing, and he liked working with Paltrow and the rest of the *St. Elsewhere* team. He also liked the chance to play each week in a world of his own invention. As much as anyone else, and even though he came late to the party, he helped to create *St. Elsewhere* and people it with likable, eccentric, dedicated, and interesting characters. He liked writing these people and shepherding the show along its long run.

What he did not like was the stuff that came with all of this. Mostly, he did not like the way the network tried to infect the creative process, and he devoted a lot of his energies to insulating himself, and the show, from network interference. In large part, he succeeded. "With *St. Elsewhere*, we turned it into such a maverick thing, which was not successful but successful enough, that the network backed off from us because they really couldn't help us," he says, trying to understand the freedom the show's creators ultimately enjoyed. "At the moment of its birth it was different enough that we were allowed to do different things. And it wasn't like the network could even say anything to us that would even make any sense. They had no idea. They tended to think in television clichés, and we were so going in the other direction.

"But they liked the show, that was the thing. They wanted to have their say, but they liked the show. They constantly wanted us to have more romance, and all that soapy kind of stuff, and every time we tried to do it, it came off as artificial. Maybe we're just not romantic guys. It always seemed like we were trying to imitate Veronica Hamel and Daniel Travanti. That's the kind of relationship they wanted us to collaborated on a second script, during the second season, and continued to impress. Eventually he was hired as a staff writer and have in there, and it was like putting, you know, a ten foot in a five shoe. It just didn't fit, it just didn't work for us. Gee, they used to say to me and John Masius when we were writing most of the shows, why do they have to die all the time? Why can't this doctor be nicer, more heroic? Heroic was always the big thing. They always wanted characters to be more heroic. They wanted them to be extraordinary. But we were not doing a show about people who were extraordinary. We were doing a show about people who were absolutely ordinary, in an extraordinary situation. That's how they became noble. It wasn't that they were smarter than anybody or better than anybody. They just tried."

As a kid, John Tinker wanted to be a cop. Or a television writer. One or the other, and he could have gone either way. He was influenced, he says, by his two older brothers—one a police officer in south central Los Angeles, the other a story editor for Bruce Paltrow. Both of them loved their jobs. It was a tough call.

He tried being a cop first. As a student at Middlebury College, in Vermont, Tinker went to the academy in Ludlow and trained to be a state trooper. "I spent a lot of time, a lot of long nights, before I realized it was just a bad job," he recalls. "The hardest thing was coming home, feeling shitty, feeling kind of dirty. You felt like you had really been, I don't know, soiled by the whole thing. I guess it just wasn't for me."

Television was more like it. This was understandable. After all, his father, Grant Tinker, had helped to change the face of television in the 1970s. The elder Tinker founded MTM Studios and there produced such landmark television shows as *WKRP in Cincinnati*, *The Bob Newhart Show*, *Hill Street Blues*, *Lou Grant*, and, while he was married to its star, *The Mary Tyler Moore Show*. In 1981, he sold his stake in MTM and brought his signature of quality programming to NBC, where he rescued the network from near ruin and gradually restored it to prime-time prominence and profitability. It was only natural that some of this rub off on some of his children.

"I did have a different perspective on television than most of the kids I knew," the younger Tinker explains now, sitting behind his desk, sweatshirted, and nibbling at a roll of Smarties tart candies. He thumps his desk as he talks, drumrolling. "Where television was very real to a lot of kids, I got to see it wasn't real."

Tinker spent most of his childhood summers on the chimerical

MTM lot, absorbing what he could, but mostly marveling at the hard work and dedication of the talented people his father had assembled. It was a magical place to be, at a magical time. "The thing that got to me was they all had so much fun doing it," he says. "Jim Brooks, Allan Burns, Ed Weinberger, Stan Daniels, Jay Sandrich, all of these guys, I never saw a group of people laugh so much. They worked hard, and they laughed hard. I wanted to have a job that could make me laugh like that."

His first job in television was as a gofer on *Knots Landing*. It was not what he expected, but it was not all that bad. He got coffee and sandwiches for the producers, ran scripts, did whatever was asked of him. He was not that crazy about the show, but he liked the people and what they could teach him. "It was a pretty typical first experience," he comments, "in that you try and osmose as much as you can." Before long, he even got a chance to do some assistant directing, enough to decide that probably wasn't the way he was going to go.

He left *Knots Landing* for another gofer job, this one on the *St. Elsewhere* pilot, where his brother Mark had become supervising producer. Perhaps he thought he would laugh more there. Perhaps he saw the future of critically acclaimed television. As Tinker remembers it, he finished at *Knots Landing* on a Friday and went to work at *St. Elsewhere* the following Monday. He did not have time to catch his breath or to shift gears. It did not take long for him to realize he had left a fictional soap opera for a real one or to wonder why. "They were working on the pilot when I got there," he says, "and it was such a mess. There was a lot of stuff going on, a lot of tension. It took a few weeks to straighten everything out."

After the third or fourth episode, Paltrow called John Tinker to his office and told him that by the end of this season he was either up or out. "You better pick something you want to do," Paltrow said. "If you want to write, that's fine, or direct, or whatever. But you better pick it, and you better demonstrate to me that you have some ability, or you're out. I don't want you getting me sandwiches again next year. It's not why you're here. You're here to learn."

Pressed, Tinker decided he wanted to be a writer. So he teamed with his brother Mark and wrote an episode that first season. Tinker liked what he wrote, and Paltrow liked what he saw. Tinker collaborated on a second script, during the second season, and continued to impress. Eventually he was hired as a staff writer and story editor. He remained with *St. Elsewhere* for the balance of its six-year run. By the time the show was canceled, it had long been someone's job to get sandwiches for him.

In six seasons, *St. Elsewhere* received sixty-three Emmy nominations, yielding thirteen Emmy Awards. It was a showcase for some of television's best writers, actors, and directors. It was one of the most talked about, least watched shows in television history.

It was also a tough act to follow.

After *St. Elsewhere*, Tinker joined Paltrow and Fontana to form the Paltrow Group. The company's stated purpose was to create quality television shows outside the Hollywood loop. The principals wanted to live and work in New York. Their first effort, the NBC comedy/drama *Tattingers'*, centered around the title character, Nick Tattinger, and his New York restaurant. It was sold largely on *St. Elsewhere's* legacy. No one was ever completely happy with the show, including its creators, and it was canceled after only a few episodes. They tried to salvage the premise, and recoup some of the start-up costs, with a half-hour sitcom called *Nick and Hillary*, using the same cast and sets, but the network gave up on this pass after only two episodes.

Tattingers' was always a problem," Tinker assesses, "and the problem with the show was inherent to the concept. Nick could not be in the restaurant all the time if he was out solving problems, and yet the show took place in a restaurant. We were always struggling to hold the show together. The ideas just weren't coming. We were always chasing it. I wouldn't throw away the experience, but it was almost more like a job. Television shouldn't feel like a job, and this felt like a job."

More than his partners, Tinker seems to think a lot before he speaks. His instincts seem to check with the rest of him for approval. He sits with his arms crossed in a tight pretzel and thinks about what he wants to say. Then he says it: "I haven't consumed a lot of television lately, and I don't mean that the way you hear people say it to someone at a party. I just mean that I haven't been able to watch it as much as I would like. I haven't really consumed much of it. All I know is the kinds of shows I want to be working on. I think *E.O.B.* is one. *St. Elsewhere* was one. We would just eat, sleep, and breathe that show. We always had ideas. It would make us laugh, or it would make us sad, or we would be pissed off at it. It just wouldn't submit. That's the kind of show I want to work on."

Three

BACK-STORIES, IMAGINED _____

☐   Good stories hang on character. This is especially so in series television, where good stories (and, causally, good characters) are sometimes harder to find than a *Nanny and the Professor* (ABC, 1970–71) rerun. There can be laughs without character, and action-adventure, and even tears, but there can be no compelling story. Viewers tune in to find out what is happening to the people they have come to care about, not to find out how the story ends. In a business built on a few basic truths, this is one of them.

Bruce Paltrow, Tom Fontana, and John Tinker are looking for characters with which to people their presidential speechwriters sitcom. They do this in any one of their windowed offices, although mostly in Paltrow's and Fontana's, where there are more comfortable places to sit. They do this as a group, or in various pairs, or individually. They do this, sometimes, without thinking. They are working a constant puzzle—trying to invent a cast of characters that will best serve their promising concept. There are a few givens. There cannot be a dozen or so speechwriters working in their imagined *E.O.B.* office, the way there are in the real world, or at least in Washington. That would be too many for the writers to write, or to care about, and for the viewers to follow, or to care about. Probably the premise can comfortably absorb four or five speechwriters, but no more. And one of these, it is generally agreed, should be the new guy, the milk-fed young novelist who never once imagined that the president did not actually write his speeches himself—in fact, never even considered that the president did not just step up to the microphone and say whatever it was that was on his mind. (There *are* some people who think that way.) It is felt that the show needs to somehow turn on this innocent, fresh point of view. The viewer, like the apprentice speechwriter, will be a fish out of water, looking to swim with the old school.

It is also agreed that at least two of the speechwriters will be female. The tenet here is that the two women are needed to play off each other, to spar. Carla had Diane, and later Rebecca, to go up against on *Cheers;* Laverne had Shirley; Mary had Rhoda; Lucy had Ethel; Wilma had Betty. Of course, Hot Lips and 99 did not have anybody, so this may or may not be a necessary convention. For now, though, it is something to go on.

Someone gets the idea that one of the speechwriters should be a Madison Avenue refugee. Tom Fontana may have had this idea first, or maybe it was John Tinker. These guys can't seem to distinguish their own thoughts from each other's. Anyway, the advertising guy, he should be a real sloganmeister, completely lacking in political and emotional sensibility, a materialist among the ideologues. Also, the office needs a gofer. After all, what is an office without a gofer? Particularly a sitcom office? Tinker and Paltrow started out as gofers, and Fontana has done his share of fetching, and the three relish the turnabout in creating someone for the speechwriters to abuse. They'll make him relentlessly ambitious, the kind of guy who volunteers for all the drek assignments and then gets passed over for all the good ones, the kind of guy they can have fun with.

All of the characters are written with actors in mind to play them, but in only one instance is this internal casting rooted in anything more than fantasy. Paltrow, Fontana, and Tinker have decided that the role of the chief of communications will be written for a friend, the actor William Daniels, whom they employed with much success for six seasons as Dr. Mark Craig on *St. Elsewhere.* They have not yet offered the role to Daniels—they do not even have a script commitment, so such a move would be premature—but they have talked to him about it; both writers and star have been looking for a chance to turn their first happy collaboration into a second, and they agree this might be it. It is not clear whether the actor will be perfect for the part or whether the part will be perfected for the actor, but the character will begin to look and sound like Daniels as it develops.

The characters, sketched in the Paltrow Group offices, begin to look like this:

Jim Smith, thirtyish (the "ish" is important because it suggests the part is right for an actor ten years older or younger), who arrives in Washington after publishing his autobiographical first novel, chronicling a Middle American boyhood not unlike the president's. His book (which the writers have saddled with the mawkish title *Amber Waves of Grain*) somehow falls onto the president's nightstand, where it somehow manages to be read by the president, who is taken by it. Jim is recruited by his First Fan to bring some down-home, earthy charm to a White House not known for its down-home, earthy charm. He will arrive at the E.O.B., bags in hand, ready for work and looking for a place to live. He is honest and trusting. There is not a scheming bone in his lanky frame, until Washington gets its hands on him. This would be the Mary Tyler Moore role, gender bended and diluted to blend into an ensemble piece. Better, the role suggests the guy from the first season of *Taxi*, the out-of-towner hack (John Burns, played by Randall Carver) who was given a few star-turn episodes to make his way in New York before being written off the show to make room for the more memorable Jim Ignatowski (played by Christopher Lloyd). The parallel may or may not augur well for the show or for this character.

Hammond Egley (get it? Ham-and-egg-ley?), also thirtyish, a former ad man who flees the bells and whistles of Madison Avenue for the pomp and circumstance of the White House. He is not here out of any born-again patriotism. He is not here because he believes in the president and wants to help him set the nation on a sure course. He is here, probably, to hunt and gather enough inside information to write his memoirs: *I am Curious (Red, White, and Blue)*, or some such. He is here to see and be seen in the Executive Mess and to use his White House credentials to meet women. He is here to stroke his own ego and to parlay this turn so that others might jump to do it for him. These are the things that matter to him. Hammond Egley is the sort of guy who could sell Hamburger Helper to a vegetarian and spend his resulting bonus check before it is even clear one will arrive. As such, he is likely one of the office's most valued speechwriters. Also as such, he will provide a cynical sounding board for his more ardently idealistic colleagues.

Sara Scadutto, mid-thirties, an avowed environmentalist and pacifist, with a keen maternal streak. She deeply believes in her president and is honored to serve him. She is also devoted to her family, which is large and ever growing. She will be seven months pregnant when the show opens, and we will learn that this is an almost steady condition for her; there are maybe three or four kids at home. Her husband carpools and cooks dinner, but she does not understand what people mean when they tell her she is lucky to have a husband who carpools and cooks dinner. She is scattered about her life but focused about her work. Sometimes. Like Tom Fontana, she will hail from upstate New York; she will be an odd mix of rural charm and cheer and cutting East Coast savvy. She will be as passionate about Italian food as equal rights. She is described, in one of the early E.O.B. drafts, as an "earth-mother type," although whether this means she will be a flower child gone to seed or an ecologically minded frontier woman is at this stage uncertain.

Marsha Katzenberg, also mid-thirties, is the counterpoint to Sara Scadutto. She is the right to Sara's left, although she sees herself somewhere in between. The center is the only place to be, she believes. Everything else is wrong. She is a staunch supporter of the president, but she does not always agree with him or take him seriously. She is sharp-tongued and cold-hearted, at least on the surface. Underneath, there may or may not be some warmth. She is a single mother from Southern California. Like a friend of the Paltrow Group, she will also be physically challenged. A big deal, this, made even bigger for the way it is so lightly decided. The producers agree they like the plot and character possibilities presented by a handicapped speechwriter, so Marsha will wear a brace. Her handicap, at this point, is nonspecific (polio? cerebral palsy? adult-onset paralysis? television-writer dementia?); whatever it is, she will walk with a cane, or a single crutch, or a really, really, noticeable limp, and it will not slow her down. The sensibility-challenged character trait seems to be assigned without a great deal of thought to its off-camera consequences or to its on-camera implications.

Steve Lawson, early twenties, the office toady. He is ambitious to a fault. He is overeducated and underequipped. As the office researcher, it will be his job to investigate obscure pieces of information at various government libraries, to cull and sort through the morass of administration programs and treaties and policies, and to make sure there is enough toner for the Xerox machine. He wants desperately to be a speechwriter, but there is no evidence to suggest any aptitude in this direction. Still, he pines openly for a break, and there is none forthcoming. Steve Lawson is Doogie Howser without an agent: he earns an Ivy League Ph.D. before his twenty-second birthday, and he can only put it to work collating White House documents and brewing decaf. And the only reason he was able to finagle this job is because his father was a major campaign contributor. He will do everything to impress, but it will never be impressive. Besides, he is kept so busy doing everything else, he will rarely get the chance. He is an easy target and a ready foil.

Connie Gibson, sixties, a lifetime civil servant, she has run the speechwriter's office since Camelot. Safire, Buchanan, Schlesinger ...even Noonan...she's seen them all come and go. She grew up in the shadow of the nation's capital, in Virginia, so she knows this town and these parts. Indeed, she has forgotten more about how the White House works than the chief of staff will ever know. She likes to point this out. She also likes to point out that she has better access to the president than anyone else in Communications. She knows who is who and what is what. Despite her functionally low position in the office, she is also the highest paid, because of her tenure. This last leaves her feeling entitled, which perhaps she is. She says what she wants whenever she wants. She is recently widowed and keeps her husband's ashes in an urn.

B. Laurence Taylor, a gruff, slick mover and shaker of undetermined middle age. As the chief of Communications, he is the speechwriters' boss. He is an odd, Cuisinarted blending of sitcom bosses—Mr. Mooney without bile, Louie DiPalma without rancor, Lou Grant without heart, and Alan Brady without vanity. Taylor comes from money, although its source is not yet clear. His path to this particular power is also not yet clear. He is, presumably, a friend and confidant of the president's. He is not himself a writer and is therefore not inclined to coddle or indulge his staff. He expects his deadlines to be met. He does not like surprises or excuses. He operates at some remove from the rest of the characters—indeed, they will all toil in a large, bullpen-type office, while he gets his own sanctum—and will serve as a kind of conduit to the unseen administration.

The character names are pulled from the phone book, from the writers' personal address books, from the New York Giants yearbook, and from breakfast. The names are helpful in investing each character with a past, a present, and a future. The writers need a foundation, and this is where they start. After this, they just have to find something for them to do.

Four

PITCH _____

◻ Paltrow, Fontana, and Tinker fly to Los Angeles to meet with
Stuart Bloomberg, ABC's vice president for comedy development, to
sell him on their idea for *E.O.B.* They are going with heavy artillery,
and greater gusto than can be found in most beer commercials. They
are more prepared for this pitch meeting than they have been for any
other in their television-writing careers. They have in head a dozen
plot possibilities, including several ideas for the pilot script. They
have explored the dynamic of their fictional Washington workplace to
where they know how any of their imagined speechwriters would
react to any imagined situation. They know more about their would-
be characters than they know about some of their friends. They know
which one of them writes the gun control speeches and which writes
for arms control; more, they know what those speeches might say and
how effective they might be. They know who gets the laugh lines and
who delivers the setups. They are ready.

Bloomberg and his staff are ready, too. They are always ready. They
fill their days with meetings like these. They have heard almost
everything. Twice. Evil twins, "blended" families, household pets
from outer space, evil twins from outer space. This speechwriters
idea, though, is a little fresh, a little different. It is familiar without
being derivative. It has got possibilities. Bloomberg has been keen
on it on paper, and he seems charged by it in person, too. He and his
minions appear genuinely interested in the Paltrow Group pitch,

which is delivered at the ABC offices on the Avenue of the Stars, but underneath their enthusiasm there is caution. There is a problem, Bloomberg allows, with the avowed topicality of the show. What happens if an attempt to be current is rendered redundant by a last-minute turn of events? There is a problem in setting real issues and events against the backdrop of a fictional presidency, while at the same time there are a host of inverse problems in playing to a George Bush soundalike, or look-alike. The writers anticipated these reservations and counter with positives. What they did not anticipate, and cannot counter, is that the network has somewhat soured on the idea of a politically driven sitcom after an aborted attempt to get one off the ground with the producers of the popular British comedy *Yes, Minister.*

The elaborate pitch suggests all kinds of possibilities, good and bad. Happily, though, Bloomberg likes the setting and the characters enough to look past his initial concerns. Besides, he thinks, it is only a script commitment. It is only one hundred thousand dollars. One hundred thousand dollars is a lot of money almost everywhere else but in Hollywood, where it is little more than loose change for the television producer trying to peddle his wares. It is significant for what it represents and not for what it affords. For the Paltrow Group and *E.O.B.*, it represents the first in a series of green lights on the uncertain road back to the prime-time schedule.

Bloomberg's decision is made easy by a nonspecific series commitment that has previously been extended by the network to the producers. A series commitment, in theory, and in general, means a network is bound to develop the next series project presented to it by a production company, with a promise to produce at least six (and sometimes thirteen) episodes of the proposed series. In practice, however, and still in general, it means that the network is consigned only to the notion of a series commitment. There is nothing to mandate which series ideas it must be committed to. Sure, we'll put your show on the air, as long as we want to, and as long as it tests well, and as long as we can't find anything better. If we don't, or it doesn't, or we can, we'll just wait for your next best shot, or the one after that, or the one after that.

And so, since ABC is already committed to the idea of doing business with the Paltrow Group, the network decides to specifically commit to an *E.O.B.* script. Actually, Bloomberg's green light has not bought a script. Yet. What he has bought is time for the Paltrow Group to write one, which they will do in much the same way they fleshed out their initial premise: individually, in various pairs, and as a group. It comes slowly at first. There is a lot of business to do in a pilot script, and all of it must be neatly accomplished in approximately twenty-three minutes' running time. They have to introduce their premise, and their setting, and their characters. They have to tell a story. They have to make people laugh. (And, because the end product is to be passed off as intelligent situation comedy, they have to also make them think.) They have to create a kind of blueprint for future shows. They have to leave their audience so delightfully spent, and comfortable, and connected that they cannot wait to find out what happens in next week's episode. They have to create an environment in which advertisers will want to showcase their products and services. And, most important, they have to convince programmers that what they have just seen will attract viewers like Velcro.

These things have never been easily accomplished; often they are not even attempted. Television is a very forgiving medium. It takes a lot for granted. It assumes a working knowledge of its own material. We are supposed to know, for example, that the character of Arnold, the black kid with gland problems, was adopted by the posh Upper East Side white family with whom he lives, and that Webster, the other black kid with gland problems, was adopted by a white teammate of his now-dead, once-football-playing father. We are supposed to know that Dr. Richard Kimble is wanted for a murder he did not commit, and the one-armed man who haunts him is not a bad traffic cop.

One of television's operating principles is that a pilot script should be written as if it were the show's fourth or fifth episode. Network people are fond of saying this. Trouble is, operating principles do not always get the job done, and network people do not always know what they are talking about. After all, how could a television illiterate even hope to make sense of *Bewitched* without an assist from the expositional animated opening? Divest *Bewitched* of its premise and imagine watching, say, an episode from the show's sixth season. The show has already gone from black and white to color, and switched Darins, and begun Tabitha, but you do not know this. All you know is some guy's mother-in-law has turned him into a ferret.

There is a kind of shared, accumulated familiarity that comes with series television, an understood but unacknowledged history. It is not clear whether this is a good thing or a bad thing, but it is a thing. Viewers have been conditioned to consume these entertainments from the middle, with no memory of the beginning and no hope of ever reaching the end. These shows, and their characters, exist on their own planes. We tune in at various midpoints, knowing what we will find there.

Paltrow, Fontana, and Tinker, eschewing conventional wisdom but embracing common sense (and a sense of story), decide to tell this particular tale from the beginning, not from the middle. *E.O.B.*, they agree, must turn on the arrival of the out-of-towner, Jim Smith. They do not want their show to be about business-as-usual in the office of the speechwriters for the president of the United States, at least not entirely, and certainly not yet. For now, they want it to be about how business-as-usual can be upset by an outside element. They want to see what this particular office looks like through a new set of eyes, how the group absorbs the individual, and how the process infects the workplace. They want to know how writing empty promises changes their characters, if it changes them at all. To their way of thinking, the business of writing speeches for the president of the United States does not have to be all that different from working in a low-rent Boston hospital. Of course, it is different, but they will get to that. At its core, and for now, they want their new show to be about people who do a difficult job, under difficult conditions, and do it well.

And so the story line for the pilot episode of *E.O.B.* begins to emerge....

Jim Smith interrupts a bustling speechwriters' office to announce his arrival. No one notices him, except to notice that he is in the way. The president is about to deliver a speech on national television, live, from the wrong cue cards. The speechwriters are distracted by the ensuing wackiness and mayhem, after which they finally notice their new colleague and put him through a kind of interoffice hazing. Connie Gibson, the civil servant secretary, makes Smith show her his temporary identification every time he reenters the room; Hammond Egley, the Madison Avenue refugee, confuses him with the guy whose job Smith has been hired to fill; Steve Lawson, the researcher, is snivelingly incredulous that he has been passed over for yet another speechwriter opening; B. Laurence Taylor, the writers' boss, fires Smith because he does not know who he is.

Smith, with grit and sugar, argues for and wins his job back, after which he is summoned to the Oval Office and given his first assignment: a comprehensive speech on disarmament, to be delivered at a summit conference the following week. His first pass does not make it past Taylor's paper shredder; the second leads to a heated exchange on arms reduction between Marsha Katzenberg and Sara Scadutto, the two female speechwriters, and to a general warming of relations among Smith and his new colleagues. (His colleagues even offer to help bail Smith out of what seems to be a hopeless situation.) In the end, the president signs off on the revised speech, which Smith has managed on his own, but the summit is postponed and the new guy's extra efforts dashed.

Welcome to Washington.

By November 1989, a first draft script is delivered by overnight mail to Stu Bloomberg at his ABC office in Los Angeles. Paltrow, Fontana, and Tinker follow their effort by plane, same day delivery. When they arrive in Bloomberg's office, it is quickly made clear that the network is wildly unenthusiastic about the script. Bloomberg is unable to articulate what, precisely, he does not like about it. He apologizes for his inability to articulate what, precisely, he does not like about it, but this gets him no further. He looks at his feet, looks at the ceiling, looks at his feet. He appears to be at a loss. He knows what he wants to say but cannot quite manage it. You guys, he fumbles. You know, you're terrific, we love you, we respect you, we want to be in business with you, you've won all those Emmys, and really, you're terrific, it's just...

It's just... what? Fontana wants to say. Tell us what it's just...

The meeting, which has gone farther south than Los Angeles, even, is adjourned with Bloomberg's promise to read the script again that evening. Maybe he is missing something. By the next morning, though, he has not found anything new to like about it. All he has found are the words to say what, precisely, he does not like about it. Over the phone, he tells Paltrow that what the network was really looking for was a script about this guy, this Jim Smith, a young, idealistic guy who comes to Washington: He's looking for an apartment, he's looking for a girlfriend, and he just happens to work as a speechwriter for the president of the United States. Bloomberg suggests a number of changes that may or may not accomplish this.

Paltrow is not interested in Bloomberg's suggestions. Come on, he's thinking, underneath his antic frustration, we told them exactly what we were going to do, they loved it, told us to go ahead and write it exactly as we pitched it, and then we went out and wrote exactly what we told them we were going to write. No surprises. Now, boom! all of a sudden, they don't love it. What's the deal?

As he did with *The White Shadow* some years earlier, Paltrow tells the network to take the pilot on his terms or to leave it. They leave it. The series commitment remains in place for the next time around.

"They wanted Mary Tyler Moore," Paltrow says after the phone call. "That was not at all the show we wanted to make. To us, it was always an ensemble show. We only want to do the show we want to do."

The writers return to New York a confused and dejected bunch. They really thought they had something here. (Or, in industry terms, they really, really, thought they had something here.) They thought they were giving the network what it wanted—or at least what it asked for. After all, Bloomberg had signed off on the pilot story line before they even wrote the script. Paltrow, who protects his partners from most network dealings, is convinced these network guys have no idea what they want. They want whatever works, but they have no idea what will work. They want to keep their jobs, that's what they want, and the way to keep their jobs is to play it safe, which accounts for the perennial star vehicles, spin-offs, and proven-formulas-brewed-in-ever-so-slightly-different-petri-dishes. The studios, too, are without a clue. In the months since he lost MTM as a financial partner, Paltrow has been shopping for another. He needs to affiliate with one of the major studios (Paramount, Columbia, Warner Bros.) in order to keep his personal risks to a minimum. He needs to do this because licensing fees paid by the networks to producers to develop a television pilot do not cover the cost of production. In some cases, they do not even come close. Typically, producers dip into their own pockets to finance the cost overages (which can run to several hundred thousand dollars), in hopes of recouping or amortizing their investments with a long series run. For this, the Paltrow Group needs a studio.

It should not be too hard to find one, given the *St. Elsewhere* legacy, but Paltrow is a careful shopper. He does not want to go into business with studio executives who think they know more about making good television shows than he does. He has a hard enough time convincing the network he knows what he is doing without requiring a second opinion from some television studio. He needs a studio for its deep pockets and its facilities; what he does not need is the aggravation. He is a hands-on kind of guy looking for a hands-off partner.

These are Paltrow's worries, and he worries about them alone. With Fontana and Tinker, he worries about the creative end. The company's energies turn to *High* and *Modern Marriage,* two of the more viable projects on its development table. They want to move forward. They fine-tune their first-draft scripts for the hip high school drama and the domestic situation comedy, hoping for a pilot deal. They have not given up on *E.O.B.* after the ABC rejection, but they are setting it aside. Perhaps the script will look different to them in a week or two, with some distance. Perhaps not.

Meanwhile, the writers must pep-talk themselves into believing they have not gone into the wrong business. They cannot convince themselves, and so they solicit enthusiasm elsewhere. Even before the ABC pass, they began to circulate copies of the first-draft *E.O.B.* script to their friends in the television community: writers, producers, studio executives. Now they send out a few more. They are fishing for an honest reaction to their work. Sometimes even a dishonest stroke does not hurt. They do this often. Most Paltrow Group scripts can be found circulating through a dozen offices, on both coasts, long before their fates have been formally determined at the networks. With *E.O.B.,* the writers want to know if they are crazy or if what they have written really is funny, and promising, or maybe both.

One of the Paltrow Group's friendly readers is Jeff Sagansky, the former NBC executive. He has been a fan, and a friend, since his tenure at NBC during the *St. Elsewhere* days. Paltrow sends him scripts all the time, even now that Sagansky has moved to Tri-Star, a movie studio, where he is not in a position to offer anything but a trusted opinion.

Sagansky calls Paltrow with his take on *E.O.B.,* shortly after the

Bloomberg rejection. It's the best pilot script I've read since *Cheers*, he gushes. They're nuts to let it go.

By the end of December, Sagansky's enthusiasm looks like it might mean something. He is named to replace Kim LeMasters as president of CBS Entertainment. A fortuitous turn, this, at least as far as the Paltrow Group and *E.O.B.* are concerned. One of Sagansky's first official acts at CBS is to announce a slate of original programming for the coming summer, a time when viewership levels are traditionally down and most network fare is second run or second-rate. Sagansky's strategy is to showcase first-rate new product against the competition's filler in hopes of getting a jump start on the fall season. It is not a new idea (see *The Smothers Brothers Summer Show*, ABC, and *Where's Huddles?* CBS, both 1970), but it has not been done in a while, and so it seems like new. In the season just ended, the network finished so far back in the ratings that industry analysts wondered if it would survive the new decade in its current form. In the season under way, the network is faring little better when it replaces LeMasters. Now, suddenly, Sagansky has got to do something drastic; and in television, doing something that has not been tried in a few years is considered drastic.

"There was absolutely no hint Jeff was gonna land at CBS," Fontana tells. "There wasn't even anything in the air about it. It just happened."

Just a few days after Sagansky's hiring, Paltrow and company meet their old friend at the CBS offices in New York, in the high-rise midtown building known as Black Rock. It is to be a good day at Black Rock for the Paltrow Group.

I want to put "E.O.B." on the air, Sagansky announces.

What, on the air? Paltrow says. We haven't even done a pilot.

In the summer, Sagansky explains. I want to put it on in the summer. He outlines his plans for a new summer schedule. He's got a reality-based cop series in mind and a quirky hour-long comedy drama set in Alaska, among other things. He sees *E.O.B.* somewhere in the mix. I've got to turn this network around, he says. I've got to try something. I need to do business with you guys. I need a show like this. I need you guys to make noise.

Fine, Paltrow thinks: Aaaaaaaaaaaaaaaarghhhhhh!!!

Sagansky offers the Paltrow Group a six-episode summer commitment for *E.O.B.* with the first of these episodes to be shot as a pilot this spring. If all goes well on the pilot, as everyone suspects it will, production on the balance of the episodes will begin a few weeks later. He also offers the producers a pilot commitment for *High*, for consideration on his first fall-season schedule.

Aaaaaaaaaaaaaaaarghhhhhh!!! indeed.

Five

PILOT SEASON _____

○   Hard to figure, Los Angeles. If you are from out of town, cab-bing from LAX to, say, Santa Monica, it is very likely your driver will tell you more than you thought possible about his Buckminster Fuller screenplay. Really. Certainly more than you could possibly have wanted to know.

"I can feel it," your driver will very likely say, with a passion you will have very likely never before heard attached to Buckminster Fuller. "Someone, somewhere, is gonna come out with a Fuller picture, and it's within me to see that it's mine."

Back to LAX, a second driver will very likely tell you that his screenplay, set in the jungles of a place, you know, a lot like Malaysia, would be a perfect vehicle for a James Woods, a young Mia Farrow. "It involves," he'll say, "some pretty weird fucking cannibal shit, sacrificing human brains, shit like that, so I need his edge, I need James for his edge, but it's got to be softened by Mia, know what I mean? That part's got to be soft?"

If you are from out of town, this will strike you as a shade unusual, particularly because you just read somewhere that James Woods is looking to break from type and pursue light comedy.

If you are local, it is just a cab ride.

Los Angeles comes through as advertised. It is choked by smog and traffic. There are pockets of clean, glorious air around this vast

38

city, and if you have lived here long enough, you will know where to find them: in the valley, on some days, when the wind is blowing out; by the beach, maybe, for no real reason. You will also know how to beat the traffic, or at least how not to let it beat you. You will know that you can leave home for the office at eight o'clock and not arrive until ten, and so you will tell yourself it makes sense to leave at ten to arrive at ten-thirty and to make your first bunch of calls by the pool or maybe in the car.

Also: People drive with bikini tops on, women mostly. And speaking of tops—at night, when it's cold, the sporting locals drive their convertibles with the tops down and the heat on full, to compensate. You will try both, or whichever one is gender- or vehicle-appropriate. You will recognize that these are not comfortable things, these tops on and down, but they look pretty good. The messages you will take in are: It is okay to be uncomfortable as long as you do not appear uncomfortable; and, You have to look the part. You will begin to wonder what the Latin is for *In cliché, there is truth.*

There is not much seasonal about Los Angeles, at least not much an outsider can pick up on a breeze through town. The weather, you are told, is always the same, and without a life's reference points, you believe it. Instead of winter, spring, summer, and fall, you have the seasons of industry. There is Oscar season—the stretch of time, usually from the first week of the New Year to middle February, when studios lobby for nominations for their top stars and pictures, and continuing in somewhat different form from the time nominations are announced until the awards are given, in late March.

There is Sweeps season—the targeted months of February, May, and November, when television programmers do their darnedest to lure viewers to the small screen. Inexplicably, network and local ratings here determine advertising rates for the entire year. And so, explicably, this is the time of year when Oprah impanels a group of transvestite midgets to talk about how they have been discriminated against and when a *Charlie's Angels* alumna finds herself trapped in a movie-of-the-week, married to a man who lights her fingernails on fire.

There is a hiatus, the downtime of the television industry. It usually kicks in around March, when returning shows break for the summer, and ends sometime in July or August, when cast and crew come back to work on new episodes for the fall. There are smaller hiatuses peppered throughout the year—Christmas, Thanksgiving—but the town seems to absorb these like legal holidays, keeping its routines in whack.

There is also pilot season. What strange weather you will find here. It is hot and cold, stormy and calm, predictable and unpredictable. It exists at some remove from the public eye, although it has lately seeped into general consciousness. And, more than any other of the industry seasons, it determines what is fed onto the assembly line of mass Hollywood entertainment: the prime-time network television schedule.

Hope and hype spring eternal in pilot season, at least in Los Angeles. Indeed, all of Southern California seems to pulse to its possibility. A film-school student approaches graduation with a song in his heart because his best friend's uncle's neighbor knows a guy who could get him a job as a gofer (Xeroxing, making coffee, Xeroxing) on a pilot with one of the people who did *Hill Street Blues;* it's not Bochco, or anything, but somebody pretty up there on the show, and, plus, you know, if the show gets picked up, it could lead to something. A fetching blond AMW (as in actress-model-whatever) quits her gig as an aerobics instructor because she is up for a part in a *Who's the Boss?* spin-off and doesn't want the negative energy from the one job to keep her from the other. A writer shops for a two-bedroom by the beach because he has just had, like, a pretty good lunch with a producer who has all but a lock on a six-episode commitment. A programming executive boasts that this season's schedule will be fresh and new and daring and unlike any other in recent memory; he said the same thing the season before.

In New York, and points between, pilot season does not register. In New York in March 1990, people are talking about baseball's spring training lockout, the sluggish real estate market, the Yusuf Hawkins murder trial. Corral ten passersby in New York and ten in Los Angeles and engage them in a game of work association. "Pilot," you'll say. In Los Angeles, you'll get back *Highway Honeys* (NBC, 1982), *Puppetman* (CBS, 1987), or variations on the theme. In New York, you'll get back gas stoves and airline strikes and some loose change.

This decade's first pilot season has got some familiar smells to it. The four networks have commissioned one hundred and seventeen prototype episodes, to fill some thirty or forty slots on their prime-time schedules. Among these is a live-action movie pilot based on the *Archie* comic book characters and another based on the comic *The Flash; Poochinski,* a sitcom about a slain cop who reappears to fight crime in the body of a bulldog; and *The World According to Straw,* which purports to pull laughs from a director of maintenance at a high-rise office complex. There is also an assortment of movie and literary spinoffs (including *Uncle Buck, Big, Baby Talk, Parenthood, Turner & Hooch, The Witches of Eastwick,* and two separate passes at John Hughes's *Ferris Bueller's Day Off*), a few resurrections of old shows (*Dark Shadows*), and returning-star vehicles for time-tested television personalities like Nell Carter, Robert Urich, Burt Reynolds, and Jackée (one of the few television stars with one name who should perhaps consider a second).

Nearly all of these same-seeming pilots are destined for the network scrap heap. Nearly all of them will be shot in Los Angeles in the first four months of this year. During that time, nearly every other nonworking actor will be "up" for at least one role in at least one pilot. Several hundred will land these roles, signing long-term deals that promise as much as twenty-five thousand dollars per episode after as long as seven years. They will work the numbers and grow rich in their heads—buying cars they will never drive, living in homes in which they will never set foot. Lighting directors, property masters, production managers, grips, set decorators, costumers, hair stylists, and even caterers will seek to attach themselves to one or more of these pilot efforts, hoping to land on a hit.

This is the time of year to jockey for position, to "do the pilot thing," as one actor calls it. It is time to enter television's revolving door, to roll its dice, to reach for its brass knockers. This is when it all happens, if it is going to happen at all.

In New York, it happens differently. As in recent seasons, it is almost possible to count the number of New York pilots on the fingers of the one-armed man's hand. There is *Law and Order,* a two-tiered crime-and-punishment drama produced by Dick Wolf, in association with Universal Television. There is an untitled Jane Curtin pilot from producer Bill Persky, in association with Twentieth Century-Fox Television. Strangely, there is a Ruth Westheimer sitcom pilot, which is being shot in Los Angeles but which will move east if it makes it to series. There is also talk of a Carsey-Warner Productions pilot based here (they produced *The Cosby Show,* from the Kaufman-Astoria Studios, in Queens) and a Mike Nichols project, but nothing firm.

The Paltrow Group enters this pilot season as the busiest production company in town. Complementing Jeff Sagansky's noise making commitments to *E.O.B.* and *High,* for CBS, is a pilot order for *Modern Marriage,* with NBC. The three shows will be produced in affiliation with Columbia Pictures Television, which becomes the producers' studio home in March 1990. If all goes as dreamed, and all three shows wind up on the fall schedule (assuming a successful summer season for *E.O.B.*) the Columbia-Paltrow union could pump up the volume of New York television production as early as this fall. Such a turn would provide the studio with an unanticipated boon to its expanding television operations; the producers with a solid foundation on which to build their own full-service, full-fledged production facility; and New York City with several hundred new jobs, tens of millions in related spending and tax revenues, and a new coat of luster to the entertainment-driven aspects of its tourist industry.

Or, not.

Six

PRODUCTION _____

○   First things second. Coordinating producer Jim Finnerty rolls
up his sleeves, switches on his calculator, and figures just how far he
can stretch a four-hundred-thousand-dollar licensing fee. Even without his calculator, Finnerty knows he can't quite stretch it to embrace
a million-dollar budget, which is just about what the *E.O.B.* pilot will
cost, even with cut corners.

But try telling this to CBS. God knows, Finnerty has. Problem is,
the network has based the licensing fees for its summer programming
on the reduced revenues it receives from advertisers for this period of
traditionally low viewership. In summer, the network makes less
money on its prime-time programming, so it naturally wants to pay
less to produce it, even though production costs remain fixed,
unaffected by the season. Producers, who deficit their programs
under normal circumstances, are being asked to dip even deeper into
their pockets to get these shows made and on the air. That producers
are willing to even consider plowing substantial chunks of their own
cash into programming that might not even make it onto the airwaves
is testimony both to the good, long odds of the television business
and to the fact that they have no choice but to do so; if they do not, the
networks will find some other producers who will.

Finnerty, a former key grip calf-deep into his second career, has
handled production duties for the Paltrow Group since it renovated

the abandoned Pier 62 office space in December 1987. In those days, the windows were all rotted out, or shattered, and the wintry breezes off the Hudson would curl through the place like ice; scripts were typed with gloved fingers; coffee turned cold between sips. These days, there are windows, and carpets, and comfortable furniture, but the office is still pretty much bare bones, just like Finnerty's budget. Here, now, he has much to figure, and he does his figuring underneath a steady swirl of cigarette smoke. He does his carping there, too. "We're using a lot of stock scenery," he reveals, in the most measured tones heard on the pier; in the din of excitement enveloping the approaching production, Finnerty stands out as a deep breath, a pause. "We're using a lot of stuff we had lying around, from *Tattingers'* and other shows," he continues. "We brought the set in for around four hundred thousand, give or take, which is a real bargain. And that's only because we were able to salvage so much of it. We didn't even have money for our set designer, Tom John, to go to Washington to see what the War Room in the Executive Office Building looks like. He had to work from pictures."

Finnerty goes to great lengths to save a buck. He spends Bruce Paltrow's money like it was his own. He even sends Kevin Richards, a production assistant and amateur photographer, to Washington to snap pictures of the White House, which Finnerty has blown up, retouched, and repainted to serve as a backdrop, to be seen through the windows of the main *E.O.B.* set. If he had the job done professionally, using stock footage, it would have cost another several thousand dollars, which more than makes up for the fact that Richards was stopped by suspicious Secret Service agents, and nearly arrested (and wrestled to the dirt?), after skulking around the White House grounds in search of the best possible shot.

The big money saver in the early going is the decision to shoot *E.O.B.* at the CBS studios on West 57th Street, on videotape. The decision makes sense, for reasons of proximity and cross-pollination, although it is met with some considered resistance. The studios are, in many ways, inadequate to the Paltrow Group's task. (Available studio space is small, and cramped, restricting the size of the *E.O.B.* set.) The plan had been to use the soundstage at Pier 62, and to shoot the show on film, until the network agreed to kick in its facilities and support personnel at a fraction of the anticipated cost. For Finnerty, the savings are too great to pass up. The difference in the price of film and video technology is substantial (perhaps 20–30 percent, by Finnerty's estimate), although the producers fear the trade-off will cost them more than the savings. The "look" of a videotaped show can sometimes seem harsher and less polished than film, and can leave the harvest of these efforts looking more like a television sitcom than the producers care to allow. Appearance counts for something in most places; in Hollywood, it counts for everything. Indeed, the by-product of these toilings can smell like a television sitcom, sound like a television sitcom, move like a television sitcom, taste like a television sitcom—it can, in fact, actually *be* a television sitcom!— but as long as it does not particularly look like one, then perhaps no one will recognize it for what it is. *E.O.B.*, for better or worse, will look like a sitcom.

The West 57th facilities, once home to some of the most glorious productions from television's glorious past, have in recent years been used chiefly for soap operas, network and local news operations, talk shows, and in-studio sports programming. The heart of the television business has beaten a path west, leaving the New York studios with the requisite dregs of network production. *NFL Today* is produced here, and *60 Minutes,* and *The CBS Evening News with Dan Rather*—money-makers all, but nothing like the glamorous, celebrity-driven productions that preceded them. There hasn't been a dramatic series produced at the network's New York studios since *Ball Four* (CBS, 1976), based on the best-selling baseball book by Jim Bouton, who also starred in this short-lived sitcom, and the somewhat-longer-lived *On Our Own* (CBS, 1977), which featured Bess Armstrong and Lynnie Greene as roommates trying to make their way in the New York advertising community.

The situation at West 57th has mirrored the decline in New York-based production throughout the television industry. There are many reasons for this. Studio space and personnel are more plentiful and affordable in Los Angeles; established television actors, writers, producers, and directors are in greater supply there, too, and in greater demand. The state of the art has also moved there. Anything confined to the East Coast by time-zone considerations (such as news and sports programming) or personnel considerations is shot in New York; almost everything else is shot in Los Angeles.

The first and biggest creative decision is the hiring of John Whitesell II to direct the pilot episode. Whitesell, a recent refugee from the world of daytime soap opera, is a bear of a man with a baby face. His silhouette is the most menacing thing about him. Even his prime-time credits (which to date consist of a number of one-shot directing credits for various hour-long dramatic series) are not yet intimidating. One of the reasons he is hired is because he costs less than some of the name-brand sitcom directors who are often recruited to help launch a new series, at directing fees upwards of one hundred thousand dollars, plus back-end participation. (For comparison, Directors' Guild scale, for a prime-time, network half hour, is $12,319, with a recommended percentage markup for pilots.) Contributing factors are his long-standing friendship with Tom Fontana, his soap-rooted experience in dealing with the peculiarities of New York technical and production crews and facilities, and a background in the theater. He was also available on fairly short notice.

"Careerwise," Whitesell says, "directing pilots is a good thing for me at this stage, particularly in episodic." Whitesell, who has flitted about from one established series to another since forsaking the soaps of New York for the prime time of Los Angeles, is the kind of guy who likes to invent adjectives by appending "-wise" to his uncommon nouns; he also likes to put imagined quotation marks around his inventions with two staccato-curled fingers from each hand, and his meaty paws lend emphasis to the gesture.

"In a half-hour," he continues, "the director always has a lot more to say, anyway. In episodic, the frustrating thing is that you are a director for hire, you tend to just be there for that episode. The pilot in episodic sets the tone, the feel, so that's a big deal. At this point, for me, I don't really want to be doing, say, episode forty-seven of a *Hill Street Blues*, or whatever. As a director, are you really that important? No. All those guys who did the first season, those are the guys who set the show. After that, you come in and it's pretty much all laid out for you. Not that it's boring, but it's less challenging. That's why, this past year, I tried only to do series in the first thirteen, because I felt I'd have much more to say. Directingwise, I'd rather do the second or the seventh episode of *Capital News* than a *Murder, She Wrote* or a *Matlock*."

With Whitesell in place and construction of the *E.O.B.* set proceeding at West 57th Street under Finnerty's tight purse, someone finally thinks to hire the actors. To a viewing audience, the actors would seem the most essential piece of this emerging puzzle, but to the producers, and to the network, they are evidently seen as extremely well paid and sometimes temperamental props. They are not quite afterthoughts, but they are close.

Pity the actors. This is what they have to go through if they want to land a television pilot: They have to sit in a room with a half-dozen other actors with whom they bear an uncanny demographic resemblance, fidgeting and going over what are usually the very same lines from the very same pages of the very same scripts, which are now telescoped and stuffed underneath their denimed thighs, which are now bouncing fitfully to a nervous rhythm that—soundlessly, magically—permeates the entire waiting area. Everyone moves to the same jittery beat, waiting to be called.

Called, they take their turns in the next room, handing over black-and-white glossies and résumés as if they were passports and entering into a few minutes of big-eyed small talk with a group of pleasant-seeming people empowered with their immediate futures, as if what was about to pass between the actors and the pleasants is the most natural thing in the world. Clearly, it is not a natural thing at all. Rather, it is like Michael Landon in *I Was a Teenage Werewolf* (or, in a parallel universe, Michael J. Fox in *Teen Wolf*) metamorphosing before an audience as affably as the strange circumstances allow. Hundreds of actors slip into character in just this way in the two weeks before the *E.O.B.* pilot is to begin production. They do this in Los Angeles, Chicago, and New York. Sometimes they do it more than once, in more than one place. In a few cases, they do it in front of a camera, for the record. During this time, Bruce Paltrow can look up from his desk to John Tinker, with whom he has been reviewing sketches for one of the two *E.O.B.* sets, and say, "Feel like a little casting?" as if these half-dozen groupings of would-be cast members were at the ever-ready, like six-packs of a favorite beverage, waiting to be imbibed. On a literal whim, a new batch of actors appears in the Paltrow Group offices to audition. Of course, some of the actors who will wind up in the *E.O.B.* cast are put through a different set of motions. For example, John Dye. This Tupelo, Mississippi-born actor—a tee-veed version of James Spader, with a user-friendly snarl that seems borrowed from Tupelo's other famous native, Elvis Presley—is currently appearing on the CBS Vietnam drama *Tour of Duty.* The network is high on him. So high that Bruce Paltrow is encouraged to audition the actor personally on a day trip through Los Angeles. John Dye, hard to get, begs off due to flu and instead does a screen test the following day. A tape of his screen test is flown to New York on Tuesday, March 28. Dye follows on the Red Eye, grabs a few hours sleep in his room at the Intercontinental Hotel on East 48th Street, and taxis to Pier 62 at one o'clock on Wednesday afternoon to read for the role of Jim Smith. Waiting for him are Paltrow, Tinker, and Fontana, natch, as well as a half-dozen suits from CBS and Columbia, including Lisa Freiberger, CBS vice president of talent and casting, and Christopher Gorman, senior director of talent and casting for the network, who had flown in from Los Angeles for the reading. Conspicuously present, also, is Jeff Sagansky, president of CBS Entertainment.

"I was freaked out there were so many people there for this," Dye recalls. "I couldn't believe Sagansky was there. It just freaked me out."

After the reading, Paltrow pulls Dye from the wowed room and into his office and says, "I'd really like you to do this. We'd all really like you to do this."

Paltrow's enthusiasm is normally communicable, but Dye seems immune. "I don't know," the actor stammers. "I have to be really honest with you. I just don't know." One of the reasons he doesn't know is because he is up for a movie, and another pilot, and leery about accepting one opportunity at the expense of another. "I really feel I have to think about it," he dodges.

In his head, Paltrow must be thinking, What schmuck would turn this down?

In his head, Dye must be thinking, New York? Why the hell would I want to live in New York? I just bought a house in Los Angeles. I can't just pick up and leave town. Maybe, if it was just a pilot, but it's not just a pilot. They want me to sign on for five years. That's a long time, five years. Plus, it's snowing in New York. It's not snowing in Los Angeles. I just left gorgeous weather in Los Angeles.

"I prayed about it a lot," Dye says later, "and I think I made the right decision."

His decision, eventually, is to enlist with the Paltrow Group, but not before his agent capitalizes on Dye's initial indecision and stiff-arms the producers into a higher fee. The other actors will be made to sign "favored nation" contracts—earning them each ten thousand dollars for the pilot and seventy-five hundred dollars for each of five summer episodes to follow—but Dye manages somewhat more. How much more, neither he, his agent (Bob Gersh), nor the producers are willing to reveal. Dye suggests he is earning twice as much as the others and worries that his high-ticket status, if known, will alienate him from the rest of the cast. Nevertheless, he makes this known. Also, he worries that the *Tour of Duty* producers, to whom he is still contractually committed, might regard his appearance as a regular on another CBS show as a violation of their exclusivity clause. On the advice of his agent, and CBS, he does not tell them about it, even though his hiring has been noted in the trade press. It is as though he made a bargain with the devil and plastered the terms of the deal on a billboard.

The rest of the cast falls into place at the same last minute. Most notable among this group is Mary Beth Hurt, the highly regarded stage and movie actress, who signs on for the role of Sara Scadutto. Hurt, a regular on the short-lived *Tattingers'* series and the spun-off *Nick and Hillary,* was eager to work with the Paltrow Group again, but she did not exactly pursue the role, just as the producers were not exactly beating down her door. For her part, Hurt didn't even know about the role. In fact, she stopped at Pier 62 to pick up some *Tattingers'* tapes to take with her out to Los Angeles, and no one even mentioned *E.O.B.* to her. "I had no idea they were doing a series, or looking for people, or anything," she says. "And they were deeply hunting for someone at the time. So I went to California and came back, and the Sunday before rehearsals were to begin, they called and said, 'Would you do this?' My first thought was 'Sure, yeah, I'll do anything for you guys,' and then I realized, of course, they could have asked me a long time ago and that in fact I probably wasn't their first choice. Of course I wasn't. Look at how Sara is described in the script. She's supposed to be Italian-American. She's got all these soft edges to her. She's not like me at all."

"In a way, Mary Beth is a compromise choice for us," Fontana explains, "at least for this role. Actually, compromise isn't the right word, but she clearly doesn't fit into our vision of what either of the two women's roles should be, the other being Marsha Katzenberg. But she's such a wonderful actress that we just had to have her in the cast. She can do anything."

Indeed, Hurt's presence in the cast sends a signal to the television community that the Paltrow Group will court New York–based stage actors for *E.O.B.* rather than the familiar faces from pilots past, but it also raises a question: Why would such a formidable stage and movie actress consign herself to the small screen for an indefinite period? "It's not practical for me to think about doing regional theater now," Hurt allows in one of the CBS costuming rooms at West 57th, where she is being fitted for a special maternity pillow designed to make her character look substantially pregnant. "I've got one child in kindergarten and one who's twenty months, so I can't go to Honduras to do a film, or Lebanon, or wherever. I suppose I could, but I don't want to. This is the best job for me at the moment. It will keep me working regular hours, and it will keep me in the city. It's a good mommy job."

Also cast is comedian Rich Hall, late of *Saturday Night Live* and HBO's *Not Necessarily the News*, to play Hammond Egley. Hall also has a history with the Paltrow Group, although it is far more limited than Hurt's. Actually, to call it a history is overstating things. He auditioned for the Paltrow Group the previous year, for a *Tattingers'* role that ultimately went to actorslashcomedianslashBobandRay'skid Chris Elliott. At the time, Hall was very admiring of the producers and their work, and he remembers that he was treated fairly, even though he didn't get the part. This time around, the producers are anxious to see him again. "He just makes me laugh," Bruce Paltrow says of the stand-up comedian with the face of Howdy Doody. "He walks out and he makes me laugh." Indeed, during his audition, Hall reads one line and Paltrow laughs. That is just about all he is asked to do. Really, Hall is in for less than two minutes, and then he is through. As he makes to leave, Paltrow gestures to Tinker and Fontana and then says to Hall, "If you don't get the part, it's because of these two guys."

Hall finds out he got the job through a sequence of messages left on his answering machine, by his agent: Rich, call me, they want you to go in and talk to the Paltrow people again, sometime tomorrow; Rich, call me, they want to set up a screen test; Rich, call me, the screen test is set for ten A.M.; Rich, call me, forget the screen test, they want you to play the part.

Hall is a little bit intimidated by the company he will now keep. "I'm just so awed by these people," he admits. "I mean, Mary Beth Hurt, come on. And even some of the others. These are actors. I've never thought of myself as an actor. I've never taken any acting classes, and it shows. You can tell. I don't know what I'm doing. I want to know what I'm doing, and I think I will, but right now I don't. *Saturday Night Live* wasn't acting. But we learned our lines, and it was kind of like acting, so I think I'll be okay."

Jennifer Van Dyck, a Princeton-born, New York–based stage actress going through a dry spell, is tapped to play Marsha Katzenberg, the vaguely handicapped speechwriter. This is what her week is like when she goes up for the part. First she auditions for a *Turner & Hooch* pilot (spun from the Tom Hanks movie) in New York, then she flies out to L.A. for four days, to audition again, and to screen test. Then she flies back to New York with her agent, and she limos with him back to Manhattan. On the way, her agent is on the car phone to L.A., and Van Dyck is thinking, Okay, like, what life is this, anyway? L.A. says she didn't get the *Turner & Hooch* part, which isn't such a terrible thing because Van Dyck is also up for a play at the Hartford Stage and she has had to string them along to wait and see about the pilot, which she was ambivalent about, anyway, but then she gets to thinking, it's like she never even went to L.A. I mean, she's there four days, she comes back, she doesn't get the part. Why did she even bother to go? And then, the next day—the very next day!—she is auditioning for a voice-over on a Maxi-pads commercial (she does a lot of cosmetics, she tells) when she happens to check in with her agent. So glad you called, he says. Get down to Pier 62 in half an hour. There's something you might be right for. Of course, the character walks with an unexplained limp and uses a crutch or a brace, and Van Dyck does none of these things, but still, she might be right for it. She has not read the script, has not heard about it, nothing, but she races down to the pier, and there are all these other actors pacing the small waiting area in the Paltrow Group offices. Everyone has just gotten the same urgent phone call.

Before Van Dyck signs on, she is asked to accept a test deal. The other actors are asked to do this as well. A test deal, in television, is sort of like a guy asking a woman for a date after first exacting the promise of a romantic nightcap.

"Really, I was thrilled," Van Dyck says, looking back. "I don't know why I was thrilled, but I was. People keep asking me why I passed up the theater for a sitcom, and I can't give them an answer. I don't even watch television. I guess there is something to the visibility that's appealing. At this point in my career, people look at my résumé and say, 'Oh, theater background, Trinity Rep, Williamstown, that's great, that's nice,' but they haven't seen me in anything. So now they can see me in something. Television gives people a handle, although I'm not sure it's the kind of handle I want. I just don't know."

Geoffrey Nauffts, a young actor from Ohio who as a kid ate his dinners and did his homework in front of the television and who is currently appearing in the acclaimed Broadway show *A Few Good Men*, is recruited for the part of Steve Lawson. There is some tricky maneuvering afoot to free him, momentarily, from his theater schedule. There are two matinees Wednesday and one Saturday that will interfere with rehearsals, as well as a Thursday evening performance that will bump into the two scheduled *E.O.B.* tapings. At this early stage, no one is too worried about the potential conflict, except, of course, Nauffts, who is being tugged in opposite directions and spread thin. Also tricky is the sequence of events set in motion by his hiring. When Nauffts accepts the part, he withdraws himself from consideration for the lead in another CBS summer series—a quirky, hour-long, fish-out-of-water comedy-drama about a New York City doctor forced to practice medicine in a remote Alaskan town— created by the other half of the *St. Elsewhere* creative team, Joshua Brand and John Falsey. ("There are more creators/writers of *St. Elsewhere* floating around these days than people who came over on the Mayflower," *Newsday* television critic Marvin Kitman soon observes of the busy production schedules of the former colleagues. "Creators/writers of *St. Elsewhere*, along with writers for *Cosby* and *M*A*S*H*, are the three leading cash crops in Southern California. . . .") The fish-out-of-water part ultimately goes to Nauffts's friend and colleague Rob Morrow, a fellow member of the Naked Angels theater company in New York; the show, *Northern Exposure*, ultimately survives its six-episode summer run and returns to the regular network schedule as a midseason replacement series, where it has consistently ranked among the Top Twenty; Morrow, its now-celebrated star, ultimately alights as the guest host of *Saturday Night Live* and on the cover of national magazines.

But Nauffts cannot see this far into the future. All he can see is that he has been offered a pilot, with the promise of five additional summer episodes, created by some of the most highly regarded writers and producers in series television. "I tend to be a little pessimistic about these things," he says over coffee at a West 57th Street restaurant called Armstrong's, a CBS hangout. He chooses his words carefully as he talks, his angular face domed by his regulation crew cut necessitated by his role in the Broadway military drama. "It takes a lot of pilots to make a series," he continues, "and it takes a lot of series to make a hit show. Sure, there's a potential here, but I don't count on it at all.

"I wouldn't mind it. I could commit to it. At least I think I could. I don't know about five years, but I could do this for a while. I hope that it goes for a summer, or even for the next year, or even for a couple years. I could commit to the financial stability, and the experience, and the visibility, all of it. But I don't expect any of these things. I hate to sound jaded, but the only way I can protect myself as an actor against that disappointment, the only way I can harden my shell, is to just do my job and not obsess about the other stuff. Either it will come, or it won't."

One of the biggest disappointments of the casting process is that William Daniels, who had been penciled in for the part of B. Laurence Taylor, has committed to another television pilot—Fox's *Life and Desire*—and is therefore unavailable for this one. The related, and smaller, disappointment is that the producers are unable to find an acceptable replacement. Jason Robards? Fred Gwynne? Jerry Stiller? Barnard Hughes? In their heads, Paltrow and company have become so conditioned to Daniels's rhythms and mannerisms that every actor they see for the role seems wrong, forced, strained.

The role of Connie Gibson, the lifetime civil servant who manages the speechwriters' office, also remains uncast, for some of the same reasons. No one has hit it just right. Peggy Cass did not test well, according to the network. Nancy Marchand? Rita Moreno? The producers see this as a crucial role and are careful not to offer it to the wrong actress. In their care, they do not offer it to anyone; at least they do not offer it to anyone who is available to them. Instead, they sit and wait for the right actress to emerge from the pack. When she does not, they sit and wait some more. To keep busy and to answer some concerns that surfaced in a standard research check of real-life civil servant Connie Gibsons, or their equivalents, they change the character's name to Bonnie Doone. Perhaps this will also appease the casting gods who have authority over these right-place-at-the-right-time matters. Perhaps not.

Preproduction is capped by a final production meeting, which is held on Wednesday, April 4, the first day of rehearsals, and which is attended by Paltrow, Fontana, Tinker, Whitesell, and twenty-one others, including the set decorator, costume designer, associate director, stage manager, and production supervisor. The meeting takes place in Rehearsal Hall #3, at West 57th, but not before the non-CBS employees are first cleared by security and allowed to enter the building. This is accomplished without dispatch in a small security command post on the ground floor, where the producers and actors—together, as a group, for the first time—are made to wait nearly twenty minutes for their temporary photo ID cards to be processed. Waiting, the group expands to include two Columbia executives, Deborah Curtan and Fran McConnell, and *Married...With Children* producer Arthur Silver, who has been brought in by the studio to "punch up" some of the jokes in the script.

Here, in these close quarters, pleasantries and introductions ricochet off the walls like misfires. Rich Hall tells Mary Beth Hurt he is an admirer of her work and eager to learn from her. Jennifer Van Dyck and Geoffrey Nauffts discover they have some acting friends in common. John Dye tells Deborah Curtan about the thirty-six-dollar hamburger and fries he ordered up from room service the night before.

When his still-warm ID is finally handed to him, Paltrow studies it and frowns. One of the security staff, noticing the producer's objection, offers to take the picture over again. "No." Paltrow laughs. "This is fine. If you took it again it might turn out better."

Before the production meeting, the temporarily ID'd Paltrow, Fontana, and Tinker are sidetracked by director Whitesell, production designer Tom John, and several of the CBS technicians for a quick tour of the *E.O.B.* set, which is still undergoing construction and last-minute tinkering in the network workshop. The set has been built almost entirely in this workshop, designed by Tom John and built under the auspices of CBS set designer Victor Paganuzzi, a man who has provided the backdrops for the likes of Jackie Gleason, Judy Garland, and Walter Cronkite in his nearly thirty years with the network. The fireplace is being made here (from plaster of paris), as are the artificial-wood trim and columns (from plastic molds), and the doors, windows, and bookcases. A separate electrical shop handles the lighting. Plumbing, which is not necessary to this script but might come into play in future episodes, is considered a special effect, which is how it is also considered in some New York City apartment buildings.

Fontana and Tinker are seeing the sets for the first time, and even though they are still clearly unfinished, they are clearly tickled at what their imaginations have wrought. They hug and shake each other in a locker-room sort of way: Holy shit! holy shit! this is it! yeah!

The objects of their enthusiasms are the show's main set (the "War Room," named for the actual War Room—once the office of the secretary of war—at the actual Executive Office Building), which is where the speechwriters will do their speechwriting, and the "Collidge Room," which will serve as the stately office of the stately chief of Communications, B. Laurence Taylor.

The sets are not yet furnished, or "dressed," but CBS set decorator Ron Kelson walks his visitors through the work-in-progress. "The War Room is an architecturally elegant room," he tour-guides, "but because it's Washington, and because it's Washington bureaucracy, the furnishings belie the architecture. It's kind of furnished with whatever everyone can find, so you have these wonderful, grand columns, and this impressive space, decorated with these old institutional desks, these green linoleum-top battleship desks, and a hodgepodge of chairs. Old file cabinets. The Coolidge Room, however, will be furnished in a more stately style."

"Warmer," Paltrow announces suddenly, inspecting the color of the walls and the trim. "I need this warmer." As he moves from the War Room to the Coolidge Room, he says it again: "We've got to warm this up a little bit."

After the tour, the producers ride the elevator to the second floor. There, facing the elevators, they are greeted by a collage of smiling promotional photos, gridded onto the wall in a happy publicity puzzle. Connie Chung, smiling. The *60 Minutes* cast, smiling. Charles Kuralt, smiling. Joan Rivers, smiling. The local WCBS-TV news team, smiling. Dan Rather, trying to smile. The cast of *As the World Turns*, smiling. And, in the bottom right corner, the nearly obscured mug of Brent Musberger, struggling to be seen underneath a fresh coat of black paint. Behind the blackout, perhaps even he is smiling, too, although it is hard to tell, and harder still to imagine he has any reason to. Musberger was fired just this week, with great shock and fanfare, from his long-term gig as host of *The NFL Today* and as a CBS sports commentator, and already someone has thought to erase even this small reminder of his recent prominence.

"They can't get a new picture up there till next week," explains the security guy assigned to patrol the second-floor corridor by the elevators, "so they just spray-painted him."

In Rehearsal Hall #3, a long, narrow room, with a floor-to-ceiling mirror along the length of one wall, there is a makeshift conference table, which seems to be made of put-together bridge tables and some plywood. Along the unmirrored wall, there is a spread of coffee and juice and bagels and danish. No one is eating, or drinking. John Whitesell, at the head of the table, is paging through the script, stopping every here and there when a line calls for a certain prop or a specific piece of staging or set design.

A scripted joke about beepers, for example, is nearly more trouble than it's worth. (Speechwriter Marsha Katzenberg, offering advice to her new, somewhat overwhelmed colleague Jim Smith: "If you want to have a personal life, don't sleep with your beeper.") Whitesell suggests that if there is to be a joke about beepers, he needs to establish that the speechwriters do indeed wear them. "We should really show them with them on," he insists, "maybe have them go off a few times or something." Stage manager Chuck Raymond, whose job it is to procure these special-business props, makes a note of this. Later, he also makes a note that a doggie bag, which is to serve as a small visual punchline in a bit following a formal White House dinner, should be emblazoned with the official presidential seal.

Most of Whitesell's concerns are set related. On the main War Room set, for instance, he is unhappy with the way the shutters rest around the windows. "We have to make sure they close flush," he presses. "Tight, solid. This is supposedly a security-tight room. The windows have got to seem substantial."

Set designer Paganuzzi makes a note of this.

"Have you found a desk yet for Taylor?" Whitesell asks set decorator Kelson.

"Yes, we have," Kelson is happy to report. "It's a good-size desk. A very aggressive desk."

"What about the colors?" Paltrow interjects, starting in again where he left off in the workshop.

"What about them?" Kelson tries.

"I don't mean to address this to you specifically," Paltrow says, "but just in general. For the walls, you know. The colors. I think we're talking about warmer colors. The pinks, the peaches, as an undertone of the white. I just think everyone will look better with warmer colors, that's all. Other than that, I leave it to you. I don't care."

Warmer colors, it is generally agreed, will be a good thing.

At the beginning of Act 2, there is a scene in which Jim Smith sweats out the response to his first speech, and is summoned to B. Laurence Taylor's office in the Coolidge Room for his dressing down. "You'll be happy to know," Taylor tells his new charge, "the reaction was unanimous." Next, Taylor retrieves a file folder from his desk and tips it open to reveal a tumble of confetti.

"The president shredded my speech?" Smith asks, incredulous.

"He didn't even see the stupid thing," Taylor replies. "What do you think, you write it and, bang, he says it? Your pen to the president's mouth?"

According to Whitesell, the exchange presents a problem, gag-wise. "Should the paper be shredded, or should we go with confetti?" he wonders. He puts this on the put-together bridge tables for general debate.

"It has a tendency to fall funny if it's shredded," Chuck Raymond offers. "It kinda clumps up and falls like a rock."

"So, confetti, then," Whitesell decrees.

"I don't know," Paltrow says. "I was kinda thinking shredding is funnier if we can make it work. You don't confetti a speech, you shred a speech."

"It's gotta look right, though," Tom Fontana says. "It's gotta just float to the ground."

"Tell you what," Whitesell concludes in the interest of haste. "Let's have both." To Chuck Raymond, he says, "Make us up some confetti and make us up some shredded stuff, and then we can go either way." Raymond makes a note of this, too.

Over the next several minutes, it is determined that someone will "dress" Taylor's briefcase (stage-manager lingo for putting stuff inside it), that a small fern will be placed by an open office window, and that an office bar will be stocked with top-shelf liquors and glassware. "No paper cups," Fontana confirms.

"Are there any other questions?" Whitesell asks in closing.

"Yeah," Paltrow says. "Are we gonna get renewed?"

Seven

REHEARSALS _____

☐   Lunch is a big deal around these parts, at least according to production supervisor Donna Isman, a bundle of such nervous energy she might even be combustible. Isman, early thirty something, with the frizzed dirty-blond locks of a misplaced flower child, is charged with everything that might otherwise fall through the cracks and some things that will despite her best efforts. If there is to be an *E.O.B.* production meeting, as there has been this morning, it is up to her to arrange for the put-together bridge tables and the chairs, as well as for the fresh scripts and freshly sharpened pencils for each attendee. She also orders the shrink-wrapped bagels and danish, makes sure the actors are assigned appropriate dressing rooms, coordinates the payroll account, arranges for stock footage of the show's Washington exteriors, designs and purchases "Camp E.O.B." T-shirts for the cast and crew, recruits the two stand-up comedians who will warm up the studio audiences during the two *E.O.B.* tapings on Thursday, April 12, and scouts and hires the audio facility for the postproduction process known as "sweetening" (Master Sound, of Long Island City). She knows where everything is, where everyone is supposed to be, and how much everything costs. In theory, anyway.

This lunch thing, though, has pretty much got the better of her. She has ordered enough food for thirty people, from the CBS in-house caterer (pasta, salad, deli meats and cheeses, and enough fruit

to encourage a Carmen Miranda convention), and when the production meeting breaks and the ensuing table reading of the script is
completed, Isman does a not-so-subtle full-body shrug as the rehearsal hall empties. She makes like a spurned hostess, losing her guests,
and she seems to take the defection personally. "There's lunch, guys,"
she says as the actors, producers, and technicians make to leave.
"Lunch. A lot of it."

No one seems to hear her, and all but a handful leave the building
for coffee shops unknown.

Worse, the food arrives accompanied by a sidecar of plastic plates
and flatware and Styrofoam cups. "Biodegradable!" a piqued Isman
shouts to the caterer as he and his staff unwrap the platters and the
plastic. "I asked for biodegradable. We talked about paper goods. I
was very specific about this."

The caterer explains, calmly, how the disposable cups that are often
passed off in advertisements, or on their packaging, as biodegradable
are in fact more toxic than Styrofoam, what with the lettering on
them and everything. "It's the difference of, like, disintegrating into
the earth in one hundred years or two hundred years," the caterer
explains, as if he is making sense. "That's how bad it is."

"Okay," Isman considers, "but, like, if somebody knows biodegradable, if somebody really knows this stuff, will he know the
difference?"

"No," the caterer assures, "he'll be happy with it."

The somebody Isman is concerned about is Bruce Paltrow, who has
left to make a few calls but who will be back for lunch. His care for
the environment is well known among those who work with them.
Indeed, the Paltrow Group support staff and Isman refer to their
boss's environmental sensitivity as his Blythe Danner cause, presumably because he inherited it from his wife.

Wherever it originates, the environmentally correct cause has built
in Isman's mind to where she is absolutely frantic about the
Styrofoam cups, but her frenzy seems fueled by more than her shared
consideration for the earth's safekeeping. She is worried about pissing
off her boss. And, by extension, she is worried about her job. Of
course, Paltrow does not appear to be the kind of boss who would lose
his grip over such as this—he does not even seem the kind of person
who would turn such convictions to extremes—but Isman will not
rest until lunch is served. When it is, she watches from the corner of

the rehearsal hall, once removed through the room-length mirror, as Paltrow sips from his Styrofoam cup without comment. The production supervisor manages a small smile and returns to her busy day.

After lunch, Paltrow, Fontana, and Tinker head back to the pier to "do a little casting," as they call it. They still have two roles to fill for *E.O.B.*, and they also have to look at actors for *High* and *Modern Marriage*. (The back-to-back-to-back shooting schedules of these three pilots will be dominoed by the *E.O.B.* shoot; delays in one schedule will necessarily impact on the others.) The displaced left-coast Columbia team retreats to their hotel rooms (or, in the case of senior vice president of current programs Deborah Curtan, to the merchants of Fifth Avenue, to "do a little shopping," as she calls it). The technicians have the War Room and Coolidge Room sets to finish, and furnish, and they disappear to the workshop and studio. Geoffrey Nauffts has a matinee to do, downtown. Donna Isman has a production schedule to put together (and some leftovers to rescue for tomorrow's lunch).

Director Whitesell is left behind in Rehearsal Hall #3 with four of his seven actors, with whom he commences his first rehearsal. It seems a doomed enterprise. After all, how do you rehearse an ensemble piece without a full ensemble? But time is money, and money is scarce, so Whitesell proceeds fitfully. On a tight schedule, even a doomed rehearsal is better than no rehearsal at all. Joining the director is his production assistant, John Feld, and his associate director, Joanne Sedwick, two familiar hands from the New York soap opera community. Story editor Julie Martin, who has written one of five additional *E.O.B.* scripts that have been stockpiled for the anticipated summer run, stays behind as the eyes and ears of the Paltrow Group and to answer any questions that might arise about the script or the characters.

"One of the things I'd like you all to think about, you know, right up front, is where you think your desks should be," Whitesell instructs the actors. "You know, character wise. And make a list of things you'll want to have on your character's desk, 'cause a lot of this is who you guys are, as people, as characters." As he talks, Whitesell looks down at the table, at his hands, which are fidgeting with the tubed end of a red wrapper from a stick of Clove chewing gum.

Before Whitesell has his half cast read through the script a second time, he tries to lead them in what he hopes will be an exploration, a discovery. He seems to fumble through this process, like it's required of him, like he would rather be doing something else. What are these characters about? he wants to know. Where do they come from? What is their "story"? (The quotations are Whitesell's, supplied by the two curled fingers on either side of his head.) "What about Jim Smith?" he pushes on. "How do you see him?" He does not direct this query specifically to actor John Dye, who will be inhabiting the role, or to anyone else in particular; he simply tosses it out for general reflection. When he gets none back, he offers his own: "I see him as naive," he tries, "but naive in a good sense. He's like a Midwest J. C. Penney's, know what I mean?"

"Yeah, yeah," John Dye kicks in with gusto. He is willing himself to get the point. "Absolutely. He's hopelessly out of it, but there's something there, you know. There's something to him."

Whitesell, sensing he is on a roll with this discovery thing, bulldozes on. "Sara," he says, thumbing through his script for clues. "Okay, she's this earth-mother type, with four kids. What else do we know about her?"

"What do you mean by 'earth mother?'" Mary Beth Hurt asks, with proprietary interest.

"I don't know," Whitesell admits. "That's just what's in the script."

"Well, I need to know," Hurt persists. Her tone is firm, professional; she is clearly passionate about her work and expects her passion to be shared by her colleagues. It is not, yet, but it will prove infectious. "It's like a throwaway line," she says, "to me. When you say 'earth mother,' I can't connect that phrase with what's written in the script. You know, it talks about how committed she is to what she feels and what she believes in, but she also wants everybody to get along. That's a contradiction." She gathers momentum, continues: "I'm reading this character, and first I knew who she was, and then I thought, Wait a minute, I don't know who she is, and then she turned a corner and I knew who she was, and then she turned another corner and I just lost it."

Hurt is searching here, trying to find something to work with; the others in the group are content to go with what they've got, at least at this point, or to follow Whitesell's lead, but she is trying to invent something real, something tangible. Slowly, the other actors appear quietly galvanized by Hurt's resolve (if such a thing is possible); they look to her for the impulse to question the authority of the script and its creators. It is not clear, from the expression on Whitesell's face, whether or not this is a good thing.

"One thing that would be real helpful to know is how my character became a speechwriter?" Hurt poses. "What was she doing before? Is she a political person, or did she just kinda fall into this?"

She looks to Whitesell for answers, but he rolls his shoulders as if he doesn't have any, so Hurt turns to story editor Julie Martin, who helped to develop these characters with Paltrow, Fontana, and Tinker. (Hurt is not aware that Martin has written one of the future scripts, none of which have been made available to the cast.)

"I don't have any more information on that, Mary Beth," Martin says. "I could find out, I suppose, if you feel it's important."

"And how many children am I supposed to have?" Hurt continues. "In the script it says four, and I'm pregnant with a fifth, but then it's not consistent."

"I can check on that, too," Martin offers.

Similarly, Jennifer Van Dyck is troubled by her character's un-defined disability. She wants something to work with here, some-thing concrete. "It's not polio, is it?" she wonders. "Car accident? Cerebral palsy?"

"It could be polio," Martin figures. "It could be. I don't know, maybe one leg's shorter than the other. but she can walk. She can definitely walk. She uses a crutch, or crutches, we'll have to see, but she can walk. Maybe it's polio." That's all she knows. She could find out more, she supposes, if Van Dyck feels its important.

"I thought it was a brace," Van Dyck says. "They told me I had to wear a brace."

"Did they?" Martin says. "I didn't know that. I thought it was crutches."

"No," Van Dyck insists, "they're fitting me for a brace."

"Oh."

That unresolved, Whitesell turns to comedian Rich Hall. "Every-thing's a jingle to your guy," he announces, meaning to the character of Hammond Egley, the former advertising copywriter. "Everything's about how you say it, not about what you say."

"Okay," Hall says, trying to understand. (He really seems to be.)

"Okay," Whitesell says, "good."

"Like 'A thousand points light,'" Hall tries, catching on. He smiles at the shtick as it pops into his head. "Hammond probably wishes he wrote that. He probably takes credit for it, you know, when he's out trying to pick up women or something." Hall switches his voice and mannerisms to Hammond's, which seem remarkably like his own, and, in character, deadpan, says, "'A thousand points of light.' I wrote that. 'Read my lips.' I wrote that."

Mary Beth Hurt: "I'm having a hard time finding the balance between, you know, that normal interoffice sniping and being an earth mother, for want of a better word. There's no balance there. It just seems to leave me with no energy, know what I mean? I don't want her to have no energy. Nurturing, conciliatory, you know, that's fine, but I don't want to have no energy."

"Err on funny," Whitesell says, presumably in response. "If there's a choice between funny and not funny, we're gonna go funny, you better believe that."

The routine for these next few days of rehearsals is laid out in a schedule, on pink paper, which the actors now have in hand. Mornings at ten, the cast will sit around this table in Rehearsal Hall #3—along with Whitesell and his directing team and the producers—for a read-through of the current script. Each morning, the new script will reflect changes made by Paltrow, Fontana, and Tinker the night before, based on the previous day's rehearsals. The rehearsals, and a run-through at the end of each day (where the cast is put through the motions of each scene, before an audience that will on some days include Columbia and CBS executives), will be the writer-producers' best indication of how their script is working, or not working. As a direct result of these run-throughs, changes will be made to accommodate the strengths and weaknesses of the actors (Rich Hall, for example, reveals a tendency to mumble when he is given too much to say, so his lines will be trimmed to where they are short and to the point), the timing of the material (the script runs about five to seven minutes too long at this early stage, so some scenes must be cut), the emerging dynamic of the characters (the dialogue of Marsha Katzenberg and Sara Scadutto, it becomes clear, appears interchangeable, and so lines and deliveries are altered to better distinguish between the two), and to ease certain bits of staging. (Exit- and entrance-appropriate lines are added and deleted to help the actors with their comings and goings.)

At just after two o'clock on this first day of rehearsals, Whitesell's voyage of discovery is interrupted by a snack, a very serious snack—

fruit, cheese, jelly beans, brownies, candy bars, soda, juice, and coffee, along with a necessary sampling of environmentally correct paper goods. Production supervisor Isman, who ordered this spread as well, apparently likes to put on the feed. There are only eight people in the room, and she has once again ordered up a banquet.

"Why don't we just read through the script one time more," Whitesell suggests, ambling over to the spread for a little something. The other actors have no choice but to grab apples, granola bars, and small bottles of Evian water as sustenance for the task ahead. Also in preparation, Whitesell turns to his production assistant, John Feld, and says, "We could use a bucket of pencils." He is, apparently, anticipating some significant and spontaneous note taking in these next moments. Feld retreats to the rehearsal hall phone and within three minutes—timed—a bunch of brand-new pencils arrive. They arrive bundled, not bucketed. Feld places them dutifully on the table, where they remain bundled for the rest of the afternoon. Whitesell, in another distraction (or, perhaps, in justification), slips one pencil loose and begins to play with it, but he does not use it to make any notes.

For this pass at the script, Whitesell himself reads the uncast parts of B. Laurence Taylor and Bonnie Doone, as well as the unrepresented part of Geoffrey Naufft's Steve Lawson, the office toady. Feld reads a brief voice-over speech by the fictional president. (The producers are negotiating with Walter Cronkite to play the recurring off-camera role.)

In this reading, as in the one this morning, the actors are not quite acting so much as they are, well, reading. They are learning their lines, getting familiar with the material, finding where the jokes are. This last does not seem as if it should be too difficult, but the actors are made to stop over a half-dozen lines, trying to see if there is a joke there. Even when they seem to stumble over one by accident, and laugh, they are not always sure.

For example: In the opening scene, it becomes known, in an antic sort of way, that the president of the United States, awaiting an appearance on live television, has been given the wrong speech. "He's standing in the Oval Office," an agitated Sara Scadutto opines, "about to congratulate the Dalai Lama on catching an eighteen-pound large-mouth bass. He's got the speech to the National Association of Fishermen."

Bonnie Doone, coolly: "These things happen."

Marsha Katzenberg, entering the War Room with an old bulletin, sharply: "The president's live in forty-five seconds and he has the wrong damn speech!"

Sara Scadutto, hopelessly: "We know."

Marsha Katzenberg, haughtily: "I ran over to make sure he could pronounce 'Himalayas,' and he gave me that look, you know, like Bambi staring helplessly into oncoming headlights. This is all your fault, Steve."

Steve Lawson, snivelingly: "No, uh-uh, I followed each draft through, from staff to bond to cards. Once it's on TelePrompTer, blame White House A.V."

Bonnie Doone, finally: "Those shitheads."

The "shitheads" line gets the only laugh in what is generally a funny scene, and Whitesell and his charges cannot quite figure it, or themselves. Of course, they are only laughing among their own small group, but they have to think their laughs are indicative of something. They laugh because they know the line will never make it onto network airwaves and also because it surprises them, in a sophomoric kind of way. This seems clear, but, still, Whitesell has them looking for the joke. "Okay," he declares, "we all agree that's funny, but why is it funny?"

The actors, eager to please but unable to answer, are made to play along with their director. It is like a silly Leonard Nimoy special: *In Search of . . . THE JOKE!*

Another example: At the end of Act 1, Scene C, Bonnie Doone approaches the newly arrived Jim Smith and hands him an official-seeming envelope. "Invitation," she says. "Ball. Tonight. East Room. Mrs. Sadat."

Sara Scadutto: "Everyone's dying to see her."

Marsha Katzenberg: "Word is she's in town for a breast enlargement."

Beat.

"I don't get it," Jennifer Van Dyck admits after she says her line. "Am I missing something? Somebody explain this to me. Does Mrs. Sadat have small breasts? Is that it?"

"Let's just go with it," Whitesell coaches, "see how it plays." This, the actors will soon learn, is their director's standard line of dismissal. Let's just leave it the way it is and see how it plays, he will say, when an actor seeks to rework a scripted line or adopt a certain piece of business or staging in some new way. He is sweet about it, Whitesell is, but it is a clear brush-off: nice idea, but it stays as written until the producers tell me otherwise.

John Dye cannot sit still during this read-through. He is all over the place, sitting on his haunches, on his seat back, or with legs kicked on the table. Once, he stands and turns his chair around and straddles it, saloon style. Then he stands and paces. He smokes, often, and he seems to do it as much to have something to do with his hands as for the nicotine. In one way, his motions suggest he is bored with this part of the process, can't be bothered, but in another he appears tense, uncertain about his place in this operation, among this group. He is, after all, a "television" actor, working a room where such a distinction is not way up there on anyone's résumé. He is, as the read-through progresses, the first among the cast to slip into what may or may not become his character, and it comes off smelling like he's trying too hard, showing off, compensating.

At the end of the read-through, Mary Beth Hurt checks in with an epiphany. "I should have lots of baby things around me," she says. "You know, my briefcase could be a diaper bag. Have you seen those diaper bags? The ones with the puffy letters on them? It could say 'diaper' or something. 'Baby.'"

"Yeah," Julie Martin enthuses, "that's great. As much textural stuff as possible."

"I could have all this stuff in my pocket," Hurt continues, "mommy stuff, like, you know, cereal, pacifiers, crayons, whatever. Toys. Maybe I reach in to pull out a handkerchief and it's a diaper, you know." She has been anxious to find something to hang her character on, and she seizes on this.

"Good," Whitesell says, "good. Anybody else?"

"Is this a homework assignment?" Rich Hall jokes.

"I think it will help us," Whitesell says defensively. "Just play with it a little, see what you come up with. Have some fun with it." (He is, the actors are quickly learning, the kind of director who also likes to say, "Have some fun with it.")

With this, the director dismisses the actors for the day. There is little point in working on any staging, he maintains, with only four of the seven cast members in place. Plus, he does not even have a stage yet. According to Isman's schedule, they will not be rehearsing on set until Monday, three days before taping. "With any luck," Whitesell says, gathering his things, "we'll have a Bonnie and a Taylor here by tomorrow morning."

As they break, the group is met by Julie Grossberg, assistant to Bruce Paltrow, and Bonnie Mark, assistant to Tom Fontana, who have cabbed uptown from the Paltrow Group offices to see how these now-stalled rehearsals are going and to check in on Donna Isman in the West 57th production office. They've brought along some papers for the actors to sign—W-4 forms, and such—and after they hand them out they wander over to the fruits and cheeses to examine the pickings.

There John Dye approaches Bonnie Mark with his completed paperwork and hands it to her, along with four or five personal letters and bills, unstamped, he would like her to mail for him. "Is that a problem?" he asks when he senses it is. "You know, on *Tour of Duty*, my other show, we have this one place where we can just leave our mail and it gets picked up. I'm still not sure how things work around here."

"No," Bonnie Mark says, taking the letters. "It's not a problem."

"If it is," Dye says, "just tell me. I could always find a couple stamps somewhere."

"It's not a problem."

But it is. Or, more accurately, it will be. Dye's request suggests to Bonnie Mark, and to the rehearsal hall eavesdroppers, a sense of entitlement, privilege. It is like a star turn, she thinks, an ego thing. Perhaps it is. Later, at Pier 62, she will mention the exchange to Fontana and Paltrow. Maybe it's nothing, she will say, but here it is. For now, though, she collects her papers, and Dye's personal mail, and stops in on Isman before returning to the pier. As she departs the CBS building with Grossberg, at about five o'clock, they pass an apparently homeless black man of undetermined middle age, leaning against the dark marble facade of the main 530 W. 57th Street entrance, huddled against the cold with two flattened cardboard boxes pressed close as blankets. The man wears a blue baseball cap with no message on it.

By the next morning—Thursday, April 5—the forward-thinking maintenance staff at West 57th has replaced the blacked-out Brent Musberger publicity square with the major league baseball insignia and the message "play ball," trumpeting CBS's high-ticket acquisition of the broadcast rights for the brand-new baseball season. Time, and outward appearances, march on.

The Paltrow Group, meanwhile, has been unable to fill the imagined shoes of Bonnie Doone and B. Laurence Taylor, and this news is met this morning with unhappy concern by the other actors. But the show must go on, even in rehearsal. The tapings are just a week away, and there is a mess of work to do. Of course, it will no longer do for Whitesell to continue reading the uncast parts himself, so for today's rehearsal, Tom Fontana has imported a friend from his workshop theater days, David Laundra, to play Taylor, and production assistant Hillary Danner, Paltrow's niece, has been recruited to play Bonnie.

"We're very tough negotiators," Paltrow says when he is asked why the producers are having so much trouble filling these remaining holes. "We're gonna make the deal that works for us." He gets a room-size laugh when he says this. Most of what he says gets a room-size laugh.

The script has been trimmed by about fifteen pages. Some of the expositional material has been dropped, some speeches shortened, and one or two scenes cut entirely, but the core of the script remains intact. The dialogue is cleaner, crisper; the jokes, funnier. Hillary Danner, reading the script for the first time, trips over Arthur Schlesinger's name as if she has never seen it before.

The biggest new laugh comes early on, in the second scene, where the writer-producers have come up with a lowly assignment to better illustrate Steve Lawson's lowly standing in this sitcom office. In earlier drafts, he has been asked to polish Taylor's car or to fetch his laundry. With today's revision, Bonnie Doone hands the poor fellow a plunger and directs him to the bathroom. "Steve," she says. "Ladies' room again. This time you may have to snake it."

The "shitheads" line survives last night's cut, and when it comes around in the read-through, Fontana and Tinker toss each other a shared smile, as if they are testing the limits of standards and practices. For them, it seems, the tweaking is as important as what will ultimately wind up on the air. It is like a special fuel, a kick. The breast-enlargement joke survives as well, but with a new target: Nancy Reagan. Here, too, the writers seem to want to get away with things for as long as possible.

"Well," Fontana assesses after the read-through, "at least it's shorter."

"The staging works for me," Paltrow mock critiques his still-sitting troupe. (He gets a big laugh with this as well.)

Paltrow, Fontana, and Tinker leave for the pier immediately following the read-through. They have some urgent casting to attend to, and Tinker has to scout New Jersey locations for the coming *High* shoot.

Whitesell, alone with his charges, finally gets down to business. He has Feld and stage manager Chuck Raymond rough out the dimensions of the set with masking tape on the rehearsal hall floor. Within these confines, they arrange loose tables and chairs to indicate the placement of the office furnishings. Then the director requests office supplies, and odds and ends, and loose papers, primarily to give the actors something to do with their hands. "We need tons of shit," he says, "spread out, so they have some stuff to go through."

"Yeah," Mary Beth Hurt seconds. "Let's start getting it." She is anxious to begin rooting her character in some kind of context. She wants to know what she is doing, or what she is supposed to be doing.

Raymond takes Hurt and Whitesell a little too literally here. In response to the actress's epiphany from the day before regarding the overflow of kiddie items surrounding her character, he checks in with a few nondescript baby toys, some diapers, and a six-pack of Kellogg's breakfast cereals, the more desirable of which will likely be reduced to munch by the end of the day by the more sweet toothed members of the cast. For the rest of the group, on short notice, he produces newspapers, cups, pens, pencils, batteries, and ice packs—batteries? ice packs?—and these are spread out over the various surfaces on the makeshift set.

Next, Whitesell sets about the painstaking task of physically moving the actors through their lines. He does this scene by scene and line by line. It takes a long time and a lot of thought to do this. Whitesell moves the actors around like puppets—better, chess pieces—concerned as much about the camera angles he will confront when he moves to the set on Monday as he is about staging the piece to best overall effect. He has a very clear vision of how he wants the actors to move through each scene and what the tempo of each scene should be. Each scene, which will run about three minutes on television, takes a half hour or so in first rehearsal, and before long the actors are struggling through this crude choreography, learning their lines along with their paces.

(Strangely, the director spends as much time on the maneuverings of Hillary Danner and David Laundra, and on their deliveries, as he does on the "real" members of his cast; the stand-ins are being made to rehearse on behalf of their successors, keeping the roles warm for those who will ultimately fill them.)

"Are we in commercial here?" Mary Beth Hurt asks in one of the spaces between scenes.

"No," Whitesell answers. "Why?"

"I just want to know what the people are seeing at home," she says. "We're changing scenes, and I want to know what goes out on the TV."

John Dye interrupts his routine by asking if there will be three or four cameras recording his every move.

"Four," Whitesell responds.

"What do you mean?" Hurt says. "I don't understand what that means."

"It means there'll be four cameras."

"I thought this was a three-camera show?" Hurt tries.

"It is."

"Then why are there four cameras?"

"There's always four cameras in a three-camera show," Whitesell explains.

Oh.

Hurt is concerned about awkward crosses, about having to worry too much where each camera is, and where she is supposed to be in relation to them. She is concerned about quite a lot of things, really.

"Let's just see how it plays," Whitesell tries. "Until we're on the set Monday, we'll just have to go through it as best we can. Let's have some fun with it."

Nobody, it seems, is having any fun with it. Except for Hillary Danner. It is like an Andy Hardy movie, the way she has been rescued from her desk at the pier and asked to playact with these professionals. The smile on her face as she goes through her motions, and fumbles through her lines, is bright enough to sell toothpaste.

There is some downtime to this rehearsal process, particularly for the actors who are off-camera for consecutive scenes. Geoffrey Nauffts, to fill his, slithers under one of the tables for a nap, using his knapsack for a pillow. That he is actually able to doze under such conditions is testimony more to the fact that he is working two jobs (remember, he played two performances yesterday, on Broadway) than it is to the sleepy pace of these rehearsals.

At 12:22 P.M., shortly before lunch (which turns out to be leftovers from the day before, dressed up for a second serving), a pair of crutches arrives for Jennifer Van Dyck. She has no idea what to do with them. None of the producers has talked to her about handicapping her character, and Whitesell has yet to be consulted on the specific physicality of the scripted disability. But the crutches are here, and they begin to take up more space in the room than they are actually occupying. They are becoming a large concern to the actress, and to the director, and to the other actors who will have to play off them.

The most difficult scene, in this early going, is a heated exchange between Sara Scadutto and Marsha Katzenberg concerning a disarmament address being prepared by rookie speechwriter Jim Smith. One of the difficulties is that no one can quite figure just how heated the exchange is actually supposed to be. It is the only substantive, issue-oriented scene in the entire script; and it is the only major scene not involving Bonnie Doone or B. Laurence Taylor, leaving Whitesell free to work exclusively with his "real" actors, to put a fine point on things.

The scene takes place at night, during the East Room ball originally intended to honor the small-breasted Jehan Sadat, but now appended to salute the also underendowed Nancy Reagan. Jim Smith has stayed behind in the War Room to finish the first draft of his speech, which B. Laurence Taylor expects on his desk first thing in the morning. One by one, Smith's new colleagues, tuxedoed and gowned for the evening's affair, enter the office to see how the new guy is doing (and, perhaps, to rub his nose in what he is missing). Eventually, Smith finds himself in the middle of an argument between Sara Scadutto and Marsha Katzenberg over what the precise tone of his speech should be.

(Realize, in April 1990, the anticipated tone of a speech on disarmament, and its context, is far different from what it will soon become.)

"Right out of the blocks," Marsha coaches, "the president has got to sound invincible."

Jim: "Ah, right."

Sara: "Marsha, this is about disarmament. The tone should be nurturing, conciliatory."

Jim: "Good point."

Marsha: "Forgive me. We're digging in our heels."

Jim: "That's true."

Sara: "No, no, no. We're extending the olive branch. In an ideal world, we'd advocate the banning of nuclear weapons for all eternity."

Jim: "That's true, too."

And so on, until the two women have built up such a head of steam, trashing their immediate surroundings to emphasize their points, that they have left poor Jim more confused about his efforts than he was before they came in to offer help. More, they leave his desk looking pretty much as it would if it had been placed in an industrial-size washing machine and run through a couple of spin cycles. Indeed, the generated mess (tossed and broken pencils, flung papers, hurled books) escalates as the rehearsal progresses, and after each pass, stage manager Raymond diligently cleans up the devastation and sets it right. He does this about a dozen times, without complaint. No one moves to help him.

The problems with the scene are unclear to Whitesell and his cast, although it is clear there are problems. Some think it should be played lighter, funnier, while others think it should reveal these women as fiery ideological opposites, establishing early on that this office is stoked by good, caring people of conviction and dedication. Either way, it is something to work on over the next few days. Maybe the writers could put in a line or two to better articulate where the scene is supposed to be going and to give the actors a better idea how to get there.

"Let's just see how it plays," Whitesell says when he is finally ready to move on.

By five o'clock on this first full day of rehearsals (held with a not-quite-full cast), the junta of producers and studio executives has assembled for a run-through of the entire script. Joining the onlookers is veteran *Saturday Night Live* comedy writer Herb Sargent, who has been drafted as a onetime script doctor and consultant and to help with the logistics of preceding each taped show with a live, stand-alone opening. This so-called cold opening is a matter of some concern to the producers and to the cast, but everyone appears excited by the prospects of live television, even if it will only be live for the moment or two leading up to the show's opening credits. Most excited, reportedly, is Jeff Sagansky, who has hugged the idea into his master plan for cutting-edge television. Indeed, the front matter to the current *E.O.B.* script includes the following explanation: "The cold opening will be shot live the night this episode airs and will be based on news events of that particular week. The scene will involve Marsha Katzenberg, Sara Scadutto, and Hammond Egley and Steve Lawson. Hopefully, this opening will be satirical, au courant, witty, and devastatingly funny. If it's not, blame Sagansky."

For now, in a fairly sound chicken-before-the-egg strategy, it is decided that the cold-opening segment will be more fully addressed after the taping of the pilot. For now, Herb Sargent is simply here to see what the producers have got to work with and to explore with them the possibilities for the opening.

Also for now, the actors retreat to a corner of the rehearsal hall as this jury seats itself along the long, nonmirrored wall. A jittery tension flows from each side of the room, and, to ease it, Tom Fontana looks across at the wide mirror, strikes an MTV pose, and says, "It's like the Paula Abdul video!"

Showtime. Or at least run-through time. The actors, working from their scripts, often moving and delivering their lines with their heads down, tackle the material in earnest. They are nowhere near ready to make a formal presentation of the work-in-progress, but for this informal pass they clearly want to make a good impression. In some ways, it is like another audition, this run-through, even though the actors and director have already won their jobs. It is an audition for the producers as well. It is the first time they are seeing their efforts spring to life, and if their vision has not quite been fully realized, at least it is getting there. The results are rough, at best. As the piece progresses, though, there begins to emerge a rhythm, a feel, a sense that underneath these stops and starts there is something here, something worth pursuing. A few of the actors, even, are scratching their ways into character. They are delivering their lines with an almost-familiar ease, as if they have delivered them a dozen times before, as indeed they already have. Certain punch lines—"Word is she's in town for a breast enlargement"—which have been given particular attention, are now voiced with the same inflection and emphasis each time out.

Between scenes, as Raymond and Feld rearrange the pretend furniture, the big room is almost eerily silent, except for the scraping and squeaking of metal against floor. Occasionally, Fontana makes to fill the silence with a laugh: "The Paltrow Group," he slogans. "We don't make shows, we make fun." Once, after the messy disarmament scene, Fontana gets up from his chair to help Raymond clean up. He does this, it seems, without thinking, but when he gets caught at it, and catches himself, he jokes it off. "Hey," he says. "I did summer stock. Once a stage director, always a stage director."

The run-through—indicative, mostly, of how little time the director has had to work with his actors and how little time they, in turn, have had to work with the material—is met with applause and congratulations all around. Fontana and Tinker stand to shake each actor's hand, and each other's. Asked about the latest efforts to cast the roles of Bonnie Doone and B. Laurence Taylor, Fontana says, "We have a plan. It's 'Plan Z,' but we have a plan."

Paltrow also works the cast, exchanging pleasantries and compliments. "You make me laugh," he is overheard saying to Rich Hall, again. He loves what Geoffrey Nauffts is doing, he tells Geoffrey Nauffts. He tells Mary Beth Hurt that even though she has done Chekhov and Shakespeare and has a reputation as a serious New York actress, he knows her for what she really is: a goof. "The bigger the rep, the bigger the clown," he kids her, with affection.

When he reaches Jennifer Van Dyck, Paltrow listens to the actress's concerns about her character's disability. He calls over one of the costumers to discuss the available options for braces, and crutches, and (resultingly) wardrobe. "I don't want to spend two thousand dollars," he allows, looking at a picture of one possible device. "That's nuts. I have a real fetish about wasting money." Even at this late date, he has offered Van Dyck no idea what to make of her character, how to brace and disable her, although it is agreed that for tomorrow's rehearsals the actress will be given three- and five-pound ankle weights to help her get used to the extra weight and develop a limp, and whatever else she might need to do to get into character.

When John Dye solicits comment on his performance, Paltrow says, "I don't think it's a good idea to give you specific notes. That'll all come through Whitesell. I think it's better if it all comes to you through one voice."

With this, Paltrow, Fontana, and Tinker join Columbia's Fran McConnell, Deborah Curtan, and Arthur Silver, in the green room adjacent to the *E.O.B.* set, to discuss what they have just seen. Whitesell and story editor Martin are also in attendance. This is called a "notes" meeting, and everyone here has some "notes" they want to pass on to each other, or to the director, who will then pass certain of them on to the cast or to relevant members. On the set of every network television show, evidently, no one ever has a comment to make about a script, or an actor, or a camera angle; they have notes. And another thing: Few people actually take notes at these notes meetings, and no one appears to read from notes they have already made, even though everyone has a great deal to say.

"I think it's fabulous," Paltrow says of what has just now passed for the show as the notes meeting begins. "It's juicy." There is tremendous energy and boyish enthusiasm to his voice, and like every other mood and emotion in television and every opinion that will surface in this green room, these will be contagious.

But despite these shared enthusiasms (or perhaps because of them), the meeting begins slowly. No one has found much in particular to criticize, or to high-praise, especially considering that the cast, and the sets, are not yet complete. The meeting proceeds around the room without much meaningful commentary. Some people speak simply for the chance to make themselves heard, even if they have nothing pressing to say. Underneath all these notes, however, there emerges a consistent concern: There is general agreement that the difficult disarmament scene is not quite playing as it should but no real consensus on how to fix it.

"I think we need to establish Jennifer's character as a kind of Mack truck," Fran McConnell says, meaning that although Marsha Katzenberg was conceived as somewhat sharp-tongued and acerbic, she has not really been given the material with which to demonstrate these traits. "You all see her this way, but I don't think the audience will."

Noted.

"Jennifer was playing the results of the scene," Deborah Curtan contributes, and the others nod not only as if they understood this but also as if this were precisely what they had meant to say.

Also noted.

When Paltrow's turn comes around, he eases into something that has been bothering him. He has to stand up to get it off his chest. "John Dye," he begins. "Is it just me, or does anybody else think we have a problem here?" No one answers, so he continues. "I think we have a problem here. I think we have a major fucking problem here." He builds up momentum as he says this, and for a moment it seems he will be carried away by it, somewhere, and then all of a sudden the rest of the room is swept up by the same momentum and transported by it to the same place. Yes, they're all nodding, in complete agreement. It's a problem. It's a big problem. It's a major fucking problem. What can we do about it?

"Let's talk worst-case scenario," Curtan tries. "How quickly can we replace him?"

"We can have someone in here tomorrow morning," Paltrow assures.

In a moment, the idea takes hold and everyone in the room has something to say:

"Who's our number-two choice?"

"He doesn't have John Dye's good looks, but he has the kind of looks that grow on you.

"His looks become good on you, they're not right away, but they become good."

"He can act the shit out of this piece."

"He's probably still available. We just saw him last week."

"There's always Peter MacNicol."

What the producers want is for Jim Smith to be a real Jimmy Stewart kind of character, all wide-eyed and naive and fresh, and not at all jaded, and they think what they are getting from John Dye is a prima donna, a cocky, know-it-all braggart who somehow sees himself as the lead in what is supposed to be an ensemble show. To illustrate, Tom Fontana shares the report from his assistant, Bonnie Mark, about how Dye wanted her to mail his bills for him. He sets it out as an indication of the problem at hand. "I told her to take them and just throw them out," he says. "Let the bill collectors come after him." He says this good-naturedly, and it gets a laugh, but within his dismissal is a clear disdain for what he, too, perceives as a star turn on the part of the young actor.

His colleagues agree. "He doesn't know who he's dealing with, this kid," Paltrow says. "This is an ensemble piece. There are no stars here. We're not about stars. We're not in the Valley."

"He's playing it like a California dude," McConnell assesses, connecting the persona to the performance.

Yes, yes, yes, everyone else agrees. Absolutely.

"I wonder if he even knows who Jimmy Stewart is," Arthur Silver says.

"You've got to rock him," Paltrow says to Whitesell. "You've got to scare the shit out of him. I want him terrorized tomorrow. Tell him Paltrow wanted to fire him. Tell him you had to talk me out of it. I don't care. Maybe that'll shake him up." Paltrow is nearly ranting, but he is not out of control, or good humor. This is a concern to him, but it is not enough to upset him. "You can do that, John, right? You used to play football. You can do this stuff. You like to do this stuff."

"Right," Whitesell says. "No, definitely, I can do that."

"Tell him we'll give him twenty-four hours," Paltrow continues. "We'll give him tomorrow."

Finally, a voice is heard in Dye's defense. "He wasn't so bad in rehearsals," Julie Martin allows. "This last reading was the worst he did all day."

"Probably he was just nervous," Whitesell figures, adding his, to make it a chorus.

Remarkably, these two eyewitness accounts turn the room around again. Now, just as suddenly as his undoing moments earlier, Dye's standing among this group is again transformed. He has become a nervous actor, someone to be coddled, coaxed, and pushed. He has it in him, folks are now convinced; it is just a matter of getting it out of him. The entire question of Dye's performance, which only moments ago seemed to determine life or death for *E.O.B.*, is now perceived as a point of fine-tuning.

To an outsider, the turnabout is troubling. No one wants to put Dye's performance into context. No one mentions that he is working opposite two stand-in cast members, one of whom is not even an actor. He has only had a few hours to try on his character. It is also revealing for the way these otherwise creative minds are so quick to second any opinion so long as it is given freely, passionately, and convincingly. In television, it appears, as elsewhere, everyone is eager to accept that everyone else knows what they're doing and more than they know themselves. If someone else bothers to have an opinion, then it deserves to be shared.

The meeting breaks with the understanding that Whitesell will talk to the actor tomorrow, on somewhat softer terms than those first suggested, and work with him to ease the producers' concerns. John Dye, unwittingly, has managed the neat trick of dodging a bullet that has never been fired.

Bonnie Doone is not so lucky. Of course, she is just a character and therefore unable to manage much of anything on her own behalf. She does not survive a long night of rewriting and rethinking at the pier, after which it is finally determined that rehearsals cannot continue with this key role uncast. It is too unsettling for the other actors, and the director. And so, at this eleventh hour, the despairing producers give up on finding an actress to play the part and instead resign themselves to writing the character out of the script. The thinking is that the show needs someone to fill Bonnie's role in the ensemble, over the long run, but that it does not make sense to cast someone less than wonderful simply for the sake of the pilot. The plan is to redirect a good deal of Bonnie's lines to Geoffrey Naufft's character, who was already performing as a kind of functionary in the speech-writers' office.

It is a decision born of haste and frustration, and it is not one met cheerfully by the rest of the cast when they hear about it the following morning. Indeed, they react as if they have lost an old friend. This morning's fresh script has got some other changes—the "shitheads" line disappears for the first time (despite this, Rich Hall playfully inserts it during the read-through and gets a bigger laugh with it than anyone else ever got when it was supposed to be there); also, Nancy Reagan becomes Margaret Thatcher, and the breast-enlargement procedure she is to undergo becomes a breast lift—and it, too, is cleaner, tighter, than the one that preceded it. But the sweeping change is what the script looks like without Bonnie in it: uncentered, without focus or tether. Indeed, after the read-through, most of the talk is about what the show has lost and not what it has gained.

"The bottom line," Whitesell soft-pedals his cast, "pilotwise, is can you live without her, and I think you can. This is not a move anyone wanted to make."

"I hate to see Bonnie go," Mary Beth Hurt says, eulogizing an old, imaginary friend. "She was the maypole to this piece, and we were all the crepe paper."

"Okay, Mary Beth," Rich Hall delivers, "you can be the maypole."

Eight

DRESS _____

☐   Jane Trapnell, a diminutive woman given to pizzazzy business
suits and tight, mid-length skirts, has been sneaking the actors aside
during these first days of rehearsal, sizing them up, taking their
measurements. She has been doing this because, as costume designer, it is her job to dress them. She has been doing this, for various
New York commercial, feature, and television productions for several
years. For the past five, she dressed the actors in the CBS sitcom *Kate
& Allie*. For the past three days, she has been dressing the *E.O.B.*
cast.

Clearly, she does not actually dress these people. Most actors are
able to put their clothes on all by themselves. What she does is shop
for them. She helps to define their characters, and set the stage, and
tone, through their wardrobe. Of course, Trapnell does not go out
and do this on her own whim. There is much more to it than that, she
insists. First she has to study the script, to learn which actors are in
each scene and where each scene is set. She must determine if the
scene is funny (bright, loud colors; flashy, trendy styles) or sad (dark,
somber colors; conservative styles). Next, she figures what kind of
clothing (casual, office, evening wear, outerwear) is situation- and
season-appropriate. (The *E.O.B.* pilot, not incidentally, is set in the
summertime.). That done, Trapnell sits down with the producers and
the director to discover what "look" they are after for each character.

She talks to the actors to find out what they are comfortable wearing; she tries to get to know them and their clothing. She makes notes. She looks over her budget.

Then she goes shopping.

It is a good job, if you like to shop, as Jane Trapnell apparently does. One of the great things about it is you get to spend someone else's money on someone else's time. Plus, you get to dress all these people up like little dolls. It is a kind of fantasy or indulged passion.

To watch Trapnell shop is to fret the future of mail order. Today— Friday, April 6—she hits Saks Fifth Avenue. She is looking to outfit Mary Beth Hurt's character, Sara Scadutto, and Jennifer Van Dyck's, Marsha Katzenberg. Each needs two office outfits and formal evening wear; they may or may not need foul-weather wear. This should be no big deal, but it is. One of the characters is pregnant; the other wears a brace on her leg due to an as-yet-unspecified handicap. Dressing the men in the cast has been easy: tuxedos, and suits and ties, and a raincoat, for John Dye's entrance as Jim Smith. But this—dressing up a pregnancy and a handicap—is where Trapnell will earn her salary. This will be a challenge.

Saks is set up for this kind of thing. It has a department called Studio Services, which is located on the sixth floor of its landmark midtown Manhattan store, tucked behind the men's department. Through Studio Services, it is possible for producers to set up a line of credit and dispatch their customers to every department in the store to pick and choose a mountain of outfits for their consideration. The outfits are then shuttled across town to the studio, where the actors will model them for the producers. What they do not like, they send back, at no cost; what they like, and keep, they pay for later. It is like running a tab at a bar that allows you to order drinks on consignment.

Trapnell calls ahead to tell them she is coming. She is met at Studio Services by a woman named Connie Buck. They know each other from countless previous shops. The plan is for Buck to escort Trapnell from floor to floor, helping her with her selections. Buck is a good shopping partner, especially on her own turf. She knows where everything is. Ask her to locate any item in the store's tremendous inventory and she can call it up from memory. She will even draw you a little map to help you get through the maze of aisles and racks and displays. Connie Buck is Saks's designated shopper and dispenser of fashion sense to the theatrical community, and while she certainly appears savvy enough for the job, she does not appear quite kempt enough. For one thing, she has a tear in the knee of her black panty hose the size of a golf pencil. It is too big not to notice, this tear, and yet she goes about her business as if she has yet to or as if no one else will. It is not as if she cannot find another pair of black panty hose in a place like Saks.

The two women sit in Buck's messed office and small-talk about the costuming business. There is a lot of production in New York this spring, they agree, certainly more than there has been. There is not a lot of work out there, but there is enough to go around. Each woman seems to know more about New York–based productions—movies, pilots, commercials, music videos—than they could have possibly gleaned from *Variety*. They know their business and their prospects.

Eventually, they turn to their notes.

"These ladies are conservative," Trapnell starts in, looking up from her papers, describing the two characters she is looking to outfit.

"Oh, this is easy," Buck nonchalants. "No problem. What kind of look do you want?"

Jane Trapnell: "I think what they're after is a Peggy Noonan look. It's based on Peggy Noonan, that's what I've been told, so that's the look we're after here."

Connie Buck: "Peggy Noonan. Okay. Great. Who's Peggy Noonan?"

"You know, the speechwriter. She's the speechwriter. Peggy Noonan, the speechwriter."

"What does Peggy look like?"

"I don't know. I haven't seen a picture of her, so I don't know. I thought you'd know. You've probably seen her. She's got a book out now, it's out now, something about a revolution. Something like that. I forget the title. You must have heard of it?"

"Oh, yes, sure. It's out now, right?"

"Right. She's on all the talk shows. You've seen her. I'm sure you've seen her."

"Oh, yes, right, sure. The speechwriter."

"Right. She wrote for Reagan, and I think for Bush. Did she write for Bush? I think so. I guess she'd be dressing, you know, like a Diane Sawyer. A little like Diane Sawyer. I think that's what they want, only maybe a little funkier."

"We do Diane. Oh, yes. If you want Diane Sawyer, we can give you Diane Sawyer. That's not a problem. She's Armani. She's very classic."

"But a little funkier."

"Absolutely."

"So that's what we'll go for, then."

"For Peggy, you're talking about?" Buck is making notes, making sure.

"Peggy? Who's Peggy? I don't have a Peggy." Trapnell is confused.

"Sure there's a Peggy," Buck maintains. "Weren't you just talking about a Peggy? There's a Peggy in here. Check your notes."

"No, no, no," Trapnell says. "Peggy Noonan. That's just who it's based on."

"So there's two girls we're dressing here, or three?"

"Just two."

"Oh." Buck shrugs. "Why didn't you say so?"

First stop is maternity, for Mary Beth Hurt's character. Trapnell wants to dress the characters one at a time, and she wants to get the pregnancy thing out of the way first. The maternity department is surprisingly small for a department store this big. There are a few racks of clothes and a couple of displays, but there is not much to choose from.

"Most ladies who shop here don't get pregnant," Buck explains, as if it were ludicrous to think otherwise.

"I'll just pull a lot of stuff and see what Mary Beth likes," Trapnell says.

And she does. When she sees something she likes, she pulls it off the rack and drapes it over Buck's outstretched arms. When she is not sure if she likes something, she pulls it, anyway. Buck pulls some outfits on her own; this is difficult, her arms laden with outfits, but she manages. Within five minutes, Buck is overwhelmed by thirty outfits. It is more than she can even uncomfortably carry, and she disappears to one of the sales desks to unburden.

When she returns, Trapnell is pressing a pink maternity outfit to her front and looking in one of the full-length mirrors. "Pink is probably a better color on Mary Beth than orange," she announces.

"Oh, yes, definitely," Connie Buck agrees, with certainty, although it is uncertain whether she would even recognize Mary Beth Hurt if she sat next to her at a dinner party. It's not like she's working from pictures or anything.

"What about padded shoulders?" Trapnell wants to know.

"They're very confident. Perfect."

"On a pregnant person?"

"Sure, on a pregnant person. Why not on a pregnant person?"

"You think?"

"Oh, absolutely."

They move out of maternity, deciding they'll have more of a selection elsewhere. They stick to loose, flowing kinds of outfits to accommodate the character's pregnancy. Five minutes and another bundle later, they have moved on to evening wear. "Evening wear is gonna be a problem," Buck predicts, "as far as the pregnancy goes. What's your budget?"

"It's good," Trapnell says. "You know, it's okay. It's good."

"Can you go high? Can you have one high-priced dress?"

"Yeah, we can go a little high. No two-thousand-dollar dresses, but yeah, we can go a little high."

"Good," Buck says. "I've got a Geoffrey Beene you've just got to see."

She ushers Trapnell to the Geoffrey Beene, but it is not there. Undaunted, Buck finds another dress, by another designer, and says this is the one she had in mind all along. Yes, this is even more stunning than the Geoffrey Beene. It costs twenty-five hundred dollars, and Trapnell chokes on the price: "Oh, no, they'll never go for that. It's stunning, but they'll never go for that."

"Shame," Buck asseses.

"Yeah."

"You would have just loved the Geoffrey Beene. It's darling. It's high-collar, and it's linen, and it's trapeze, and it's just darling."

The "trapeze" look to which Buck refers is wide-shouldered, and tapered in toward a slim waist. It does not suggest the ideal look for a pregnant person, but the two women are sold on the idea. They know what they want, and this, for now, is it. They seek out another trapeze dress, white, by the designer Isaac Mizrahi. Both pronounce him one of their absolute favorite designers, but neither can pronounce his name.

"I can never get it right," Trapnell allows.

"Oh, it's Mizzirahi, Mirahi, something like that," Buck tries. "What's the difference?"

Continuing, Buck suggests an outfit for Jennifer Van Dyck's character, but Trapnell does not even want to think about it. "I'm not concentrating on her yet," she says. "I haven't set my mind to it. Let's just shop for this one character and then move on to her."

She is pulling every outfit that catches her eye; some she pulls simply as contrast. She overloads Buck two more times in the next fifteen minutes. Buck pooh-poohs some of Trapnell's choices, but they are added to the pile just the same. Occasionally, though, Buck will discard one of Trapnell's outfits on her own. Sometimes she does this without saying anything (she simply returns the offending outfit to its rack after Trapnell moves on), and sometimes she voices her disapproval. Of a black-and-red suit with a sequined diamond pattern, she says, "It's too wintery looking, with the argyle and everything, and the colors. I don't think this is what you're looking for." It, too, gets returned to its rack. Trapnell does not protest or does not notice.

Also occasionally, Buck selects an outfit for consideration that Trapnell does not like. Maybe it just doesn't look like what she's looking for, or it costs more money than she wants to spend.

"Oh, but it's good on," Buck counters when this happens. "It's good on."

"Yeah?" Trapnell says, her interest invariably revived, as though these three words—"it's good on"—are enough to make her rethink her taste.

Ten minutes later, Trapnell has grown tired. She will shop for Van Dyck later in the day, she decides, or perhaps tomorrow. She has done enough for now. For now, she has pulled nearly one hundred outfits—representing roughly thirty thousand dollars' worth of Saks's inventory—to be sent back to the studio, by messenger. Buck has left piles of her selections on three separate floors, at five separate sales desks. Even Trapnell realizes she has set aside far too many outfits—the producers, she knows, will just be overwhelmed with indecision—and so she goes through her piles again, trying to decide against the outfits she does not absolutely adore, the ones that might not look so good on.

She trims, in little bits, but she is still left with a deep stack of clothes.

Trapnell steps out onto Fifth Avenue and flags a cab. She was inside the store for less than an hour. She wants to get back to the studio to get Mary Beth Hurt into some of these clothes.

Nine

CAST _____

○ John Dye spends his Friday lunch hour in what passes for his dressing room at West 57th Street. He does not know it, but he is waiting for the first shoe to drop. The other shoe he does not have to listen for. Not yet. He does not know this, either.

The row of dressing rooms for the *E.O.B.* cast is rather depressing and institutional seeming. The rooms are tucked along a maze of dormitory-green, cinder-blocked hallways made narrow by lengths of high-school-style lockers and stacked folding chairs. The paint on the hallway walls is cracked, and peeling in spots. Light bulbs could use replacing every here and there. The only noticeable attempt at decoration is a faded drawing of the cast of *M*A*S*H*, which looks like it has been hanging on these otherwise naked walls since before the novel on which the movie was based, on which the series was based, was even conceived.

To get to these dressing rooms, it is necessary to first pass a wizened old security guard with too many stories to tell. If you stop to listen, the actors are cautioned, you will never get where you are going. The actors are also cautioned against leaving any valuable personal belongings in their dressing rooms, and as a result they have already made it a practice of keeping their Walkmans and their Dayrunner date books and their changes of clothes with them in the rehearsal hall, in knapsacks and miniduffels. (In his, Rich Hall keeps

85

a copy of the Martin Amis novel *London Fields,* along with running shoes and shorts for his lunch-hour jogs.) Indeed, it is such a dispiriting chore for the actors to snake their way upstairs, along these cluttered corridors, and past the chatty guard to their dressing rooms that most choose to pass their brief periods of downtime in the rehearsal hall or in the hallway just outside. This is one perq they could have done without.

The actual dressing rooms are done up like sleeping compartments on a decrepit railroad. Sort of. They are tiny, thin rooms. Each has a small couch, a half bath, a couple of straight-back chairs, and a phone. Some have showers, but most do not. Dye's room does not even have an ashtray or a wastebasket, and he has to douse his cigarettes in the sink and stand the wet butts on their filtered edges to dry. He seems tired and out of sorts, although he is not yet aware of last night's green room drama in which he figured so prominently. His funk is coming from someplace else.

"I'm pretty much the thumb on this set," he allows with eery prescience, between smokes. "New York actors are different from L.A. actors. They just are, and I'm constantly aware of that. It's right there in front of me. Plus, the whole system is different from what I'm used to. I come from theater or film, right, so this is a little different. In theater, of course, you have weeks of rehearsal, where the changes to the script are mostly a honing. In film, you rehearse a scene and you get it right, and you make whatever slight, subtle changes, and then you shoot it. Here we have, you know, six days of rehearsal, with a script that is majorly overhauled every night. We go home and come to work the next day to a script that barely resembles the one from the day before. Of course, it's not structurally different, and the essence is usually the same, but not always. Like today, the essence changed. We lost a character, and it really did tilt the balance a little bit. It affects the whole.

"Film is a director's medium, and television is a producer's medium. The only thing the actors can control are those little moments, you know, the pieces that make you go home and say, 'Yeah, that's great.' Those are the things that make it sparkle for us. I don't have that yet with Jim. I don't think Jim is an entire person yet. I don't even know if we're close, because you can't really get into the whys, why does he say this, why does he do this, why does he feel this, why does he think this, you know, until the words are set. The feelings aren't there yet. It's not about acting at this point. It's about that little last drop of red paint that makes it just the perfect color blush, you know. That's the fun stuff, the good stuff, but I'm not there yet. I don't know if any of us are. Some of us are closer than others, obviously. I look around the cast, and there's a lot of talent, and they've all got the basics. The basics, for people like them, that's a given, that's where you start. The things that make them artists, like Mary Beth, are their ability to transform the basic into the strange, yet the familiar."

John Dye, asked, seems the sort of actor who could go on and on about his craft, and his career. At the age of nineteen, he landed his first film role, in Memphis, the nearest big city to his small hometown. He auditioned for a walk-on part—"like, you know, the waiter who goes to get the Diet Coke or something"—in a cable-ready campus comedy called *Making the Grade* and wound up with one of the leads. He moved to Los Angeles on the crest of this and has been working ever since. "When you look like I look," he assesses, "and you're in your twenties, you do a lot of teenage campus comedies."

He is interrupted from his career highlights by a pounding at his dressing-room door: Whitesell, with bad news. Or at least a watered-down, sugar-coated recounting of last night's notes. Whitesell, going in, does not seem to relish his role as messenger. Coming out, ten minutes later, it seems not to have been too bad. In fact, it went better than expected. The actor took it pretty well, considering.

Dye is downstairs in the rehearsal hall before he has a chance to digest what has happened or what Whitesell has had to say. He emerges from this closed-door session somewhat shaken but also stirred, pumped, challenged. He has taken his second chance to heart. He concentrates fully, or at least he makes a show of concentrating fully. Here and there, throughout the afternoon rehearsal, he peppers his remarks with self-deprecating comments like "Yeah, if they don't fire me" or, at the end of the day, in response to a fellow actor's "See you tomorrow," "I hope so." His asides are like little Post-it notes, to remind himself how close he came, how close he still is.

The rest of the cast is unaware of their colleague's dilemma, and they do not notice these asides for what they are. They have got their own problems. Geoffrey Nauffts has a slew of new lines to learn (most of the lines that belonged to the written-off Bonnie Doone are now his), and he has to absorb the new turns and traits his character has taken, and taken on, but more than that, he has to shoulder some off-set difficulties as well. The producers of *A Few Good Men* are giving the actor a hard time about getting out of his matinee performance tomorrow and the two performances next week that conflict with the *E.O.B.* tapings and the final day of rehearsals. The play is up for a Tony Award, and with the anticipated increase in ticket sales, the producers would like to keep the original cast in place for as long as possible. Nauffts is signed to the production for three months, which are about to expire, and he is being made to accept three months more as a condition for this extra time off. In the end, he agrees to work an extra three weeks, taking him up to and through the Tony ceremonies, and he is made to kick back a portion of his Broadway salary to defray the cost of his understudy, but the petty negotiations are a distraction to him, to the work.

"I don't think I'm doing my best work here," he says, handicapping his performance to date. "I'm not comfortable with what I'm doing. It's a different medium for me. When I do a play, I like to do all this research, but I don't have the time to do that because I'm doing a play at night. What we're doing here, in essence, is putting together a sort of miniplay, and at the end of the day we show it to the producers, a miniaudience. We only have a week, and we're putting on these shows right away. I have to make good choices and put some energy into this right away. I'm not comfortable with this yet.

"I hate to say this, but I could be having more fun if I knew where this was going. Every day it's something different, it takes another turn. It's like we haven't had a chance to concentrate on the material yet, because the material keeps changing. I just have to focus."

Jennifer Van Dyck has a pair of metal crutches she is working with, and she has developed a bit where she uses one of them to make an emphatic, final point in the still-troubled disarmament scene. (She sweeps Jim Smith's desk clean with the thing, and it gets a big laugh.) The producers have also settled on a four-hundred-and-fifty-dollar brace, which she has begun to wear. Her concerns, as she paces the rehearsal hall, practicing her limp, becoming proficient with her crutches, are all over the place. Some of them have to do with her decision to be here in the first place. "I'm pretty dumb when it comes to television," she admits. "It really wasn't a part of my life when I was growing up. I watched *The Waltons* and public television specials. I mean, I'm aware that there are smart sitcoms. I've been talking to a lot of people over the past few days, trying to learn what the good sitcoms have been, because, again, I don't really have the vocabulary. *M*A*S*H, Cheers, Rhoda,* never saw it. *Mary Tyler Moore.* I guess that was a half hour, right? Some people said *Murphy Brown* as far as a recent one. So I'm still trying to learn the vocabulary."

Van Dyck is also, and mostly, still trying to figure out how to make Marsha Katzenberg a complete person. "The part is very barbed," she says, "and we all know people who are like that, who are really witty and make us laugh but who are also really caustic, so I have to find a way to make it so that's not her only way of communicating, even though that's her most efficient way of communicating. She has to have something else to her, know what I mean?

"I spent the whole first two days thinking, I hope they cut the crutches, because this is a waste of time, but then I realized this morning that this was just my way of resisting it. The brace is in, and I have to make it work. I have to make the whole character work. I'm not at all like Marsha Katzenberg. The descriptions they have in the script? Out the window. They have nothing to do with me. I'm about as un-Jewish as they get. And on top of that she's crippled, and all those things. It's sort of like putting on pieces that don't really fit but having to make them fit."

She grabs her crutches and limps away, lost in thought.

Rich Hall is also lost in thought. Or maybe he is just lost. He walks the room as if he is in a maternity ward. He talks to himself as he does this. More accurately, he mumbles. He swallows his words, the way he has been told he sometimes does in his performances. When he notices he is being watched—pacing, scratching his head, mumbling to himself, pacing some more—he turns his meanderings into a routine. "It's my imaginary friend," he improvises, and then his eyes flash as a better line registers. "It's my imaginary acting coach."

When he finally sits still, he says this: "At a certain point today, I realized that this has become like an opera. You know what to say, and suddenly you just play it for the rhythms. You get past the point of having to remember what you're gonna say, and it's gonna come out whether you think about it or not, so you start thinking about, Well, how am I gonna make little subtle changes and nuances to the thing?

I mean, I feel like we could go on the stage now and do like a halfway decent sitcom. That's all it would be, halfway decent, but that's better than most of what's on television.

"I don't even like sitcoms. I've seen every joke in the world, many times over. Unless a sitcom has got something different, unless it's like *Garry Shandling,* or *Tanner,* or something, then it's not something I'm gonna watch. But this is a challenge. Obviously, this isn't *Tanner* or anything. That's cable. That's fringe. There's no question, this is a prime-time show, a network show. I don't mean to put it down, but that's what it is. We've got to concentrate on the characters, find the sympathy, you know. I think for people who want a politically aware show, this'll be a letdown, but I don't think that's what most people want. I think people want a show about characters. We've got a pregnant speechwriter. We've got a crippled speechwriter. We've got the new guy and your basic boss. We've got a nasty researcher. And I'm supposed to be the yuppie that everybody loves to hate. That's what we've got to work with."

Mary Beth Hurt, for her part, would like a little more to work with. She has had some experience with the creative processes of Paltrow, Fontana, and Tinker, and she worries about the differences this time out. She worries about what she is not getting from the producers and what she needs. "I think they feel like *Tattingers'* bit the big one," she figures as she drops to the rehearsal hall floor and allows herself a break. "And it bit it twice, if you count *Nick and Hillary,* so they're a little gun-shy right now. That's the way it looks to me. They're probably not as confident as they were when they were doing *St. Elsewhere.* When they left *St. Elsewhere,* they knew exactly how to do it, and they could do no wrong. Well, that's not the case now. And they've got these two other shows going, too, so they're not around as much. So we're seeing a lot of, you know, asking other people for approval, and reassurance, and direction. And they're less likely to ask the actors now. They're not asking us at all.

"We're treated as kind of dumb, sometimes, as actors, but I find that very much less from Paltrow and these guys. I like these guys a lot. I find them very unthreatened and much more honest than most of the people I've met in television. But they're not giving us very much to go on here. They've got these other scripts, for the other five shows we might do, but they're not giving them to us. Even if they never shoot them, they would be helpful. If I could read them, I could learn about my character's background, the way the writers want the characters to interact. But these guys have lost their confidence a little bit, they're not showing us what they've got. They're listening to too many other people. I don't know that that's wrong, but when you lose your confidence, your game is not as good.

"As far as my character is concerned, I'm less there on that at the moment, but I'm not too worried about it, because if this pilot goes, I think that's the sort of thing that will become more clear. I mean, these are not Shakespearian characters or Arthur Miller characters. They're not that at all. It's half hour, and right now a line doesn't get changed because a person or a character wouldn't say that. It gets changed because someone physically is coming in the door or somebody has to get behind the desk. So at this point you can't say, Well, Sara wouldn't say that. I don't know whether Sara would say that. I don't know what she would say. I'm resigned to that.

"This is a whole new format for me. It's kind of like doing skits, I guess, like a pep skit, you know, from a high school pep rally or something. That's what this feels like to me. For some people who do it well, who have done it for a long time, like Penny Marshall, she knows absolutely how to do it. I hope it's something you can learn. I used to do a lot of pep rallies, so maybe it will come back to me. Right now, I'm trying to find the balance between the actors and the director. He calls a certain number of shots to try to get your character set and going. You know, he'll say, Go here, go there, and I just hate that. It doesn't leave me enough to do. That's when the job gets very boring. Just the fact that you can say a line well, that doesn't make it interesting. But if you can get the character going, and the relationships going, then it can really be fun. Then it gets a life of its own, and it can fly."

E.O.B. is not quite ready for lift-off, but it does have runway clearance. Today's run-through is smoother than yesterday's, more practiced. Afterward, a ponytailed Bruce Paltrow is the first to applaud John Dye's performance. "Night and day," he enthuses. "Night and day."

Once again, the green room moves to Paltrow's beat. All anyone wants to talk about is Dye's performance, and what is remarkable about this is that his performance does not seem that much different from the day before—at least not to an outsider. The entire piece is more polished, the character of Steve Lawson has been rendered more prominent than anticipated as a result of the Bonnie Doone axing, the disarmament scene has been refined to where Whitesell's staging has managed to fill in some of the blanks in the script, Rich Hall seems to have finally found a way to hit his lines without swallowing them, and even David Laundra is beginning to do some interesting things with the borrowed part of Taylor. Dye's Jim Smith, though, looks basically the same. He looks fine, actually, but there are no new notes to him, no revolutions. It is not just more of the same, it is better of the same, but it is still the same. The component parts are what's new and improved, and Dye looks good against these new surroundings.

Still, it is like he reinvented the wheel, to listen to the folks in this green room. John Dye's reputation is transformed, and born again. He has, judging from the mood of the room, turned it around completely, nailed it, saved his ass, one-eightied it, and pulled it out of the shitter.

Dye's treading-water turnaround leaves the producers with only one near-term crisis: B. Laurence Taylor. They are now desperate to fill the role. Writing this character out of the script, the way they did with Bonnie Doone, is not an option here. His weight and authority are integral elements of the script and the scripted workplace. Without him, the E.O.B. office will have no paternal core, no fulcrum, no link to the presidency. It would just be a bunch of thirtyish speechwriters toiling in a vacuum. Later on, it might be possible to write an entire show without a scene in it for Taylor, but by then his presence will have been established; he will be a part of the dynamic of the piece even if he is not in it.

The producers have arranged for "a little casting" immediately following the notes meeting, to be conducted in one of the rehearsal halls at West 57th. It is the first such session they are conducting here, and there is hope that the change of venue will bring some good luck along with it. It does. Finally. Of the four actors who come through the double doors of Rehearsal Hall #2, one hits the notes the producers have been looking for: William Duff Griffin, a veteran New York stage actor with a smattering of big- and small-screen credits and a stentorian voice that could sell mutual funds. He walks into the audition thinking E.O.B. is a drama series about the White House. He has prepared a whole Nixon *Final Days* bit with his part, but when he is finally corrected on this, he manages to find the tone and temperament the producers have had in mind.

"We had a miracle." Tom Fontana exclaims later this evening. "A goddam Christian miracle."

In fact, it appears the part of Taylor would have been cast even if Griffin never showed up to audition. Another of the four actors was good enough to land it. He was okay, the producers agreed. Not great, but okay, and good enough, and if this guy had the good fortune to audition the day before, the part would have been his. With Griffin, though, there is a feeling among the producers, and the network and studio executives, that they have gotten exactly what they wanted, that the wait has been worth it, that the last, hardest-to-find ingredient for their strange brew has been unearthed and placed in the pot.

"He's lock and load," Tinker declares of his new Taylor, meaning, perhaps, that in Griffin the producers have found a seasoned professional, someone who will hit his marks, hit his lines, and hit the ground running.

To celebrate, Paltrow, Fontana, and Tinker decide to call it an evening. There will be no rewrites tonight. Better to wait, they figure, and see what Griffin does with his part before making any additional changes.

The next morning—Saturday, April 7—before the cast gets the news of Griffin's hiring, they get the news of Mary Beth Hurt's fish. It died. More accurately, it was her kid's fish, and it is the second one she has lost in the last few days. Evidently, these are tough times for tropical fish on Riverside Drive. Good mom Hurt Ziplocked this second casualty in the freezer along with the first one. She is waiting for the chance to give the fish a proper burial in the Hudson, but she has been pretty busy with rehearsals, and her daughter has been pretty busy with her own stuff, and, plus, the weather has just been lousy.

The new Taylor, William Duff Griffin, sits off to the side, oblivious to Hurt's domestic bulletin. He is wearing a plain red sweatshirt, tan slacks and sneakers, and doing what he can with the *New York Times* crossword. (There is a little thing going on with exclamation points in today's puzzle, and Griffin picks up on it right away.) There seems to be a slight air of professorial authority about the actor, although his

physical appearance—short, stocky, and built low to the ground—
somewhat belies his manner. As such, he seems a peculiar fusion of
The Flintstones's Barney Rubble and *M*A*S*H's* Charles Winchester.
Even silent, and aloof, he is a very definite presence in the room—at
the very least, he is a new presence—but he is left alone by the
others. No one moves to greet him, not right away. There is a swirl of
activity around Griffin that he chooses to ignore, and in this swirl
there are whispers: The part's been cast, that's him, he's here, Taylor's
here. Through this, Griffin makes no effort to introduce himself, to
peel himself from the one puzzle and place himself in the other.

Griffin works the *Times* to the last possible moment, and Whitesell
actually has to lean over and ask him to join the others to commence
the morning's table reading. Introductions are made all the way
around the table, and by the time they reach Nauffts and Hall, they
have been parodied into opening sitcom credits: "And Rich Hall, as
the Beaver."

The table reading proceeds slowly and to a new rhythm. Over the
past two days, the cast has grown accustomed to Laundra's pace and
inflections, and Griffin's new take has got them off their timing. He,
and they, will take some getting used to. Throughout the morning,
Griffin does not seem to realize how closely he is being watched, and
measured, or precisely what his impact is, or will be, on the other
people in this room. His manner is professional, straightforward, but
he seems a little removed from what's going on, from what's gone on.
He is like the new kid in school, except he is not a kid and this is not
school. (Other than that, it's just like it.) Of course, from where
Griffin sits, the situation—joining up with an up-and-running cast,
in an up-and-running rehearsal—must be unsettling. Already, these
people have a history, with each other and with the material. Even a
short history is something.

As Raymond and Feld move to set the tables and chairs along their
marks on the masking-taped floor, the others lapse into their
distractions. Geoffrey Nauffts picks up a paddle-ball toy from the
asked-for assortment on Sara Scadutto's desk and begins to tool with
it. He cannot get the hang of it, but keeps at it. It is a good time to
him, and he is determined to master the motion. When he does, he
suggests to the room at large that he might try to work it in as a piece
of business for his character. He soundtracks his play with borrowed
snippets from the sitcom themes of his growing up. He seems to do

this without thinking, as though these familiar themes are so much a part of him, and a part of this process, that they belong in this room, as a carrot and a red flag, both. "Come and knock on our door," he sings, mimicking the opening bars from the *Three's Company* theme.

"Da da da da da dum," John Dye joins in, in synch to the music. He knows the tune but not the words. For the first time all week, Dye is loose, laughing, having a good time. He seems to have recovered from yesterday's notes, and from his other uncertainties, enough to put him in a singsong, carefree mood.

Rich Hall, inspired by Griffin, pulls the day-early Sunday *Times* crossword puzzle from his bag and sets to work at it. Griffin, across the room, notices and says, "Tomorrow's puzzle, today? What are you gonna do tomorrow?"

"Finish it," Hall says.

Later this morning, the cast is taken by Chuck Raymond for their first look at the *E.O.B.* sets, which have been moved from the workshop to the studio down the corridor from the rehearsal hall. They are excited by all the room they will have to work with and by the way the entire production seems to be taking shape. They have been rehearsing in such a cramped, makeshift setting that the actual War Room and Coolidge sets appear liberating to them, validating.

Nauffts, inspired, does a mock Mary Tyler Moore twirl, tosses a baseball cap into the air, and sings out, "You might just make it, after all."

"What's that?" Jennifer Van Dyck wants to know, looking on. "What's he doing?" Her television reference points are, by her own admission, "in the dead zone."

"Mary Tyler Moore," she is told. "That's the theme song. 'Who can turn the world on with her smile.'"

"That was a good show, right?"

Ten

REWRITE

☐   It is Saturday evening, close to six. The sun is shimmering its last over the murky waters of the Hudson River. Soon, through Tom Fontana's Pier 62 office window, it will be possible to catch the glare of moonlight against the water. Mostly, this will be possible with a rich imagination.

Now, on the inside of the office window, Paltrow, Fontana, and Tinker are putting their rich imaginations to more disciplined use. They are revising their *E.O.B.* script yet another time. They will do this several times more before the Thursday taping, but they are joined in this night's effort by *Married...With Children*'s Arthur Silver (whom the producers have come to regard in the past few days as a good, funny, and sitcom-savvy friend), director John Whitesell, story editor Julie Martin, and assistant Bonnie Mark.

The revisions begin on the script's title page, as they have on almost every other night. Even at this late juncture, no one is completely pleased with the name of the show. The producers are happy with *E.O.B.* as a title, but not as happy as they would be if they had network support and enthusiasm to go along with their own. The network is worried no one will know what *E.O.B.* stands for, that maybe someone will mistake it for a show about obstetricians, or off-track betting, or equal opportunity employers. It has been a tough sell, and the transaction is not yet complete. Sagansky is reportedly high on the title *Lip Service,* which smells to this room like something from the Aaron Spelling/Fred Silverman school of mid-1970s jiggle programming. The producers are not wild about this prospect. Instead, they are pushing *The War Room* as a second choice because of its strength, and splendor, and history and also because they cannot come up with anything they like better. *E.O.B.,* they like better, but it might have to go the way of Bonnie Doone. They kick around a few other ideas (*Speech,* for one), before setting the title aside. After all, even the perfect title will not cover up any holes in the script, and so they seek to fill these.

This group has got its routine down, by now. The writers go over the script page by page and scene by scene, stopping over perceived trouble spots or wherever they think they can make something tighter, funnier, or just generally better. Tonight's first trouble spot is in the first scene. Arthur Silver is concerned about the Steve Lawson line "Once it's on the TelePrompTer, blame White House A.V.," a frazzled explanation for why the president is about to read the wrong speech.

"I don't know what A.V. is," Silver says.

"Audio visual," Tinker responds. "In high school, remember? A.V.?"

"Oh, okay, but I don't think this is gonna be clear. People don't know A.V."

"What do you think, Tommy?" Paltrow asks Fontana.

"I know what it is," Fontana says in a hard deadpan. "We all know what it is. That's why it's there." Fontana has turned serious. All week long, up at West 57th, he has been a funny, cutup guy, but here he is quiet and thoughtful. This comedy writing is serious business to him. That, or he's tired.

"Maybe Arthur's right," Paltrow tries, "maybe we should come up with something else."

"What you need there is a joke," Silver offers. "There's no laugh there. You need a laugh there."

"Okay," Paltrow agrees, "good, I like that. The train's really moving here, and then it just stops. Let's give Steve a joke here."

This is easier decided than accomplished. Everyone suggests a line or two to make the scene funnier, but nothing seems right. Some things seem flat. They try out the lines on themselves, and each other, but not much can be made to fit, and what can is not funny.

"We can have Steve refer to White House A.V. as something else," someone suggests.

"As what?"

"Videophiles."

"Techies."

"Media munchkins."

"Media maniacs."

"Vidiots," John Tinker submits.

This last elicits a general nod of approval and is then bent to audio-vidiots, which Tinker thinks might be clearer, and maybe even funnier.

Ultimately, the Steve Lawson line remains intact, but a new line, for Sara Scadutto, is added to immediately follow it. The exchange, altered, now reads:

Steve Lawson: "Once it's on the TelePrompTer, blame White House A.V."

Sara Scadutto: "Those audiovidiots."

It is not the sort of comeback likely to leave the Nielsen family rolling in the aisles at home, but it succeeds in clarifying what White House A.V. is, and does, and in smoothing everyone's concerns for this moment.

Bonnie Mark, whose job it is to record these changes and transfer them to a fresh script in time for rehearsals on Monday, scribbles frantically to keep up with the rest of the room. She makes the changes in longhand, in pencil, in and around the margins of her script. She races to keep up. When she misses something, Julie Martin leans over to help fill in the blanks.

Next, the writers fish for an alternative to the "shitheads" line, but nothing bites. They lose the beat and move on.

For several days now, the producers have been toying with adding another scene, set in the White House Executive Mess. They are planning to build a mess hall set for future episodes, so this move is hobbled not so much by the expense as the timing. There is little chance they could mount the set and rehearse the scene in the five days until taping. Still, this is discussed.

Also discussed, as a point of information, is whether B. Laurence Taylor would accurately be called chief of staff, as he is in the current draft, or something else. Fontana consults a stack of books behind his desk for the answer, and while he does, someone offers up the fictional title of media czar for consideration: "There's a drug czar, so why can't there be a media czar?"

Fontana finds the answer in a book called *Reagan's Ruling Class:* chief of Communications. Bonnie Mark makes a scribble of this, too.

As they work, the producers break out their own personal snacks. For this special task, they require special fuel; and, this being their full-time office, they have conveniently got a kitchen full of stuff they like to eat. First, Tinker disappears for a bag of tortilla chips and a jar of salsa. Next, Fontana leaves for some chips of his own (potato), which he eats dry. Paltrow, also hungry, reaches for a pack of trail mix. They are good, serious snackers these guys. Watching them—munching, concentrating—it is easy to see the three men sitting in front of a television set, snacking at same. There is a skill to eating in front of a television set, just as there is a skill to eating in the middle of an informal spitballing session (which, hopefully, will yield a television show on the other side of which there will be many million snackings more), and these guys seem to have mastered it: head up, face forward, the hands moving from chips to dip to face, chips to dip to face, without any help from the eyes, without dripping a drop, without missing a beat.

They are good sharers, too, or at least they try to be. They offer their snacks all around, but no one reaches for them, perhaps because such a move would encroach too much on the producers' private snacking space. Plus, Paltrow, Fontana, and Tinker are enjoying themselves so much that no one seems to want to deprive them of their provisions.

"What about the braces line?" Paltrow wonders, between fistfuls of trail mix, when he comes to an exchange concerning Marsha Katzenberg's handicap.

(Hammond Egley, to Marsha, begging to swap one of his issues speeches for two of her Rose Garden addresses: "Will you do the speech on gun control?"

Marsha Katzenberg, insistent: "For the last time, no, never...."

Hammond Egley, pleading: "Why? You love snub-noses, magnums, bazookas. The feel of cold steel against your flesh."

Marsha Katzenberg, defiant: "You making a crack about my braces?")

"Is it brace or braces?" Paltrow weighs. "Which is funnier?"

"Braces sounds like braces," Silver says, flashing his teeth.

"And it's just one brace."

"But brace isn't funny. Braces is funny."

Whitesell says he can get Jennifer Van Dyck to kind of gesture to her character's bad leg when she says this, to keep people from thinking about teeth, and everyone agrees this would be a good thing. So braces it is. For now.

Much of tonight's discussion is along these same lines. "Yippee," it is agreed, is a funny word, particularly coming from the mouth of out-of-towner Jim Smith. "Sniveling" is also a funny word, according to this group, as is "cummerbund." The writers actually try to add a line or two to the scene that takes place during the East Room ball to accommodate the word *cummerbund,* seeing as how they have already got the speechwriters dressed in formal attire, but when nothing seems right to them, they abandon this.

"Abe Lincoln always gets a laugh," Paltrow confirms when the group is brick-walled on an exit line to help Steve Lawson leave Jim Smith alone in the after-hours office with a rim shot. As the scene is now written, Steve is cleaning the coffee grinds from the pot and finishing up for the night, while Jim is sweating out the official response to his first speech. The others have all left for the East Room ball. To pass the time and to remind himself that he can indeed turn a phrase, Jim reads aloud from his novel, *Amber Waves of Grain,* which he happens to have handy. As he reads, he discovers to his horror that he agrees with Steve's harsh earlier assessment of the work. "Oh, my God," he realizes. "You're right. Overwritten Sinclair Lewis."

"More like overwritten Jerry Lewis," Steve responds.

"The *New York Times* called my novel 'an ideal gift,'" Jim defends.

"Sure," Steve concludes, "who'd take it on any other terms?" Then, as he makes for the door, Steve turns over his shoulder and adds, "Remember what Abraham Lincoln once said, 'If you were any good, you wouldn't have to work this late.'"

"It's a non sequitur," Silver challenges. "It just hangs there. It doesn't mean anything."

"But it's funny," Tinker insists.

"But it's a non sequitur."

"It's funny because it's a non sequitur," Paltrow responds, thinking it through. "You've got Lincoln, and Lincoln is always good for a laugh, and then, boom, you get this thing from out of nowhere. Boom. 'If you were any good,' Boom. I think it's funny. It makes me laugh." The line stays.

The rewriting is put on pause while Paltrow takes a phone call from John Dye. The actor is contemplating a haircut, and he wants to check with the producers before proceeding.

"You mean a trim, right?" Paltrow says, making sure.

Yes, Dye says. Nothing major, just clean it up a little.

"That's fine," Paltrow allows. "If you want to get a haircut, get a haircut. Just don't come in with a mohawk."

Moving on. "The dry-cleaning moment doesn't work for me," Fontana weighs, referring to a scene in which Taylor sends Steve Lawson to fetch his laundry.

"Maybe dry cleaning isn't funny," Martin tries. "Is laundry funnier than dry cleaning?"

Fontana mumbles the line to himself, over and over, and ponders this. "I don't know," he says. "I think the moment's not working, the exchange. I don't think laundry helps it."

Whitesell: "I think we should have these people say 'speech' as many times as possible. As a reinforcer."

There is some agreement on this, and the director suggests a couple of spots where this can be easily accomplished.

Paltrow worries that Marsha Katzenberg is becoming a one-note character and that the one note is too harsh. "We've got smart Dorothy Parker, smart Dorothy Parker, smart Dorothy Parker, and that's it," he argues. "I think we have to soften her."

"Not yet," Fontana cautions. "You're right, but it's too soon. Let people know her first, this way, then soften her."

Arthur Silver finds a spot in the script where Marsha can at least be put on the defensive, which might make her seem less acerbic: immediately following the Margaret Thatcher breast-lift sequence. Even after all these readings, the puerile line still generates a smile, but by now it is agreed that it probably works better as a setup than as the joke itself. Here Silver proposes that the next line go to Marsha. "Have her come back," he tries, "after Sara says, 'Word is she's in town for a breast lift,' with something like 'You'd never say that to a liberal.'"

After it gets kicked around some, it comes out looking like this:

Marsha Katzenberg: "We're honoring Margaret Thatcher. Everyone's dying to see her."

Sara Scadutto: "Word is she's in town for a breast lift."

Marsha Katzenberg: "Why do you only take shots at conservatives?"

Sara Scadutto: "Because I know it annoys you."

"Okay," Paltrow says, "good. That works for me." It works for everyone else, too.

At the front end of the disarmament scene, Silver picks another spot where they might punch up Marsha Katzenberg's character. Marsha, in the current version, intending to jump-start a reluctant Jim Smith into reading from his speech-in-progress so she can get back to the White House affair: "Would you hurry up? My lobster Newburg is stiffening."

"It's not a great line," Silver says. "It's okay, but it's not great."

"Soft or hard?" Paltrow wants to know. "You want to see her sweeter or, just, you know, really lean into this guy?"

"I think you could go for Dorothy Parker here."

"Yeah?"

"Yeah."

"Okay, Arthur, you're the pro."

"But not too Dorothy Parker."

The first stabs at revision all follow the existing form, with slight variations—lobster Newburg becomes veal Oscar—until a light bulb flashes over Paltrow's head. "I've got it," he announces. "I've got the line. Someone said this to me once. It's perfect."

What? what? what? the others say, in a real-life sequence to oddly mirror the fictional one this group is trying to fix.

"You have the rhythms of a man waiting for a harvest." Paltrow delivers. He gets a big laugh with this.

"Someone said that to you once?" Fontana says.

"Yeah, someone said that to me once."

"When?"

"When? I don't know when. Someone said that to me once. I thought it was a great line. I've been saving it."

Comments and suggestions flit about the room faster than Bonnie Mark can keep track of them. At one point, after Paltrow suggests a new bit, Mark asks him to repeat himself. It got away from her before she could write it down.

"Yeah," Fontana joins in the confusion, "what are we talking about here?"

"I have no idea." Paltrow shrugs. "It only comes out once."

A lot of what comes out is never intended for Bonnie Mark's scripted page. Rather, the room moves to a telegraphed shorthand;

even Silver, who has only known these folks a few days, fits himself into it. Paltrow can look at a line and say, "Single, single, bang, a two-shot to a single," and everyone else somehow knows what he means. Similarly, Tinker can say, "It's gotta be boom, boom, boom," and have it also make sense.

Most of tonight's revisions are minor, more tune-up than overhaul, with two exceptions. The first is the decision to shift the end of Act 1 to where Taylor dumps the shredded first-effort speech in front of a disheartened Jim Smith and to cut to commercial as the shredded paper drops to the floor.

"Whump, whump, whump, whump," Tinker trombones, parodying the standard sitcom background noises that usually accompany such moments of melancholy and hopelessness. "Boom, you're out of it, right there."

The second exception is a decision that never gets made. No one is happy with the one scene that remains in Taylor's Coolidge Room office. The consensus is that the script is still too long, and that this scene is flat, stilted, and that the story-necessary aspects can be redirected elsewhere, on the main set. The concern, again, is not about the money wasted on an unused set, because the Coolidge Room figures in the future plans for the show. Rather, the producers are worried that the show will suffer if it is played against the same backdrop throughout.

"Arthur," Paltrow says, turning to Silver, "are we violating any rules if we do that?"

"If you kill the set?"

"If we kill the set."

"Shit, no," Silver says emphatically and then, less emphatically, "I don't know."

"Are we fundamentally, based on your experience, making a mistake? Tell us?"

"I don't think so."

"Good," Paltrow says, "because I hate that fucking scene. It's a drag on the whole show, that scene."

Everyone hates that fucking scene, it turns out.

"That'll save us a few minutes," Whitesell considers. "We're still way over, timewise."

Arthur Silver: "If you ask me, you're better off with a conference-room set, or something, rather than an office. Know what I mean?

Ultimately, a conference room will be much better for you to play down the road. You're gonna need a place where these people can go, where they can have a private conversation. You know, like Lou Grant's office or Sam Malone's office."

"We should be so fortunate," Tinker says, looking upward, hands clasped.

After much deliberation, it is decided that the Coolidge Room scene will be cut. Everyone appears firm on this, and they remain firm for four minutes. After four minutes, the group's resolve turns to pudding.

"We spent the money," Paltrow resigns, "we'll show the sets. What the fuck."

Eleven

RUN·THROUGH _____

◯   The sets are up and dressed. Mostly. Where they are not dressed, they are mostly presentable. And where they are not presentable, they are at least covered with drop cloths and scaffolding.

Rich Hall, also dressed (and mostly presentable), arrives on the *E.O.B.* set early this morning—Monday, April 9—and he wanders over to what will be his character's desk, which sits in the back-center of the War Room, in front of a pseudomarble fireplace and mantel. He wants to see what he will have to work with, and at this moment most of what he has got is a bunch of collectible political artifacts, which dot his institutional desk like a memorabilia show. The most prominent items are a fluffy pair of Ronald-and-Nancy-Reagan-headed slippers (she, strangely, is the model for the left foot, to the president's right) that have been donated to the cause by the senior producer of *CBS News*, Susan Zirinsky, who has just relocated to New York from Washington. There is also a set of what appear to be brand-new golf clubs. (Well, they are certainly golf clubs; what they appear to be is brand-new.)

"How do you feel about a pen set?" John Whitesell asks Hall as he wanders over for his own inspection.

"Generally, I'm opposed to them," Hall responds.

"For your desk," Whitesell tries again. "I think there should be a pen set on Hammond's desk."

"Oh," Hall says, "fine."

By this time Whitesell has brought stage manager Chuck Raymond in on the conversation. "I want to Japanese-up this desk a little bit," the director tells Raymond. "You know, very sleek, efficient, lose all this crap."

"Yeah," Hall seconds, pretending at serious, "get rid of it. What were you thinking?"

Within minutes, "all this crap" is gone, including the Reagan slippers, which have been relegated to the mantel, and the golf clubs, which are now leaning against the fireplace, sleeping off the last round. In their place, Raymond has found an elegant enough desk assortment—blotter, pen set, "in" box, Rolodex—none of which has to jockey for space on the now-Japanesed surface. Everything is stacked and arranged neatly. From this outward appearance, Hammond Egley appears the very model of fastidiousness and efficiency.

Mary Beth Hurt and Jennifer Van Dyck, examining their own digs, are looking to make their characters more comfortable, or themselves more comfortable with their characters. This may or may not be the same thing. Van Dyck picks up a small, sad-looking cactus, which has been left on her desk as dressing, and *tsks* at it; then she looks across the War Room set to Hurt, who appears to be doing the same at hers. "How would you feel about trading cactuses?" Van Dyck asks.

And they do.

Also on Hurt's desk is a framed picture of the actor Alec Baldwin, which no one will admit to having placed there, and the pack of assorted Kellogg's kiddie cereals, which has followed her here from the rehearsal hall. "If those are still there tomorrow," Julie Martin vows when she notices the cereal, which she seems to think is probably the most ridiculous thing you could possibly put on the desk of a speechwriter to the president of the United States, "I'm just gonna go and take them off myself."

John Dye, perhaps tellingly, does not have a desk to call his character's own. According to the script, Jim Smith arrives on the scene with his worldly possessions in an overflowing cardboard box and two suitcases, which means that the War Room set is not yet dressed to accommodate him. The other actors all have these new, vaguely defined personal spaces in which they seek to find their characters and lose themselves, and all John Dye can do is hug close to Jim Smith's cardboard box. Throughout today's rehearsal, he will stand closer to these props than he has to.

Whitesell prowls the stage for one of those neat podium-on-wheels things he is used to working with out in California. With these, it is possible for the director to spread out his script on an angled surface, line up his freshly sharpened pencils alongside, place his morning paper on the shelf underneath, rest his something to drink on the flat edges framing the angle, and then wheel the whole collection around from one set to the next. "Do we have these here?" he asks Raymond. (They do not.) "In California, we have them." Like the actors, he wants a space of his own, only he wants his to be portable.

A great many of the sets' dressings are recycled or on loan. The large, round conference table that dominates the War Room is a graduate of the *Tattingers'* set. The water cooler, which helps to frame the main entrance to the War Room, is transplanted from CBS set decorator Ron Kelson's office. Network management, on a tight budget, will not let Kelson order refills for the water cooler, so he figures, what the hell, he might as well put it to use here.

The War Room bookcases are filled with innocuous titles, most of which have been salvaged from the CBS property department, where they are stored by size and weight and where boxes of them are sometimes used to support shelving. Some of them have been purchased, also by size and weight, from a local remainder warehouse. Most of these books have nothing to do with Washington, or politics, or speechwriting. If they do, it is by accident and not by design. *Poodle Springs,* by Raymond Chandler and Robert Parker, has somehow managed to sneak onto these shelves, as have the autobiographies of talk-show host Phil Donahue, baseball umpire Ron Luciano, and some guy who claims to have been Elvis Presley's spiritual healer.

One of these salvaged books, *FBI Codename Tennpar: Tennessee's Ray Blanton Years,* by Henry Hillin, has been plucked from this literary chorus line and tapped for a cameo in this production. It has been propped as a stand-in for Jim Smith's autobiographical first novel, *Amber Waves of Grain.* For this make-over, art director Victor Paganuzzi photographed a Thomas Hart Benton painting of wheat fields and had it reprinted on a dummy dust jacket, which he designed himself; the ersatz book cover, emblazoned with the pretend title, even includes an author photograph of actor John Dye posing as author Jim Smith. Paganuzzi makes ten copies of this, at a total cost of about four hundred dollars, exceeding his budget by an uncomfortable margin. "We thought the artist was dead," he explains, to justify the runaway cost, "but Columbia said we have to pay for it, so I guess he's not."

Between the hard covers of the mocked-up book are some morning-talk-show droppings. "To Mariette Hartley," the FBI book is inscribed, "whose work I enjoy. With every good wish, Hank Hillin, 4/14/87"—a remnant from the actress-turned-hostess-turned-actress-(again)'s stint on the network's *The Morning Program*.

When the producers arrive, at about ten, discussion turns to whether enough exits have been designed into the War Room set. "The doors upstage are not really helpful to me," Whitesell says. "I need to get these people into the room and out of the room."

"I really, really, don't have any money for this," Paltrow finagles with Paganuzzi and set designer Tom John. "Can we do this really, really, cheaply?"

The changes to the set, which begin after the producers' initial inspection this morning, will ultimately cost nearly fifty thousand dollars and will include a fanning out of the back walls (to give the actors more room in which to work), the rehinging of a secret-paneled door (which was supposed to have led directly from the War Room to the Coolidge Room, but which at first swings in counterdirections on each set), the constant rehanging of the replicated artwork, and the various repainting and refinishing touches made over the next several days.

Because the producers are using CBS carpenters and painters and because CBS is a union shop, they are made to pay arms and legs, through the nose, by the hour. "If something costs fifty dollars an hour, then something that should take five hours is taking ten," laments production supervisor Isman. "They're supposed to give us a breakdown, how many men, how many hours, but right now they're just giving us figures, without any breakdowns. There's a lot of padding going on."

The sets smell of fresh paint during this morning's table reading, which production associate Feld clocks at twenty minutes. It is the timeliest reading so far and confirms that the nightly revisions are at least moving in this right direction. "With the laughs," Fontana heckles, "we'll be nineteen minutes."

Fontana and Tinker depart quickly after the reading for some urgent business on *High,* and Paltrow returns to the pier, leaving the director and his cast to act their way around the set for the first time. Most of the work this morning is physical: there are now very definite marks for the actors to hit and very definite camera angles for the director to explore. After a while, the floor is taped with so many marks for the actors, and for some of the wheeled-around props, that it is impossible to tell one piece of tape from another. The floor looks like a hard-to-figure grid of the constellations. Later, to soften up the set, the designer will place a large area rug in the center of the room, which has the dual benefit of obscuring all of these original marks and upsetting the actors' timing.

Rich Hall, who proudly boasts that he has the least stage experience of this troupe, has some difficulty with Whitesell's stage directions, and Whitesell, with some proud bluster of his own, has some difficulty making himself understood.

"I want you upstage of the table," he says to Hall at one point.

Hall, trying, moves to where he thinks upstage of the table might be and says, "Here?"

"Upstage of the table," Whitesell says again, louder.

"Here?"

"Upstage of the table," Whitesell bellows. The director does not point or otherwise explain himself. He simply repeats himself until he is understood. The only reason he eventually is understood is because one of the other actors generously offers Hall a clue, else the actor might never have gotten where the director so unclearly wanted him to go.

Throughout today's rehearsals, the set is visited by dozens of CBS personnel, on break or on lunch, anxious for a stare at the prime-time excitement in their midst. Secretaries, news writers, technicians, security guards, local station managers, free-lance hangers-on . . . everyone wants to rub up against whatever it is that is going on here. The building is truly buzzing with this production. Realize, it has been nearly fourteen years since any kind of theatrical television series was produced here, and most of the by-now-turned-around staff has never set foot on a sitcom set. Dan Rather and Andy Rooney are old news to them, but this is a goose, a thrill. The visitors come from news and sports, network and local, to see what all the fuss is about and to make some of their own. Their CBS IDs are like backstage passes to the glitz and glamour of Hollywood, the same glitz and glamour that used to pulse throughout West 57th like no big deal.

Two of these visitors, in suits and ties, linger long enough to watch a few scenes, and when they have had their fill, one of them turns to the other and wonders, in a literal stage whisper, "Is this a drama?" His friend, also whispering, does not know, and neither one of them can tell from what they have just seen. This is not a good sign.

Columbia's Deborah Curtan looks on and tries to imagine a future for *E.O.B.* She has been doing a lot of this over the past several days, she says. Mostly, she does this because it is her job, but it is also the sort of thing she would do, anyway, if she happened to be hanging around the set of a start-up series for some other reason. (Apparently, she is the sort of person who would not mind hanging around the set of a start-up series for some other reason, or for no reason at all.)

"We weren't really involved in the development of this show until last week," she says as she settles in to one of the too-narrow seats in the grandstand overlooking the stage. As senior vice president for current programs, it is up to Curtan to nurture developing shows into hits. She has done this for shows like *Married...With Children*, *Who's the Boss?* and *227*. During this pilot season, she is trying to do the same for *Baby Talk* (a spin-off of the movie *Look Who's Talking*), *Married People* (about three generations of married couples, each of which occupies a floor in a three-story, three-family New York brownstone), and for the three Paltrow Group efforts. "We still don't know what we've got with *E.O.B.*," she assesses. "Obviously, we're hoping to be the next *Murphy Brown*, the next *Designing Women*, but the network is number three right now, and they don't have too many successful time slots in which to program it. The time slot can make or break the show. Our hope is that they put us on Monday nights, right after *Murphy Brown*. Actually, it's a good partner piece to it.

"When I look at a pilot, I look for characters that tell me, Yeah, I can see a series here. It's like *Married People*, when I tell people that premise, they can kinda see the series there. You don't need to build a *Hollywood Squares*–type set to see each floor, but the minute the producers pitched this, I said it was like *Knots Landing* in a brownstone. It is. It's three different couples, sometimes they'll interact, sometimes they won't, but they're all connected by where they live. So it was easy to see the series there. With this, it's not so easy. It's a difficult premise, presidential speechwriters, it's about a job that people don't know about, it's Greek to a lot of people. It's a good, solid cast, but there's nobody the viewers really know, there's no real breakout character. What we have to hope for is that the writers can fill the show with likable, identifiable-enough characters, because unless it gets more commercial and relatable, then it won't be successful. It needs a good time slot and good writing. These guys, Bruce and Tom and John, can bring smart, God knows they can bring smart, but I think they need someone to come in and bring funny. They haven't shown me that they can bring funny."

This afternoon, after rehearsals, the actors gather for a costume parade during which they are made to model the wardrobe assembled by costume designer Jane Trapnell. The cast members, spiffed, walk around the variously lit War Room set and allow the producers to watch them, in assorted groupings and against assorted backdrops, through the half-dozen camera monitors suspended around the studio. Trapnell, whose efforts are on formal display for the first time (she has earlier shown the producers individual outfits, on an as-purchased basis), appears a little bit nervous. She has found one of the brand-new not-sharpened pencils and nibbles the eraser between her hardly clenched teeth. (Perhaps she is worrying if she can bring style.)

"It's all too dark," Paltrow says from the grandstand, where he is seated alongside Fontana, Tinker, Whitesell, Curtan, and Silver. "This is a comedy," he leans over to tell Trapnell. "It's much too severe."

"But it's formal," Trapnell counters, losing the eraser. "It can't be formal and not be dark."

"Call Gay Talese," Fontana sallies. "Find out what he's wearing and we'll put them in that."

"Look at Jennifer," Paltrow says, signaling actress Jennifer Van Dyck. "She's much too severe looking. Right now, she looks like she's in *The Killing of Sister George*."

"We've got some other outfits," Trapnell offers. (Indeed, if her other sprees were anything like her Saks outing, this could be the understatement of the production.)

"Then let me see the other outfits," Paltrow says. "These, I don't like. The tuxedos, I like. Rich Hall, his tux, that's a home run for me. That I like."

Today's run-through tells the producers what they already know: The actors have only had a day to work on the set; William Duff Griffin is still feeling his way into his part and into this ensemble; and the script is still too long, despite this morning's breakneck reading. It is tomorrow's run-through they are concerned about. Tomorrow the producers will be visited on the set by CBS president Howard Stringer, Jeff Sagansky, and a lineup of heavy hitters from CBS and Columbia. Of course, tomorrow's performance is expected to be rough and unfinished, but it still looms as a great big deal to the cast and to the producers. It is the first look-see for the folks who are paying for all of this and who will determine its fate. As such, it is not to be taken lightly.

"If I were you," Arthur Silver advises Paltrow, "I'd give notes personally to the actors, before the network gets here."

"We've been going through Whitesell," Paltrow explains.

"You're better off doing it yourself," Silver insists. "For this, you don't want anything lost in the translation."

"I could do that. We could do that. I got notes up the wazoo. My notes are taking notes."

And so, one by one, Paltrow sidles up to his actors and offers them his notes. Jennifer Van Dyck is playing Marsha as too angry. He doesn't want anger, he says. What he wants is importance. Rich Hall is still swallowing some of his lines, and he has got to do something about his frantic hand movements. All week long, Paltrow and company have watched the actor flail nervously, like a windmill, and now that they are watching him do more of the same on the set, and on the monitors, the movements are more pronounced and more troubling. Paltrow suggests Hall spend some time in his pockets. To Geoffrey Nauffts, he says to keep the energy up, he has a tendency to lose the energy in his performance. If he keeps it up there, he'll be fine. John Dye is a hundred percent better, a hundred percent better. All Paltrow wants to see is a little more texture to this character, some different colors to him. William Duff Griffin has yet to learn his lines, or his paces, but Paltrow does not seem too concerned about this. It'll come, he tells the actor. It'll come. But Paltrow sees every one of Griffin's lines as a "bash" line, and he warns the actor that if he "bashes on a bash line, you won't be a likable character."

Finally, to Mary Beth Hurt, he says, "What, I'm supposed to tell you how to act?"

"Is it okay?" the actress wants to know. "Is Sara okay to you?"

"She's okay to me. Is she okay to you?"

"Not completely, no."

"Good," Paltrow ribs. "That's what I like to hear."

"And can we do something about that rug?" Hurt asks.

"What about it?"

"It affects how I move," she says. "If it's gonna come off, then it should come off. I need to know if it's gonna be there."

For Tuesday's run-through, which is held early in the afternoon in consideration of the first night of Passover, Fontana and Tinker seat themselves in the bullpen of folding chairs off to the side of the studio's grandstand seating area. Paltrow works the rest of the room, which is soon top-heavy with CBS and Columbia brass. There is a palpable hush on the soundstage as CBS president Howard Stringer and Sagansky stroll in; cast and crew clearly know who these men are and what they represent. The two men are followed by Steve Warner, CBS vice president for special projects, and a half-dozen other network executives, and what is palpable during these secondary entrances is the way the bustle of the studio returns to normal. With the exception of vice president of casting Lisa Freiberger, the network contingent is outfitted in the same blue suit, with only slightly different ties. Scott Siegler, president of Columbia Pictures Television, climbs into the grandstand seats without commotion, accompanied by Curtan, McConnell, and Rick Jacobs, the studio's senior vice president of talent and casting.

In all, there are twenty-five important-looking visitors to the set, and Paltrow, in a sport coat for the first time since rehearsals began, somehow manages an ingratiating word for each one of them. With some effort, he small-talks these two groups as if he belongs, or wants to belong, although what he would clearly rather be doing is sitting off to the side in the bullpen of folding chairs with Fontana and Tinker, quietly jeering at the power plays in the grandstand seats above. But someone from the Paltrow Group has got to hard-sell the company's wares, and Paltrow has had more practice and is better suited to this task than his partners. That, or he has simply drawn the short straw.

The run-through moves along without glitch, but also without spark. Fontana and Tinker lead the hoped-for laugh track with huge guffaws intended to start a trend. Whitesell, too, laughs long and loud at bits and pieces he has by now seen at least a hundred times. Sagansky, getting comfortable, slips his brightly stockinged feet from his black loafers and simply smiles uncomfortably where the laughs should be. In fact, the only laughs from Sagansky are heard between scenes, when the overhead monitors are switched to the bedroom set of the CBS soap opera *As the World Turns,* which is being taped in another West 57th studio. Perhaps it is the juxtaposition—from sitcom to soap, from prime time to day time, from the War Room to the bedroom—that Sagansky, and an in-cahoots Stringer, find so amusing. Perhaps it is simply a release of tension or a distraction. Whatever it is, the monitored soap holds their attention in a way that the fits and starts of the *E.O.B.* run-through does not.

Stringer makes an early exit, before the end of the first act. This, also, is not a good sign, unless of course Stringer is heading for the *As the World Turns* set, where things seem more interesting, in which case it is still not a good sign, although not as bad.

The run-through itself is actually smoother, tighter, and more seamless than it has ever been. Scenes that have not quite been working, such as the belabored disarmament scene, seem to fall into place for today's pass. Other key scenes, like the frantic opening in which every character is given a busy entrance and introduction, are played cleanly for the first time. The actors, although admittedly nervous before this performance, appear energized by their high-profile, high-powered audience. They have kicked it up a notch. Only William Duff Griffin misses enough of his lines and his marks to cast doubt on his performance, and even this is dismissed, still, as owing to his late entry into these proceedings.

As the piece progresses, Curtan and McConnell let themselves laugh out loud, here and there. They have not laughed out loud all week, but it has not mattered until now. Now, apparently, it matters a great deal. They cannot quite muster any belly laughs for the cause, but they check in with a few impressive tight-lipped-smile laughs that seem to do the trick. It is as though the network folks will not realize the material is funny if it is not underlined as such by the producers.

After the run-through, Nauffts makes a quick exit with Hall, and the two actors walk together for a few blocks, heading east on West 57th Street. Neither is too happy with his performance, nor with the perceived extra pressure placed on the cast to do well, nor with the bad fortune that their first fresh audience for the show was also the toughest possible audience for the show.

"It's their fucking jobs," Hall says of the network suits who descended on the set for today's run-through. "They're not like a real audience. Their asses are on the line. That's why they don't laugh. I don't think they can laugh. It's their careers. We can always get another job."

"I don't think we played it with enough confidence," Nauffts figures, without a whole lot more of the same.

"No."

"It didn't fell right."

"Yeah."

"Maybe I should start looking for other work."

Meanwhile, in the green room, sequestered from yet another Donna Isman spread of meats and cheeses that will go untouched in the room next door, Paltrow, Fontana, and Tinker confer with their partners from Columbia and their customers from CBS. There is some haste to this meeting—the first Passover seder looms as a deadline and lifeline—so the notes are exchanged as quickly as possible.

Quickly, then, Sagansky and his charges rough out what they like about the show and what they do not like, what works and what doesn't, and what should be done about all of it. Their comments signal a long night of revisions for the Paltrow Group, Passover or no. They also suggest that what the producers had hoped would be an intelligent, adult, politically aware, situation comedy is about to become standard network fare.

Twelve

STRIKE _____

○ "This sucks," John Dye gripes, riffling through the fresh script
on Wednesday morning, April 11. He is sitting in the green room
with the other actors, looking for the asterisks in the right-hand
margins of his new pages. The asterisks indicate a change to the
previous day's material, and this morning there are seventy-one of
them.

Most of these, according to the cast's early read, are not for the
better. Three bathroom jokes have been grafted onto the front end of
the script; elsewhere, the characters have been made saccharine and
predictable; the show's teeth have been extracted; even the title has
been changed—to *The War Room*, the consensus second choice.
About the only good thing this group can say about today's new script
is that the title has not been changed to *Lip Service*.

To the cast, it is emblematic that today's revisions have been
printed on yellow paper, reflecting what they understand to be
cowardice and timidity on the part of their producers. Of course, the
actors did not attend last night's notes session and could not possibly
know what the impulses were behind each change or what passed
between the network and the producers, but this does not shake
them from their considered opinions. The general impression holds
that the graceless hand of prime-time television has reached down

and grasped the throat of this show, squeezing most of the life out of it, and its creators.

For a moment, the actors even contemplate mutiny. At least John Dye does. He seems to think that Bruce Paltrow and Jeff Sagansky can (and should) be made to listen to his opinion about what this show should be. "Maybe if we all told them we hated it," he tries, and then abandons his insurrection mid-sentence, after it occurs to him that perhaps this is not such a good idea.

"They've got to know this sucks," Jennifer Van Dyck reasons. "They don't need us to tell them that. They're intelligent guys. They're smart. I'm sure they didn't like this."

Mary Beth Hurt, conspiratorially: "Let's do it badly. If we do it badly, they'll see." She is particularly upset by last night's changes because they significantly impact on her and on how her character will be seen. Now, suddenly, the pregnant Sara Scadutto has been burdened with a perpetually full bladder and seems in almost constant need of a rest stop. "We've gone from believable satire to bathroom humor in less than twenty-four hours," the actress opines. "It's not at all the script we started out with."

"I think the whole thing is getting a little bit pedantic," asserts Rich Hall, who has to learn to live with the fact that his favored sobriquet for the show—*Working Title*—has not been chosen to replace *E.O.B.* "We've lost about twenty IQ points since last night."

John Whitesell barrels into the green room, and the small talk is put on pause. The director is not good-humored today. More, he is not all here. He is confounded by what he has still got left to do as tomorrow's taping nears. For now, he recognizes the displeasure with the new material, but he does not acknowledge it. It is there, but it is not important. "Let's just see how it plays," he tries, again, as he settles in for this morning's reading. "Let's have some fun with it."

Hurt and Van Dyck, not really trying to have some fun with it, trip noticeably over a new, full-bladdered exchange between their two characters:

Sara Scadutto: "I gotta go, I gotta go."

Marsha Katzenberg: "Why do you have to go so often?"

Sara Scadutto: "Because I'm pregnant."

Marsha Katzenberg: "Then just go."

Sara Scadutto: "I can't. You ruined it for me."

"This is funny?" Van Dyck moans. "Somebody tell me this is funny."

"Yeah," Hurt says. "We're supposed to play this? How are we supposed to play this?"

"Let's just get through it," Whitesell coaches, "let's just see how it plays," but he is unable to muster any enthusiasm, or patience. Soon he gives up on either and cuts the reading short at its midpoint. "How about we'll work on the rest on the set?" he says when they reach the end of the first act. "Let's just take five and get it all together and then get to work."

William Duff Griffin, who has yet to land in lockstep with the rest of the cast, takes his five on one of the green room couches while his costars disperse. "Every part, for me, is an adventure," reflects Griffin, who has been acting professionally for twenty-two years. (Before that, he worked for eight years as a programmer for IBM.) "If I told you I was having fun right now, you might think my mind was a little bizarre, but yes, if I take a half step back and look at it, it is fun. It's much different than anything I've done. It is an adventure, and I take it as just that. The others have some problems with these changes today, but I'm not worried about that. I don't mind that. For me, I suppose it's easier because none of my lines were changed. Things were taken out, but none of them were changed. I don't have to learn anything new. So if things don't fall apart, if my pants don't start to fall down as I'm saying my lines, then I should be okay.

"It's sort of like an Ethel Merman thing. I'm ready. I'm wandering through this thing like Candide. I don't know what's at stake. I don't know who anyone is. I see all these people in suits and ties, there must be nine thousand people walking around, and I haven't a clue who they are or why they are here. I don't care. In some respects, I don't even worry about the material. I just worry about my lines. If I know my lines, I don't even have to know what I'm saying. It's all there in the material, so I don't have to think about it."

Whitesell has made a quick exit for the control booth, a compact sliver of a room situated to the left of the stage, replete with several dozen monitors connected, individually and collectively, to the four cameras out on the floor. Today's exacting job of camera blocking—positioning his actors, and his four cameras, for each shot—has got the better of Whitesell. He seems frayed, distracted, and he spends most of this late morning arranging his cast and crew from the dim comfort of this small control room. From here he can do what he is paid to do without having to worry about smoothing the actors over their revised script or holding anyone's hand. From here, in the booth, Whitesell is in complete control. He snaps his fingers to jump-cut from one camera shot to the next, barking out instructions through the intercom that links him to the set. He is Big Brother with a sitcom to direct, and he is so busy with the mechanics of his job that he barely notices the actors, except to see where and how they are standing and in which directions they can be made to turn.

"You know," he observes as he snaps his fingers and watches the on-line monitor flit from one camera angle to the next, the switches choreographed to his beat, "if you do this long enough, this isn't exactly brain surgery."

Occasionally, Whitesell ventures out from this high-tech cocoon to offer a hands-on solution to a particular staging or blocking problem, but he seems to prefer working things through from a distance. On one of these outings, to troubleshoot a sound problem, he bounds onto the stage to help test the boom microphones. "How's it coming in there, audiowise?" he says, hoping that the boom will carry his already-booming voice into the booth next door. He stands in the middle of the War Room set as he says this, looking (inexplicably) ceilingward for a response. "Hello," he tries when he gets nothing back. "Hello. Hello." Again, he does not bend to make himself heard or understood. He bellows until he is. "Hello. Hello. Hello." The problem is eventually solved without him.

Assistant director Sedwick is plugged in to the four camera operators through a headset. As Whitesell snaps, she interprets. She could do this in a near whisper—the headset microphone rests a quarter inch from her lips—but she does this louder than she has to. Whether she does this unconsciously or for effect is not clear. Also, she talks fast, like a carnival barker, and it is hard to imagine she is making herself understood. But she is. "Camera one," she fast-talks, louder than she has to, "that's you, pull in tight, not too tight, we want him full body, we need all of him. Good. Pull back. Go to three, wide shot...." Her directions are reflected on the monitors as the images go full and wide, tight and close, depending.

Before the actors are put through the paces of each scene, Sedwick steps out onto the set and goes over the blocking with each of the cameramen, who write her instructions on little pads taped to the back of their cameras. Their marked-up scripts and these little note-pads tell them where to be at each moment.

The War Room's gun-metal desk tops turn up too shiny on the monitors, and Whitesell dispatches Chuck Raymond to see about a spray to dull the finish. A couple of stagehands begin to unshine the desks during the afternoon break with a foul-smelling aerosol spray that hangs thick in the still studio air, and by the time the actors return from lunch the set stinks like a science experiment gone bad.

"Ooooooh." Mary Beth Hurt holds her nose as she comes back in. "We probably shouldn't be breathing that. That's got to be carcinogenic."

Perhaps, but at least the desks are no longer shiny.

There is a clear division of labor on the set, although this has not been clear until today, when the set is filled for the first time with stagehands and carpenters and camera crew. Chuck Raymond cannot unshine the desks himself, because there are others present whose job it is to do so. A cameraman cannot inch a chair from the path of his machine; he must sit and wait for a prop man to come and do it for him. If Whitesell wants the venetian blinds decorating the set's back window to rest at a more open angle, Mary Beth Hurt cannot simply lean over and tug on the toggles to achieve the desired effect; there is a designated venetian blinds guy. (Apparently, this is a special effect.)

When the producers arrive for the late-afternoon run-through, the blocking and lighting are still not complete. The sets, too, are not fully dressed. Tom John and Victor Paganuzzi are unpacking books on the Coolidge room set, filling in the empty spaces. Paganuzzi wants to know if some of the books can rest askew on the set's window seat, but John is not wild about the idea. Michael Foxworthy, another set decorator, is busy assembling a model of the space shuttle, which is to be displayed in Taylor's office. A technician is painting one of the phone cords white. And the make-do War Room bar, which will be hidden behind a double-doored metal file closet, is stocked not only with top-shelf liquors and respectable glassware, as previously discussed, but also with Doritos, pork rinds, and (oddly) eight canisters of Cheez Whiz.

The run-through is really the first front-to-back rehearsal the cast has had all day, what with the lighting, and camera blocking, and all the other last-minute details that have occupied their director's attention. Considering the sweeping script changes of the night before, the actors have not had a lot of time to spend on the new material, and Whitesell has not bothered to help them through their final paces. He has got his own paces to worry about, and he is still at them.

The producers watch the run-through from the control booth, which is now nearly crowded to capacity. When viewed on the monitors, the up-tempo of the opening scene is exaggerated to where it is difficult to watch without gasping for breath. The scene is busy, hard to follow, almost claustrophobic.

"Someone is gonna want to laugh here," Arthur Silver observes, "but where're they gonna fit it in? There's no room."

Indeed, the opening scene moves at such a frenetic pace, with jump cuts and slapstick and overorchestrated mayhem, that a good deal of it is lost in the blur of activity. "Who's gonna want to laugh at this pace?" Paltrow says, his straight face underscoring the animated irreverence everywhere else. "I'm just hoping to cash the check. I hope the check clears." He is clearly unhappy with the look and lighting of the show, with the performances of some of his actors, and with the hurried direction, but underneath his unease there is still characteristic good cheer and an unflappable sense that he and his partners will pull this off.

There is always tomorrow.

Regrettably, tomorrow does not quite turn out according to plan. Thursday, April 12, is like a half-dozen worst-case scenarios all rolled into one really, really, harrowing scenario. Everything that can go wrong does, as do some things that could not possibly go wrong.

The day begins without incident, but it quickly unravels. First, without incident, the cast members are awakened from their beds with elaborate flower arrangements, courtesy of CBS. A nice touch, this, and Griffin, nicely touched, leaves his arrangement off at his local police station, a gift for the cops. "The police never get to smile," he explains of his beneficence. "They deserve to smile. What am I gonna do with flowers?" The actor seems totally unruffled by today's taping and the opening night, ass-on-the-line excitement that surrounds it. He is just here to do what he is told and, hopefully, to remember his lines.

Still without incident, Mary Beth Hurt busies herself around Sara Scadutto's work space. She has brought some of her daughter's finger paintings from home to use as personal set decoration, and she sets these out with a mother's care. She also stares long and hard at the framed photos the prop department has displayed on her character's desk. She wants to know who these people are in relation to her character, to figure some connection. Of course, there is none, but she is happy to invent something. She notices that the same girl shows up in three different pictures. Perhaps she is one of Sara's children. Alec Baldwin is still here, too, but Hurt has determined he is not Sara's husband. Maybe a brother who lives out of town. The Kellogg's Variety Pak, which was on her desk through yesterday's run-through, is finally gone, thanks to a take-charge Julie Martin.

Also, Hurt consults a scratch pad she has fixed to the desk as a kind of cheat sheet, on which she has made notes to herself about each scene and on which she now makes some more. She has given each scene a nickname to help her remember her role within it, and she goes over these one last time.

At eleven-thirty, the actors proceed two at a time to the makeup room on the third floor. There CBS makeup artist Rosemary Zurlo does what she can with blush and powder. Also, she is quick to dispense "Paul Newman drops" to the blue-eyed members of the troupe. "They just make the blue eyes bluer," she tells. This, too, passes without incident, although Zurlo also tells how one time she dispensed too much of the stuff to an actor whose nose began to run blue. Some of the actors, told, have heard of this happening. It is not an uncommon thing.

Set decorator Foxworthy turns up with a bulging plastic bag filled with water and five hearty-seeming goldfish, which he has purchased along with a bowl at a neighborhood pet store and which he has been asked to place on the round conference table in the center of the War Room. Tom John wanted a little something to soften up the institutional furnishings and to fill some of the bare space on the large tabletop, and the goldfish answered both needs nicely. Foxworthy names the new props Hammond, Sara, Marsha, Jim, and Steve.

And then, incident: The day takes its first bad turn across the Hudson River from the West 57th Street studios, in New Jersey, when Columbia suddenly pulls the plug on the Paltrow Group's other CBS pilot, *High*, just as the producers are completing preproduction. This happens in midafternoon, shortly before taping is to begin on *E.O.B./The War Room*. It happens without warning, although in retrospect it has been some time in coming. For the past several days, there has been a heated back and forthing between the studio and the producers over the *High* budget, and the studio, up against it, finally begs off the project. To the Paltrow Group, it is a kick in the groin where what was needed was a shot in the arm.

Despite this unexpected turn, CBS is still anxious to proceed with the pilot, but the network will not spend additional monies to get it made. It is up to the Paltrow Group to cover the difference between the network licensing fee and the actual production costs or to find anouther financial partner willing to do so (or to abandon the project themselves).

It is also up to the Paltrow Group to determine its future relationship with the studio, or if there will even be one. If there is, it does not promise to be smooth. A vengeful Paltrow vows to wrest *The War Room* and *Modern Marriage* from Columbia and shop all three shows to another studio. Under normal circumstances, as before, the producers and their pilots are an attractive package, but these are not normal circumstances. On principle, it is still a viable option, although it is not a sensible one. It is not sensible because one of these three pilots is due to tape this evening and another is fully cast and scheduled to begin filming on Monday. The third is partially cast and in preproduction for an early May shoot. By the time Paltrow is able to untangle his company from one studio and sign on with another, the air will have gone out of all three projects, and the producers could emerge at the other end of this pilot season with nothing to show for their efforts.

Clearly, the producers will not let this happen. They have come too far to take these particular steps backward, even on principle. Plus, *The War Room* and *High* cannot realistically absorb any delays—director Whitesell begins another shoot in Los Angeles next week, and one of the *High* locations is a real-life New Jersey high school that will not be on Easter break forever—and so the producers' next move will likely not interfere with these already-tight schedules.

"The most ridiculous thing is it's not a lot of money," Paltrow says, suggesting that the disputed bottom lines are less than a hundred thousand dollars apart. "That's what's so ridiculous. It's nothing. And they knew what the budget was, going in. No surprises. We're not over budget. But, boom, they wake up and say, 'Nah, we don't want to pay,' and we're supposed to say, 'Oh, okay, thanks, anyway.' It's just nonsense."

It is, also, an unadorned negotiating ploy, gotten out of hand. Gary Lieberthal, chairman and chief executive officer of Columbia Pictures Television, simply wants to keep production costs down, and this is the way he argues his case. It seems like a bad strategy, to alienate his under-the-gun partners, with whom he is already in bed on other pressing projects, but it is a strategy.

Meanwhile, a second disaster lurks around a second corner, and this bad turn could prove more damaging than the first, at least to this production. Local One of the Theatrical Stage Employees Union, which represents the stagehands, set decorators, makeup artists, wardrobe handlers, and lighting technicians currently toiling on *The War Room* set, has threatened a strike against the network for five o'clock this afternoon. This is unsettling, but it is not news around West 57th Street. The only thing new about this information is that the strike deadline happens to come around on the calendar today. By proximity, then, it is something to be taken seriously.

Curiously, the producers have known about the possibility of this strike since before production began, but they have done nothing to guard against it, even though the potential crisis could have easily been averted with a simple schedule change. In sliding the entire production ahead by one day, the producers would have been guaranteed a wrap before the strike deadline. They did not do this mostly because they could not have been ready one day sooner (as it happened, the show was not fully cast until the fourth day of rehearsals, and the sets were not mounted until three days before taping) but also because they were told it was not necessary. For two weeks now, CBS officials have been assuring the Paltrow Group, coordinating producer Finnerty, and Columbia executives that network and union negotiators would certainly resolve their disputes before the current contract expired. Not to worry, they said, everything is under control. And besides, this particular union has never staged a work stoppage throughout its long association with the network, so there was no reason to suspect they would engage in one here. Of course, there was also no reason to suspect they would not.

For the next several hours, *The War Room* cast and crew go through their motions as if nothing has happened. Indeed, as far as they are concerned, nothing has, even though some things might. They are, with the exception of the could-be striking union members, oblivious to these high-stakes dramas, and Paltrow would like to keep them that way. There is no reason, he figures, to let anyone know this whole project can implode, at any moment, for any number of reasons. Most people already know this, or at least fear it, on one level, but they do not need to base their knowledge or fear on anything tangible. When word of the impending strike ultimately does reach the actors, during a break, it is dismissed with incredulity. Such a thing—a strike? come on—is too preposterous to be believed, and therefore it is not.

Donna Isman turns up on the set with a couple of stacks of white Camp *E.O.B.* T-shirts, which no longer seem relevant but which she distributes to the cast and crew as if they were. If she knows about the pending strike, or about Columbia's sudden defection from *High*, she is not saying. She hands out the shirts, but no one puts them on. The actors, naturally, are in costume for the taping. The camera operators and technicians, who all week long have been dressed in jeans and T-shirts, have donned jackets and ties in honor of today's taping, in a bow to tradition. And the shirts are nothing special: black block letters against a plain white background.

At two o'clock, about an hour behind schedule, Whitesell leads his troupe through a taped run-through. This is done to work out any last-minute problems with the camera blocking, or lighting, and to bank at least one take of each scene as a safeguard against glitches in tonight's two tapings. As they work on the first scene, there is still a painter doing touch-up work on the adjacent Coolidge Room set and a scenic artist transforming a photo blowup of the Washington Monument from daytime into dusk.

The producers sit in the first row of the audience grandstand, which is otherwise empty. Between takes, Paltrow keeps saying, "This is a good show, it's a good show, it's a funny show." He says this, first, to Tinker, and then to himself, over and over, until it becomes like a mantra: "It's a good show, it's a funny show."

Fontana, when a joke falls flat, stands and taunts the offending actor: "You killed the joke. You'll go to comedian's jail. Instead of Sing Sing, it'll be Ha Ha."

At the close of the first act, it takes five minutes for two stagehands to clean up the confetti of Jim Smith's first speech. One guy holds the broom, and one guy holds the dustpan. They've got a system. By now, the two (actually, four) hands have tidied this scene at least fifty times, and each pass has been followed by this too-long maintenance pause. By conservative estimate, figuring each of these guys earns about twenty dollars an hour, the cumulative man-hour cleanup cost for this one scene will approach two hundred dollars. This seems like a lot.

The taping moves slowly, in fits and starts. Whitesell frequently stops to reposition his actors, or to find a new camera angle, or to have the lighting adjusted. Only a few of these delays have to do with how the actors are delivering their lines or interacting with each other; fewer still are to help the actors to discover new aspects to what has now become familiar material; rather, they are mostly about where the actors are standing and how they look in relation to everyone else and to the set itself.

During these downtimes, the producers putter nervously about the set. One moment, they are zipping around like kids in a candy store, only it is their store and they have paid for all of the candy; the next, they sit and fret over the sour developments the day has brought, and still might bring.

Tinker spends some of this time in the control booth, his feet crossed against the control panel in front of him, his reclining/swivel chair doing a good job of both. "This is what the Paltrow Group symbol should be," he says when someone catches him in this position, and then he mock poses: hands clasped behind his head, seat back, feet up. "My father used to say, 'First be best, then be first,' but we've got our own motto. 'First be stupid, then be lazy.'"

Paltrow escapes from this madness by dealing with the chaos on *High*. He is on the phone to Pier 62, to the network, to Columbia, to his lawyers, trying to salvage his show.

Fontana finds his peace and quiet on the Coolidge Room set. Here, amid the bustle and clamor of this pretaping, he also finds a sigh. He leans back against the cool leather of B. Laurence Taylor's desk chair, puts his feet up on the aggressive desk, and takes it all in.

At 4:16 in the afternoon, as he sits and reflects, one of the stagehands approaches him cautiously. "Are you the producer?" the man says.

"Yes," Fontana responds, still reclining. "I'm the one who doesn't make decisions."

The guy does not get it. "But you are one of the producers?" he tries again.

"Last time I checked," Fontana says.

"Well, I'm the shop steward, and I'm supposed to inform you that my people are striking at five o'clock."

Fontana leans forward with the bulletin. "Oh," he says, and then, pleadingly, "Take me with you, please."

Alarmed, Fontana hurries to the control booth to pass this news on to Paltrow, who is huddled with Whitesell, making some last-minute changes to the still-busy opening scene. "We're being struck," Fontana announces solemnly. "Five o'clock, they're going out."

Paltrow falls back hard against the soundproofed wall at the news. "Shit," he says, slapping his hand against the wall for emphasis. "I knew this would happen. I fucking knew this would happen." He starts out calm, but he whips himself into a small rage. "Shit," he says again.

Shit, indeed. Clearly, tonight's two tapings can proceed without the set decorators, stagehands, and makeup and wardrobe people; most of their work is complete, and what remains to be done can be easily delegated to others. But the lighting is another matter. The intricate maze of fixtures and beams that hang from grids and catwalks suspended high above the set are too elaborate for a lay person to master. It is not simply a matter of flipping a switch. There is more to it than that, and by five o'clock, Paltrow is convinced, the still-on-the-job technicians will have had nearly an hour to undo the lighting figurations that have already been set into the system. Whoever he can find to troubleshoot the lighting will be forced to start from scratch, without a clue. They might as well light a candle. At least they'll get a prayer out of the deal.

Thirteen

TAPE

○   At five o'clock the *War Room* sets go dark. Literally. A minute later, also literally, CBS sends in reinforcements. Specifically, the network dispatches a half-dozen former technicians from the ranks of middle management, who descend on the soundstage to see what they can do with the lighting, if they can do anything at all.

As these born-again technicians approach, the left-behind camera and technical crews make an arrow for the safety of the control booth. Their union has instructed them not to go out in sympathy with the stagehands, but nobody has said anything to them about sanctuary. The thought of all those overweight and out-of-touch middle managers snaking around on the grids and catwalks up above has got these cameramen and technicians concerned. More, and worse, the thought that a striking lighting technician has snipped a few wires, or loosened a few screws, to undermine the production and stand a few hairs has got them unnerved. They have all seen too many old movies, where someone is sandbagged on an opera-house stage by a spiteful saboteur, not to be concered about this.

"It's probably not a good idea to stand under the lights," advises a seeking-cover Mary Cody, one of the boom operators. "It could get ugly." She moves as she says this, out from under.

It has already gotten ugly outside on West 57th Street. Here, within shouting distance of the main entrance to the CBS Broadcast

Center, the picket line has swelled and grown heated. An hour ago, some of these picketers were rigging a hose to shower pretend rain outside the War Room window or helping to position a silly campaign hat on a presidential bust decorating the set, but now they are outside, angry, chanting, "First in profits, last in wages!" and "Scabs will die in hell!," to the arriving members of the studio audience they were only recently working to entertain.

Inside, at 5:06, the cast is closeted in one of the backstage rooms for a final notes session, which turns out to be nothing more than a pep talk. "Make it like it's brand-new," Whitesell cheerleads, sidestepping the mounting technical problems now facing the show. He does not mention the strike, and when someone else does, he peps on: "Make it like you've never done these scenes before."

Despite noises to the contrary, the actors know tonight's two tapings cannot possibly yield a pilot of broadcast quality. They know that something terribly unusual and perhaps even untenable has happened. They can see all of the harried middle-managers-turned-lighting technicians, running around as if they do not know what they are doing. They can see the shadows on the set. Too, they can hear assistant director Sedwick doctoring the lyrics to the Cat Stevens song "Moonshadow" ("I'm being followed by a boom shadow...."), in what has quickly become a familiar refrain. They can see their producers huddled nervously behind B. Laurence Taylor's Coolidge Room desk. They can smell the doom.

"They should get Greyhound drivers to do the lights," Rich Hall jokes, referring to another group of now prominent strikers. "They're not doing anything right now. 'Leave the lighting to us.'"

The audience—mostly friends and family of the cast and crew, with a complement of network and entertainment-industry types—is loaded onto the stage at 5:30. There is also a smattering of tourists and just plain folks who were given free passes (to a "brand-new CBS sitcom!") on the midtown streets surrounding Black Rock earlier this afternoon. There are not enough chairs to accommodate this disparate crowd, and a few people are made to sit on the aisle steps. This is a fire hazard, but probably no more dangerous than positioning these good people underneath the suspect lighting grid.

Mark Cohen, a stand-up comedian who has been hired (for five hundred dollars) to warm up the studio audience before tonight's show, and during the sometimes long pauses throughout the taping, keeps referring to the strike in his routine and suggesting that the cameramen on the floor below him are scabs. This generates some anxious titters from the audience but puts the cameramen on boil, until one of them, finally, turns back to the audience and caterwauls, "We're not scabs!" and then to the comic, "Stop tellin' everyone we're scabs!" He does this in a tone that normally precedes fisticuffs.

The comedian gets the message, loud and heated, and shifts to lighter fare: He describes an Irish wake ("closed casket, open bar") lampoons a geriatric Mick Jagger (currently on the road in the Rolling Stones' "Steel Wheelchair Tour"), and wonders why there is not a more realistic form of auto racing, with tolls ("The New Jersey 500"). The strikers had already agitated most members of this studio audience as they entered the building, and Cohen's references to scabs and union busters has got them on edge to where their laughs do not come easy. At least, they are not coming easy for him. "You're all looking at me like you're the cast of *Children of a Lesser God,*" the comic bemoans when a string of his jokes have missed their intended marks.

The crowd, not quite warm, is also stymied by the constant flash of the PLEASE APPLAUD signs, which hang from the lighting grid every here and there. "Why are the applause signs on all the time?" Tom Fontana asks Donna Isman.

"I don't know," the production supervisor says. "I don't even know who to ask."

"Can we just turn them off, then?"

"You mean off instead of on?"

"Off, I mean off. Is there a way to turn them off? If we can't get them to applaud without the sign, we're in trouble."

Isman disappears to see about disconnecting the signs and is bounced from middle manager to middle manager, looking for clues. Nobody knows how to work these things, or not work them.

At 5:58, Fontana takes the microphone from the comedian and introduces the cast. He also introduces notable members of the studio audience, including Ed McNally, John Tinker's real-life presidential speechwriter friend, and a real-life Steve Lawson, for whom the show's fake one is named. "I know it's a stupid name," Fontana says when he presents Lawson, "but somebody has to have it." Then he gives away a Camp *E.O.B.* T-shirt.

During the taping, Fontana paces in the corner, stage left; Tinker sits in the front row of the audience, his arms pretzeled tight to his chest; Paltrow watches through the monitors in the control booth, standing next to Whitesell and Selwick, who are sitting down. The actors, when they exit their scenes, retreat to the nearest monitor to see how their costars are doing. They cannot tell from the audience, or from the mood backstage, or even from their positions opposite during their shared scenes. It is as though they need to experience the show secondhand, on a television screen, in order to judge it for themselves.

Firsthand, there is more energy to this performance than there has ever been in rehearsals. The actors seem fueled by the crowd and by a kind of show-must-go-on ethos that permeates the soundstage. And yet despite their best efforts, certain of the material falls flat, and when this happens the actors seem to lose their stride for a moment. They do not expect this or know what to do with it. For example, when the formally attired speechwriters return to the War Room to check on Jim Smith's progress and Marsha Katzenberg boasts about having her picture taken with the president and Margaret Thatcher, the cast bumps into a darkly funny barb that has managed to pull laughs all week long, until now:

Marsha Katzenberg, gloating: "Tomorrow morning, my face'll be folded by every paperboy in America. I've got to phone my folks."

Sara Scadutto, upset at being excluded from the photo opportunity: "Thank you very much."

Marsha Katzenberg, solicitously and with some swagger: "I tried to get the president to include you in the photo. It's not my fault I'm his favorite writer. He loves my style. He loves my politics."

Hammond Egley: "He loves your crutches. It looks good to be photographed with the physically challenged."

Audience members do not know what to make of this exchange. Are they expected to laugh? moan? let it slide? They are not accustomed to jokes about handicapped people, and this, along with others like it peppered throughout the script, has got them clearly unsettled. Ton Fontana laughs, as does the now-unpretzeled John Tinker, but few follow their lead. Perhaps a PLEASE LAUGH sign, in working condition, would be helpful here.

A second show, which was to have started at eight o'clock, gets under way about an hour late. Another comic, Billy Garan, is brought on to keep this second crowd at bay, but the biggest laugh of the warmup goes to boom operator Hal Schur, who swivels on his perch to face the audience and says, "Hey, want to hear the fish?" and then swivels back and stretches his boom microphone out over the goldfish bowl.

This second pass is more slow-footed than the first. The actors seem to be dragging. William Duff Griffin keeps missing his lines, and the ones he manages to remember come out as if he is reading them and not thinking them. John Dye is inordinately distracted by the houselights, which no one can manage to turn off between scenes. He wants to wrap himself in character, in the extra darkness, to shield himself and what he is doing from the studio audience.

At the end of the first act, CBS production supervisor Richard Reinhardt, in short sleeves and tie, cleans up the mess of confetti left behind by what is left of Jim Smith's speech. Reinhardt is doing most of the work of the striking stagehands for these two performances— misting down the War Room windows to suggest rain; tidying up the mess of the disarmament scene—and to save time for this task he deploys a vacuum.

Why didn't the union hands think of this?

Paltrow is on the phone for most of this second show, trying to salvage this production and the one in New Jersey. It is clear to him, and to the others in the control booth, that the lighting for these two *War Room* tapings has been either too light or too dark. Where it falls somewhere in between, it still looks generally unprofessional. He knows that if he has to rely on scenes pulled from these two tapings, plus the material from the taped run-through this afternoon, he will wind up with a pilot looking like something shot in a friend's basement, for cable access, and he is scrambling to arrange a second set of tapings for tomorrow. Actually, the second set of tapings is arranged easily; the scrambling comes in determining who will pay for them. Finally, the network agrees to eat the cost of the additional tapings because it has failed to deliver the services and facilities it promised for the first.

A great deal is riding on this *War Room* pilot, for Paltrow and company. True, there is a summer-series commitment in place from Jeff Sagansky for five additional episodes, but this is loosely contingent on the execution of the prototype. If the pilot self-destructs, as it appears to be doing at this moment, then it will be easy for the network to rescind its series promise. If the pilot is merely serviceable, then there is another door left open for the network to back through. Paltrow knows the pilot has to live up to expectations if it is to continue on as a summer series; and if it is to steamroll into the fall season, it has to be better than expected.

This, so far, is not better than expected.

When the second show wraps, the pitching-in Reinhardt hands out CBS pens and luggage tags to the cast. He is spent, and flush with camaraderie. He does his distributing with great fanfare, as if he is dispensing game-show prizes, and the actors accept these parting gifts—the home version of this particular fiasco—as if they are worth having. The ridiculous gesture signals a ridiculous message: Hey, we know we screwed you guys tonight with this strike, but at least you get these great pens and luggage tags out of the deal!

There is some concern about the actors having to cross the picket line for tomorrow's taping, and to circumvent this problem a plan is hatched for the cast to meet at Columbus Circle at ten o'clock in the morning, in front of the New York Coliseum. From there, they will embark, by shuttle van, for one of the backdoor delivery entrances at West 57th. Of course, there is no hiding that they will still be crossing the picket line, even with these maneuvers, just as they have crossed it today, but no one will notice, and they will be spared the confrontation in doing so.

This turns out to be a good plan. The actors are shuttled into the studio the next morning—Friday, April 13—without incident, while outside the striking stagehands are still predicting an early, fiery death for those who cross their path. ("Scabs will die in hell!" they are still chanting, desperate for new material.) The actors, saved from the picket line and from themselves, go through the same motions as the day before, except this time around they appear drained, thrashed. This week has taken its toll. They had been gearing up for yesterday's performances, and when they passed, they took something with them. There does not seem much left for tonight. Too, they know last night's effort will likely be scrapped (although Whitesell claims much of it is "pretty usable") and that tonight's will be hobbled by some of the same technical problems.

As the cast tries to regain its footing, a new group of technicians seeks to restore the lighting. The middle managers have been replaced by nonunion lighting experts, who are busy undoing the damage of the night before. A group of them are fidgeting about the set, necks craned, and poking at the high-up spotlights with incredibly long, pointy sticks, which look like something a gondolier might use as a barbecue tool. With these, it is possible to open and shut the blinders on the individual fixtures, to redirect the spots, and to generally move things around along the grid without having to actually climb up there.

Mary Beth Hurt watches all of this lighting activity and begins to feel for the plants on her desk. She fills a small watering can and starts to feed her swapped cactus. At first, she pretends to do this for the cameras (she watches herself on the monitors and makes a couple of housewifey twirls, as if she is endorsing a kitchen product), but then she really gets into it. She does it for real. When she finishes with the plants on and around her desk, she attends to the others on the set.

"We don't usually water the props," chides Columbia production executive Debbie Penchina, looking on. "We just throw them out."

"But these lights are hot," Hurt justifies, as if she has to. "These guys are thirsty. I can't just sit and watch them suffer."

Tonight's first show is listless, and off. A few of the props fall apart to the touch—the telephone on Steve Lawson's desk loses its mouthpiece; a television cart loses a wheel—and the actors are flubbing their lines as if it is the first day of rehearsals. Most of these mistakes are ignored, and the cameras left to roll, but occasionally Whitesell's voice comes booming over the intercom—"Cut!"—and brings the scene to a halt. During one of these pauses, Tom Fontana, wearing a Day-Glo orange CBS baseball cap, turns to the audience and says, "Let's all do a Rosemary Woods. Let's forget the last eighteen seconds."

But Whitesell cannot stop and restart every scene. At least not yet. He worries that he loses too much momentum with each pause, that the audience grows quickly impatient during the downtime it takes for the crew to reposition the props, and the cameras to return to speed, so he keeps it moving, forward whenever possible. He does this knowing tonight's second show will be his last chance to get it right, to get it down. The endless stops and starts can wait until later, if needed.

The time between tonight's first and second shows seems interminable to the actors. The producers' unease about last night's taping and the general unraveling of this production has somehow filtered down to them, and it joins with the pressing weight of tonight's last-chance performance to leave them on edge, tentative. To fill the time, some of them—Hall, Nauffts, and Van Dyck—are huddled in the greenroom, fixed on an episode of the ABC blended-family sitcom *Full House*, which is coming in on one of the monitors. The show, about a widowed father raising his three young daughters with the help of his brother-in-law and his best friend, filters into this room as a promise and a warning. To this vigilant bunch, this standard domestic sitcom represents conventional network television; they look on, terrified, imagining their futures within it. This is easier for Hall than for the others. He began his stand-up career twelve years earlier on the same Philadelphia stage with actor Bob Saget, the star of *Full House*, and he has seen, from the sidelines, how the power of the medium can transform an actor's career, persona, and lifestyle. He is ready for it to happen to him. It almost has, from time to time. He knows what to expect.

The others are not so sure. They seem to have a certain fear of what might happen to them, a disdain for what they are about to do, or become, and these feelings find a target in this too-typical ABC show.

"Let's get some pointers," Nauffts says derisively, pulling up a chair. "Let's see how it's done."

Van Dyck does not bother to sit, but she is pulled closer to the set, as if by fate. "Is this gonna be us?" she says, inching to the screen. She reaches out her hand to touch the film of static emanating from the set. She really does this. "Is this what we're about to do?" she continues, mostly to herself. "I'm watching this and I'm about to retch. I can't believe this is what I'm about to do." She looks at her hands to see if any of this has rubbed off on her. She really does this, too. She is horrified by what she sees, but she is also drawn to it, pulled. She is wanted on the set, but she cannot bring herself to leave.

In the quick-change room behind the set, Hurt is waiting on a last-minute touch-up from hairstylist Annette Bianco. Someone makes a joke about working without Annette.

Also backstage, Arthur Silver works with Tom Fontana on a last-minute piece of business for the show's only "extra"—a U.S. Marine security guard stoically positioned at the War Room entrance for the duration of the script. They are trying to get actor Trevor Wallace, who was cast as the marine hours before yesterday's first taping, to spin on his heels in a regulation quarter turn and to do an about-face. They work on this for some time, but the movements do not come easily to the actor. In fact, Wallace is completely awkward at them, and Silver and Fontana eventually abandon their bit. It is too late to find another extra to fit their marine uniform, so they go with what they've got.

On the set, Jonathan Solomon, tonight's second warm-up comic, has got the final studio audience primed. (His definition of charivari: "an Italian word that means 'over your head.'") With his assist, the crowd is giddy, eager to laugh and to be entertained.

The crowd gets what it wants, by chance. In the first scene, Geoffrey Nauffts reaches for the phone on his character's desk and falls backward in his swivel chair. It is a classic pratfall, although unintentional, and the audience howls. For a moment, it appears Nauffts has hurt himself, from the way he falls—back and over, onto his head—but he hasn't, and he pulls himself up and dusts himself off and continues on with the scene, trying to stifle some howls of his own. His energy is all the way up when he returns, and he keeps it there. The audience, still laughing, helps him to keep it there. And the rest of the cast is pulled up to this turbo level. This last performance is clearly the loosest, most animated and on target of the four, and it all seems to flow from Nauffts's pratfall.

(Oddly, the recline mechanism on Nauffts's swivel chair turns up frayed and worn on later inspection, marking yet another prop-related mishap on the set. At first, these separate pieces of bad luck are lightly dismissed; later, they are blamed on the date—Friday the thirteenth. By the end of the night, though, there is whispered speculation that the set has been vandalized by the striking stage-hands. This is never confirmed, but it is widely believed.)

After the second taping, the cast is made to wait around to see if any scenes need to be shot again. "Pickups," these are called. The producers, and Whitesell, are still not happy with the complicated disarmament scene, and they quickly review the four performance takes and the taped-rehearsal take to see what they have got to work with. The Columbia executives are lingering, too, but with the exception of Silver they are not openly consulted. They seat themselves in the now-empty grandstand and fill the time by not making eye contact with the producers, with whom they still have the unresolved business of *High* to discuss.

Whitesell orders a few tight shots of actors Dye and Griffin, leading into and out of their shredded-speech encounter, and he picks up a few other shots here and there, but the disarmament scene is allowed to stand.

The cast is finally dismissed at just before midnight, and they leave for a hasty wrap party at a nearby bar. They are joined by some of the crew, and members of the Paltrow Group office, and in the din between their toasts and hugs and backslaps there are the conflicting emotions of relief, regret, and uncertainty. Everyone in this group seems glad the ordeal of this particular pilot is over, although they are sad to see it end. Mostly, they are sad to see it end badly, as they fear it has.

The party does not last beyond a couple of rounds. The actors are tired. They want to go home. For nearly two weeks, from the moment they were cast, they have immersed themselves in the fortunes and rhythms of this show to where they are now anxious to think about something else. Or nothing at all.

And so they return to their own lives, and careers, not knowing whether their efforts have have been enough to bring them all back together for a summer run, if this has been the launching-pad effort to a long, successful association, or if it has been simply a protracted audition, another in a string of disappointments.

They disperse, in separate cabs, thinking maybe they will be seeing each other again soon. Maybe they will be seeing a lot of each other here on in. Maybe not.

Fourteen

EDIT _____

○ It is Tuesday, April 17, and there is still a good deal of work to be
done. Most of this work will be done in a small, dark room. Actually,
it will be done in any number of small, dark rooms, scattered around
New York City, depending on availability. Today it is being done in a
room that is particularly small. It is also particularly noisy. This last is
not the sort of feature most people look for in an editing room.

Assistant director Joanne Sedwick is crowded with videotape editor
Carl Woitach in a small bunker of an editing room adjacent to the
under-renovation CBS News Radio offices at West 57th. They are
surrounded on all sides by hard hats and blueprints and unfinished
containers of coffee with sipping Vs punched out of their lids. Here,
even behind closed doors, they have to struggle to hear themselves
think, surrounded as they are also by the drilling and pounding of the
neighboring construction.

They are doing the best they can. They are working from John
Whitesell's rough cut, which the director slapped together before
skipping town for Los Angeles and another assignment and which is
still about six minutes too long. It will take Woitach and Sedwick the
better part of a week to lose those six minutes. It will take them
longer if they have to do all of this work here, unable to concentrate.
Today, for one thing, their progress is stalled by Woitach's precaution:
He is constantly backing up his master tape, fearful that all of the

138

exposed wiring outside this editing room might leave him exposed to some kind of power zap inside.

This is what Woitach and Sedwick have to work with: four tapes, from each of four cameras, of all four shows, plus a quad-split tape of each show and various pickups. From these they are hoping to quilt a seamless sitcom of approximately twenty-two minutes in length, which can then be sweetened, laughed and soundtracked, and forwarded to CBS. To accomplish this, they pop these tapes in and out of six Sony videocassette recorders, which are connected to six tiny black-and-white television monitors, two larger color monitors, and one quad monitor, and then they mix and match from among this group as if they were ordering off a Chinese menu. The entire operation is controlled by a computer keyboard at Carl Woitach's busy fingertips, and he jumps back and forth, from one tape to the next, looking for the biggest laughs, the cleanest takes, the best performances, and the least objectionable lighting. He loads in the good stuff, leaves off the bad, and sets aside everything else. He enters each command with a flowery final keystroke, which appears to put an exclamation point on things for him.

Woitach and Sedwick are on their own, for now. Paltrow, Fontana, and Tinker are off in New Jersey, on *High*, where the budget impasse has been bridged by some hard-to-swallow cuts and production begun on schedule. The producers will check in on the *War Room* edit at the end of the day and sit in on another all-day session tomorrow.

"This scene is aggressively bright," Sedwick suggests when she screens the otherwise best take of a scene. "It's too much."

"None of the others are clean," Woitach laments.

"Can we bring it down at all?" Sedwick asks.

"Bring what down?"

"The lighting. Can you do something with that?"

"Not much. What's there is what's there. It's harsh."

A clean take refers to a single scene, pulled from a single taping, that is polished enough to be transferred onto the master tape in its entirety. Within this clean take, an editor might make certain revisions or cut away to different reaction shots, but every image will be drawn from one of the four camera angles of the same performance. They do not have too many clean takes to work with here. Almost everything will have to be polluted. Either Rich Hall has got his hands flapping around like he's trying to land a plane, or William Duff Griffin has mangled his lines, or the shadows on the back walls of the set make it look like the scene was lit by headlights. In fact, only one scene—the until-now-troubled disarmament scene—will be transferred onto the final edit precisely as it was performed (in this case, during the second taping on Friday night). Every other scene will be cut and pasted together, with Woitach and Sedwick robbing from one take to make another one richer.

The work is precise and exacting and proceeds slowly. Woitach and Sedwick have been at it for two days, and they are astonishingly calm and straightforward about the maddeningly painstaking process. They are each chewing gum, courtesy of Sedwick, and their gum chewing neatly matches the separate ways they go about their shared business. She chews like she is distracted, like she has to remind herself; he chews like he means it, the duck's ass of hair at his collar lifting noticeably with each chomp. Sedwick, who appears to be in her middle to late thirties is thoughtful, and sure; she circles the material until she can spot the clearest path through it. Woitach, late twenties, is aggressive and eager to try anything; he attacks the material, pounding out commands on his keyboard like he is being paid by the flowery final keystroke. They are alike in that they seem not to mind the long hours ahead, or those just passed, because they know their efforts here will be integral to the success of the finished product. They also know that no one will fully appreciate the extent of their contributions. But they will know, and this is important to them.

Remarkably, Sedwick can locate every shot from every scene almost by memory. She does not work from notes or from any elaborate indexing system. The abundant images from these four tapings have been burned into her to where she can call them up in her sleep. She knows that during Thursday's second performance, for example, John Dye did a little something with his mouth when he made his entrance at the top of the show. She likes this expression and would like to work it into the show. The problem is that the rest of the late Thursday performance was particularly off and poorly lit, so she also knows where she might be able to inject Dye's little something with his mouth into another version of the same and have it look like it belongs there. Watching her work, it is difficult to imagine how she is able to internally track every angle of every scene. (There are one hundred and forty-four takes of the show's nine scenes, plus pickups and certain scenes from the taped run-through.) Either she has already screened these dozen-plus tapes too many times for her own sanity, or she is very good at what she does. Or, maybe, both.

Trick of the trade: When Woitach and Sedwick attach a segment from Thursday's late show with another from Friday's, they screen the edited effort with the sound off to see if the connection seems jarring or false.

"You can see it so much better with the sound off," explains Sedwick, who claims she sometimes rents movies and watches them with the sound off at home. The effect is muted here by the persistent sounds of the adjacent construction, but she still swears by it. "It forces you to see if there's a good match, a good fit. It's right there."

They shave bits and pieces from Whitesell's rough cut until they have pared down the master version to where it is only four minutes too long. They are not cutting any scripted material in today's edit—that will begin tomorrow, with the producers—but they are letting the air out of each scene, eliminating the awkward pauses, tightening the reaction shots, cropping the dead spaces between the actors' lines. In this way—by shedding a couple of seconds here, a couple of seconds there—they will bring the show ever closer to its broadcast length. And when they finish one pass, they go at it again, and again, until they have sandpapered it down to size.

"Let me just laugh these two things," Woitach says when Sedwick asks him to take a look at another take. The laughs he lays onto the master audio track are not canned. They are genuine, studio-audience laughs, and they are usually attached to the same punch lines for which they were so freely given. By the time the audio is mixed and sweetened, these laughs will be doctored somewhat, but for now they are the real thing. Occasionally, when he comes to where the laughs were supposed to follow the jokes about Marsha Katzenberg's handicap, he borrows them from someplace else.

On Wednesday, the operation is moved to another editing room at West 57th Street, this one quieter and more spacious. Here there is room for Tom Fontana and Bruce Paltrow, who arrive in the afternoon after working all morning on *High*. John Tinker has stayed back on the *High* set; he will put his fingerprints on the *War Room* edit tomorrow.

"Can you get in cleaner?" Paltrow asks Woitach, at the top of one scene. He does not like the way the camera picks up Geoffrey Nauffts in mid-sentence. It seems abrupt, clipped.

"I think so," Woitach responds. "We can try."

"Good. Try. If you can get in cleaner, you can get in cleaner."

Paltrow is on the phone at every other moment. There is no window in his day to return his mounting messages, so he sneaks this time open a crack to make a few calls. "I can't talk now," he says whenever he is put through, "I'm editing." And then he talks, a little. Sometimes, listening, he puts his hand over the mouthpiece and asks Woitach to tighten a reaction shot or to cut a long cross of the War Room set—"Just establish Jim at his desk," he tells, "that'll give us the geography, and then you can lose that other crap"—and then he slips back to his schmooze.

When he is off the phone and waiting for Woitach to effect one of his changes, he spars with Fontana. The producers are on each other like kid brothers in the backseat for a too-long car ride. They are frazzled, these two friends. They have jumped from one production directly into another, without a breath, and the relentless pace has caught up with their relentless good cheer to where neither one is willing to let anything slide. They are not quite on each other's nerves, but they might be getting there; and, on the way, they seem to enjoy ragging on each other.

"What's with this glass half-full, half-empty crap?" Paltrow says when Fontana approaches an editing problem from a philosophical perspective.

"That's the fundamental difference between you and me," Fontana figures. "Everything is half empty to me, and to you it's half full."

"No," Paltrow disagrees. "My glass has no water in it. There's not a drop of water in my glass."

They also rag on Whitesell, who is not here to return the parry.

"He directed this?" Fontana says, in a routine, at his friend's expense.

"Yeah," Paltrow returns, "from the inside of a coffee can, he directed this."

Mostly, though, they rag on themselves. Paltrow does this most of all. When an assistant leaves to get a second cup of tea for Fontana, after the producer accidentally spills the first while making a point, he asks if there is anything he can get for the others in the room as well. Paltrow does not want anything. "I want to be thirsty," he says. "That's what I want."

What he also wants is to deliver the strongest twenty-two minutes possible to the network, given the material he now has to work with. He does not like all of what he has to work with, but he is determined to make do. Mostly, what he does not like is the lighting, which is incredibly inconsistent from take to take. The master version of the show, patched together, looks as if it were shot in six different places at six different times of day. This is not a good thing. It is hoped that a typical television viewer will not notice the glaring differences, but it is acknowledged that a more careful viewer will certainly be bothered by them. And the most careful viewers—in network programming— will hopefully look past these technical difficulties and judge the show on its content and its potential.

"Let's do a lift," Fontana says at one point, meaning that it is finally time to trim some of the material from the show. There is still a lot of time to pare, and they have to start somewhere. They start with the bathroom jokes. They both hated the running gag sending Mary Beth Hurt's character on repeated trips to the bathroom, and they are happy to see it go. To achieve this, they simply lift the offending exchanges from the screen, along with the relevant pieces of abutting dialogue, and tighten the scene to where a fresh viewer will not notice the now-absent middle. It is not unlike the way they would have excised the same passage from the scripted page, except that now they can see what they are cutting instead of just imagining what they are cutting.

They also lose the Abe Lincoln nonsequitur Paltrow fought to keep during one of the rewrites. They lose it because it is a nonsequitur, and it is dispensable. "We'll use it again," Paltrow says of the now-thrown-away line. "We'll put it in another show. We don't waste anything around here."

On Thursday, John Tinker joins the process, while Paltrow drops out to attend to *High*. As Woitach loads today's changes into his computer, Fontana and Tinker watch the monitors of the network news feeds. When a story comes on about the apparently imminent release of the American hostages in Lebanon, the producers turn to each other in a shared shrug, because the prospect impacts in a benign way on the *High* script: One of the teenage characters has been back-storied with a father who is one of the American hostages in Lebanon, and this ongoing personal crisis is to be an important element to the show and to the student's story line within it.

"These guys have been hostages for fucking seven years," Fontana says, darning his luck, "and they have to let them out now?" He is not at all serious, of course, but it is hard for him to pass up a good line.

The edit continues for several days. The master tape is forwarded to Los Angeles, where Scott Siegler, president of Columbia Pictures Television, suggests that the producers eliminate the jokes about Marsha Katzenberg's handicap. The studio also advances the notion that perhaps this pilot episode should not introduce the series to a television audience, assuming *The War Room* is offered its promised slot of the CBS summer schedule. It is not good enough. From a technical standpoint, even the least objectionable lighting is objectionable; and, from a commercial view, it is felt that this particular script does not provide the best launch for a new series. Suddenly, there is talk that if the series is picked up, the pilot will be partially rewritten and reshot, and run as the fifth or six episode, as a kind of flashback to explain how Jim Smith came to be working in the speechwriters' office.

The final polish is more of a spit shine than a professional job. No one pays serious attention to the opening credits until it is nearly too late. At first, it was thought that the show would begin with its live, cold opening, to be followed by credits displayed against footage of real-life presidential speeches, taken from CBS News or from available archives. Logistically, the producers could not have prepared a live, topical opening to append to their pilot presentation (because the pilot will have to be as salient in May, when it is presented to the network, as it will be in July, when it is scheduled for broadcast), but they are still in need of opening credits.

Tinker, whose job it has been to produce these opening credits and to commission a theme song, has been so distracted by *High*, and *Modern Marriage*, and everything else, that he has somehow left these opening credits to produce themselves. When it finally appears they have not, he shows up in the editing room with the theme song from the Paltrow Group's canceled *Nick and Hillary* sitcom. The peppy music and innocuous lyrics seem suited to almost any situation comedy—"One thing's for sure, nothing's for certain. . . ."—and they are made to fit this one. Strangely, they do. Sort of. Anyway, they are close enough and will have to do. Underneath the borrowed song,

Woitach will lay in outtake clips from the two tapings, and when he is through, the credits will be better than nothing, although not by any significant margin.

"Can we go thicker on the lettering?" Tinker wants to know when he screens Woitach's first pass. He wants the lettering of the opening titles to appear bolder and more presidential.

"We can go thicker," answers Columbia's production supervisor Debbie Penchina, who has overseen most of the postproduction and seems to know her way around an editing room.

"Good, so let's do that, then."

"Do you want a different color?" Penchina asks.

"Good, yeah, I didn't know you could do that."

"Oh, yeah, we can do anything."

"Well," Tinker says, "then let's play with a couple things. Let's see what looks good."

Woitach punches up a bunch of different type styles on his screen, and he makes them go fat or thin, depending.

"We tried to use something that was as close to a typewriter face as we could find," Penchina says.

"Good," Tinker says. "I like that. That's good. I just think it should be a little thicker."

Woitach makes it a little thicker.

"What about the color?" Penchina wants to know.

"What are my choices?" Tinker says.

"You can do any color you want, but probably only white and yellow will read."

"Just white and yellow?"

"Probably. Yellow's a good sitcom color. Go with yellow."

A messenger interrupts this color scheming with an audiotape of a President bush soundalike, which is to be inserted onto the master tape in the opening scene, as an off-camera voice-over. Negotiations to sign Walter Cronkite to read the show's fictional presidential speeches have fallen through, as have backup negotiations with Harry Reasoner, so the producers have reluctantly agreed to mimic Bush, according to Jeff Sagansky's suggestion.

Woitach loads the tape onto his machine and dubs the voice onto the master tape. He turns the volume up as he does this, and Tinker, giving the speech his first listen, wonders how it is that his show has a bad Bush impression in it.

Nearly one month after the tapings at West 57th Street, the pilot is finally finished and ready to be sent to the network. The producers kick back in Tom Fontana's office and watch it one more time, before letting it go.

"It's a sitcom, "Fontana declares, watching. "I can't believe it. They turned it into a sitcom." He sounds dejected when he says this. He looks it, too. "You can't get married to any of this shit," he says later, after he has had a few moments to get used to this idea. "This is television."

Fifteen

BRIDGE _____

☐ BRUCE PALTROW (co-writer, co-executive producer, *The War Room*): "What went wrong with this pilot? Everything. Every single thing that could go wrong went wrong. Obviously, there was the technical stuff, the strike, and the lighting, but there was also the fact that we were so naive we got talked into a physical space we should never have agreed to go into in the first place. It was so small, it limited the amount of sets we could use and the size of the sets we could use. We had no flexibility at all. We had a very small studio audience, and they were too close to everything. So right away, our first decision was a bad one. Okay, we can shoot it here, sure. We can save some money? Sure. What we should have said was, No, we can't shoot here. If we have to shoot here, we can't shoot the show.

"And we went downhill from there. Everything fell from that. And then, because we were trying to get onto Sagansky's summer schedule, we were pushing, we did it earlier than we would have done it. We were still casting as we were in rehearsals. Bill Daniels fell out at the eleventh hour. His agent was cutesy pie. So we couldn't cast that part. And then there was the Bonnie character, Connie, whatever her name was, we couldn't cast that part, and we gave those lines to Steve. We were chasing. All along, we were chasing.

"And then there were all those other problems. All we had were problems. The director did not have pilot skills. He had replicating

147

skills. You know, if someone else had done it first, he could replicate what they'd done. But he did not bring any vision to it. And we were doing *High* at the same time and getting ready for *Modern Marriage,* and there just weren't enough hours in the day to sit over the director and see that it got done the right way. There were only twenty-four hours in a day, you know, and we needed thirty-six.

"So we were casting, and running back and forth, and location scouting, and everything else, and they shut us down on *High* for those few days and then put us back up. The budget was cut, and then we had the strike over at CBS. It was a complete, horrendous time. And it was a brand-new partnership, with Columbia, and it got off to such a horrendous start. Lawyers, everything. And then, on a personal level, and on top of everything else, my nephew was dying. He was diagnosed with cancer, he went into Sloan-Kettering, and he never came out. So I was racing from the set every night to go see him in the hospital or going back to the pier to do the rewrite and then to the hospital. It was the darkest, lowest point in my life. I don't know how I got through it. My focus wasn't as good as it should have been. I wasn't really there, you know. The responsibility is mine.

"And then *High* didn't make it onto the schedule. All along, Sagansky was telling me what a great show it was, and it was. It was exactly the show they asked us to make. Exactly. No surprises. They were talking about putting us on Thursday nights at eight, against *Cosby.* I didn't care where they put us on as long as they put us on. People would find us. They would find us. And then the schedule comes out and, boom, *The Flash* is on at eight o'clock on Thursdays, and we're not on the damn thing at all. *High* was, and is, an extraordinary program. I think it was groundbreaking. You know, they asked us to make some noise in a high school show, and that's exactly what we did. I think it's a fabulous hour of television. This was before *Beverly Hills 90210,* remember. They'd be off the air by now if we were on. *Beverly Hills 90210* is bubble gum. We gave you the real meal. I think we maybe went too far, which is why they didn't pick us up. The network was terrified of the program. The sales department said they couldn't sell it. The research department said that no one would watch it. Standards and practices had problems with a scene we had in there about bungee-cord jumping. We were just ahead of it all. Sagansky was a big supporter of the show, but everybody was against him. He'd only been in the job five months. And he just basically came to me and said, I'm sorry, I fucked you. I haven't had the job long enough. There are too many battles to fight."

DEBORAH CURTAN (senior vice president, current programs, Columbia Pictures Television): "I think what we saw in New York never had a shot. And I think we knew that, but we had to do it. Bruce Paltrow told me it was their out-of-town tryout. There were moments when it seemed like it would come apart, but we couldn't afford to be negative at that time. We had just gone into business with these people, we couldn't just go in and say, Well, maybe we shouldn't do this, after all.

"I'm sorry, but I just didn't think this show would ever make it on the air. I don't know if other people felt that way. I have a lot of problems with it. It's just not relatable. I don't know if the subject matter is that interesting. I could be dead wrong, but if we get those summer shows on, then what? Where will CBS put us on the schedule? I don't think they will. If these guys can punch it up and make it funnier, then maybe they can stay on the air, but that's not their strength. That's not what they do. I tried to talk to these guys, but they happen to be very good at what they do, and I think it's difficult to give them notes. They're very resistant to notes. That's been a problem for us."

TOM FONTANA (co-writer, co-executive producer, *The War Room*): "I don't think I'm resistant to notes. My way of dealing with notes has always been the same. Even when I was a playwright. I always look at them the same way. If there are fifty people in the audience, at the end of the play you say to each person, What do you think is right? What do you think works? What do you think doesn't work? You will get fifty different answers. You will get fifty different solutions to the problem. Well, the grandmother really should be a five-year-old boy. Well, I think the second act should be in the first act. You'll get as many different answers as there are people. The key is not to listen to a specific note. The key is to listen to all the notes and get a general sense of what's not working."

GEOFFREY NAUFFTS (actor, *The War Room*): "At first, I'm thinking, you know, definitely, we'll come back and do these summer shows. I felt like it would get picked up. There were good people involved.

The project basically had integrity, and I thought somewhere down the line it would turn into something good, even if the pilot was a little weaker than we had all thought. I thought it would go someplace. And I kept hearing, from agents, or people in the business, or at CBS, It's a go, it's a go, it's a go.

"But then, as we got further and further away from it, it seemed less likely that anything would happen. From a distance, the pilot didn't even seem as good as I thought it was when I was already admitting that it was a little weaker than we were all hoping. I started to think about the project in terms of what I'd learned from it. You know, I wrote it off. What I learned from it was that television is very different than stage work, for me. It's less spontaneous, there's less room for failure, or exploration, a lot of time. Sometimes you make safe choices, but that would be the interesting thing for me, if we ever got to do this as a series, is to try and do things, even little things, that get me off as an actor, to try to expand those boundaries, take those risks. But it will always be safer than the stage. Ultimately, the basic acting animal, the truth of acting, is still there. You can't lie to the camera. It's so right on you.

"Doing this show, I found it very strange that there's an audience there. And you're in front of them, as yourself, and then you count down, five, four, three, two, one, and you're in the scene. I found that very strange. I felt very vulnerable doing that. I think it's a very private moment, for me as an actor, it's not like you're walking on stage as a character or you're doing a film so you're just surrounded by the crew. You're actually in front of an audience, and they're seeing you fool them, in a sense. They're seeing you turn on your act. I'm not really this guy, but now I am."

JOANNE SEDWICK (associate director, *The War Room*): "One of the things that hurt the pilot, that might help them if it ever gets to series, is that there's an ensemble feeling to the cast. You need to have a point of view in a pilot, and it's hard to have a point of view in an ensemble. I don't think they had a point of view, or if they did it got diluted. And there weren't any interpersonal moments between any of the characters. So I don't think the pilot has a shot, no.

"The set, too, was also a problem. There was that huge center area, in the War Room, with six or seven desks, and it was difficult to work it the way you normally work comedy. Normally, comedy is looser shots, group shots, staying longer on shots than you do in drama, which is tighter and quicker cutting. Trying to get all seven people in a group shot, on this set, that's going to be tough. And trying to do stereo sound is rough on that set. It's just not a good set.

"Most of the problems with the pilot were probably technical. Like in the editing, we had such a limited amount of material to work with, because of the lighting, that we basically had to take whatever wasn't too bad. On film, you can cut on the line, or on a movement, or on a reaction. You have to find the rhythm of the scene. There's a tendency to cut back and forth much more rapidly on tape than on film, so that you find the rhythm of the scene and sometimes it's not on the line, sometimes it's on the pauses. There's no rule of thumb. Sometimes the reaction is much more interesting than the person who's speaking. But on the pilot we didn't even worry about finding the rhythm of the scene. That was a luxury we did not have. We just worried about cutting two pieces together and hoping the lighting looked similar enough so we could fool people into thinking there was a good match.

"What would I have done differently? I would have replaced the crew with soap people, that's the first thing I would have done. Soap people can do anything, especially in camera work or in boom. I would have worked with William Duff Griffin more. He needed the most help. And I think I would have pulled the desks in just a little bit closer, which would have given us the looser shots to work with, the group shots. John Dye turned out not to be a problem. He was going to do exactly what he did. You could shave him a little bit, you could bend him a little bit, but that was what you were going to get."

TOM FONTANA: "We've got these five other scripts, and they are far more dangerous than the pilot. Certainly, they have an edge to them that the pilot doesn't have. If anything, the pilot suffers from too many cooks. I think we moved the show closer to a more traditional sitcom and further from our original intent, and in the editing I think we subconsciously worked very hard to move it back to what our original intent was, but by that point there was not a lot we could do. You know, it was already gonna be what it was gonna be.

"I'm sure a lot of people have a lot of opinions that matter. But we have to say, This is the show we're making. Right or wrong. On *St. Elsewhere*, we weren't making *Dr. Kildare*, and everyone knew not to ask us for *Dr. Kildare*. Here we weren't making *Three's Company*, but that's what some people wanted, and we're saying, Okay, we'll try to make it a little more like *Three's Company,* if that's what you think we should do. It's like the Mary Beth peeing stuff. Intellectually, I understood why everybody thought we needed it, and I went along with it. But when I saw it, for the very first time, I thought, Oh, God, I am in the first act of a show that has three jokes about a woman peeing. That's not the show I want to write."

JENNIFER VAN DYCK (actress, *The War Room*): "I think television can be smart. This just wasn't very smart. The jokes were on the surface. There was nothing more. The whole thing just looks sort of cheesy to me. I think it needs to respect more of its audience. This script initially assumed people were smart, which I liked. But the product doesn't really reflect that. And this business with my character's handicap? I still don't know what that was all about. It was never really explained to me. I've always taken it to be that she has some sort of MS, or something. And, in the finished pilot, none of those references are in, so you don't understand my brace. You see it, but you don't know what it's about.

"But it was good for me, this pilot, even if nothing happens with it. Working with John Whitesell wasn't as productive as I'd hoped it would be. He wasn't really a creative force, he was more of a traffic controller. It was good for me in other ways. It was good for me because it taught me that my diction is really out of control on television. My character just sort of spits these things out. It just sort of hits you in the face, and it's just too much. So, technically, that's something I learned and want to figure out a way to deal with. I want to sound like a normal person. I'd like to find a way to have the words come out of my mouth without sounding like I have barbed wire attached to my larynx, or whatever."

JOHN TINKER (co-writer, co-executive producer, *The War Room*): "The pilot didn't work because we cast it too quickly, and we shot it badly. Simple as that. I like all those people, though. We wouldn't have cast them if they weren't good actors. But some of them were just so wrong for their parts. And the script wasn't as good as it could have been. And we should not have agreed to shoot it at CBS. The facility was all wrong for us. And I hate the fact that we did it on tape. I hate the look of tape. Other than that, though, I think everything went pretty well."

RICH HALL (actor, *The War Room*): "I don't think about it that much, now that I'm done with it. It was just a pilot. When the camera's on you, or you're in rehearsals, you have to be convinced it's the greatest thing. But it wasn't. It was just another week out of my life, doing something. If it goes, it goes. Maybe it will. Maybe it won't. Maybe it just sucked. That's generally the main reason why a show doesn't get on the air."

BRUCE PALTROW: "Finally, we had all this stuff going on, but when they rejected *High*, I decided to pull *The War Room*. The network was prepared to go ahead with the summer episodes, but we just pulled it. We were all very upset about *High*, because it was really terrific, and we all put a lot into it, so maybe we pulled *The War Room* out of spite. Maybe it was spite. But, mainly, it wasn't good. It wasn't what it could be. We could have fixed it in time for the summer shows, but the pilot wasn't any good. Sagansky kept telling us, I want it on, I want it on. I was thinking, Don't do us any favors. It was clear they thought the pilot was terrible. They didn't even want to use the pilot, when it came down to it. They wanted to use parts of it as a flashback episode or something, because it was paid for, but they didn't want to run it.

"We were cutting corners to get it on, and it just didn't seem like the way to go. We didn't want to do it to fail. I just don't think we were good enough. We were wide of the mark. It wasn't personal enough. The casting wasn't right. And then that whole thing with the handicapped character. No one, we found out, was comfortable laughing at a handicapped person. Those were big joke lines, but people just looked at each other. It was uncomfortable.

"So, maybe out of spite, or maybe pride, or who knows, we pulled it. They didn't put *High* on. That's their business, but we've also got our business. Look, you go make your television shows, and we'll make ours. We'll make ours with networks that treat us nicely. Listen, this is my sample. This is my sample, Mr. Feinstein, this is the blouse. You know, we make it in green, we have it in purple. We do it in all these sizes. But this is the blouse. This is exactly what it is. And I want to make the best blouse I can. That's my goal. Not every blouse is for everybody.

"Meanwhile, during this whole time, the relationship with Columbia was pretty bumpy. Jeff Sagansky and I patched up our differences over the next couple of weeks, but we didn't know Columbia, and they didn't know us. I'd say 'red' and they'd say, Paltrow said red. Does he mean red-orange, or red-fuchsia, or does he mean red-red? That's the way things were. It was like a shotgun marriage, just to get these pilots going. They didn't know us. We didn't know them. We certainly had no experience working within a large corporate setting. MTM is a small place. That's what we knew.

"So we pulled it, and we thought, you know, that was it. Dead. You know, maybe we'd come back to it at some point and try it again, or in a different way, but it was basically dead. And then, a couple months later, Jeff comes back to us and says, you know, What about *The War Room*? He said he thought he owed us because of *High*, because he didn't deliver what he promised. I think he really felt bad that *High* didn't get on the air. He loved that show. But this was a dead project, *The War Room.*

"But Sagansky still wants to make it, and we still want to make it. He wants us to go back and write another script, and then we'll think about a new cast. And then we'll shoot it again. Someplace else. We won't let them talk us into West 57th Street again. We'd like to do it in New York, but I think we'd let them talk us into Los Angeles. L.A. makes sense for a show like this. There's more flexibility out there. There's more talent, more facilities, more options available to us. Here we're limited.

"I still think we have a tremendous opportunity to do something very special, very different. I think it's a smart idea. It was a smart idea when we started, and it's still a smart idea. I like the setting, the work. I'm curious to see how these people function. I think it gives us an opportunity to talk about the ills of our society and do it in a funny way. All we can do is make the best show we can make, and hopefully the audience will come to it."

GEOFFREY NAUFFTS: "Now they're talking about reshooting it in a couple months. Nobody has said anything to me about it. If I'm not doing anything else, I would love to be in it again. My career right now is about waiting to see if other guys ahead of me are taking other jobs. I'm second choice for a few things. I guess that's what always happens to people in this business."

Sixteen

L.A.

○ To a kid, this is a do-over.

After several months getting used to the idea that *The War Room* (CBS, 1990) has likely gone the way of forgettable series like *Heck's Angels* (CBS, 1976) and *Fraud Broads* (ABC, 1984), Bruce Paltrow takes a call from Jeff Sagansky. The programming chief wants to know what has been happening with the producer's presidential speechwriters sitcom, which he still thinks about from time to time.

"Nothing's been happening," Paltrow replies. "We're trying to make a living. Why?"

Sagansky says he is just asking.

"Are you just asking because you're interested, or are you just asking because you're asking?"

Sagansky says he is asking because he is interested in looking at the material again, from a fresh perspective. Paltrow, whose own interest is suddenly squared by Sagansky's, goes back to his partners and convinces them to work with him on a new pilot script. This does not take too much convincing. Fontana and Tinker are eager to return to the speechwriters idea; the very elements that first drew them to it— the dynamic of the office, the opportunity for smart, political humor, and the ground-floor view of our nation's capital—are still very much in place. Too, the *Modern Marriage* pilot episode has been put on hold at NBC, in the fallout from the too-busy 1990 pilot season, and the various other Paltrow Group projects are still early in their development stages. The writers are anxious to get a project up and running and on the air.

They do not jump-start *The War Room* from scratch, although it is suggested that perhaps they should. Instead, they work with what they have. They do this because they know it will be easier to rewrite the material than to start all over again from nothing, but also because there are many pieces to the earlier script they think are worth saving. They like the characters they have already created and see no reason not to revisit them, to see what they are still up to. Also, they like the conceit of introducing an outside element into the speechwriters' office, and so the new pilot episode will begin, as before, with the hiring of Jim Smith. What they do not like is what they did with all these people once they brought them together, and so they kick around a few ideas intended to change that.

By December 1990, they have kicked things around to where they have taken new shape. They have borrowed the frame from the first pilot and filled it, essentially, with a different print from the same artist. The key difference in this new script is in its heart. It has one, for one thing. Another key difference is in its soul. It has one of these, too. One of the repeated criticisms of the first *War Room* effort, according to what the writers have gleaned in the intervening months, was that its characters were detached, without emotion, that there was no tug and pull to the story line, no reason for the viewer to care about these fictional people or what was happening to them. To correct this, the writers abandon the disarmament theme, which was intended to provide the pilot with its bite and to establish the dichotomy within the speechwriters' office, and replace it with a softer focus on the issue of homelessness.

"Homelessness," the character of Hammond Egley will be made to slogan, as if he is still on Madison Avenue. "It hits us where we live."

In the major new plot twist, a dislocated Jim Smith will be set off to wander the streets of the capital on his first night in town. He has worked all day (and most of the night) on a speech the president is to deliver at a Philadelphia soup kitchen, until he is finally chased from the after-hours War Room by a Secret Service agent. His temporary ID, good for one day, expires at midnight, and he is roughly escorted onto Pennsylvania Avenue. With no place to stay, Jim lands on a nearby park bench, where he makes a pillow of his luggaged possessions and curls up for the evening.

Next, the writers determine that this particular park bench will also be the temporary bed of a surprisingly lucid homeless man called Emperor Norton. The character is named for a real-life San Francisco merchant, Joshua A. Norton, who gave away all of his worldly goods to his neighboring less-fortunates more than a hundred years earlier, while declaring himself emperor of the United States. Outwardly, *The War Room*'s Emperor Norton could be the poster boy for the homeless: He is dressed in tattered, filthy clothing; he looks as if he smells really, really bad; and his eyes reveal the hard, vacant gaze of the emotionally disaffected. But underneath these familiar trappings there is the unfamiliar, or at least the unexpected.

"Please don't kill me," a startled Jim cries out when he is awakened by the homeless man.

"Kill you?" Emperor Norton replies, "I don't even know you."

The two men wind up sharing the same bench, and the same perspective, and by first light Jim Smith is back in the Executive Office Building, redrafting his speech to incorporate this shared viewed.

The other major change on this second pass is the reincarnation of the office's civil-servant secretary, who is now named Bonnie Cole. She is returned to her position of acquired authority in the speech-writers' office, and her reappearance in this new script fills the void left by her removal from the earlier draft. Once again, she becomes the glue to this ensemble piece, the axis.

After reading the revised script, Sagansky green-lights a second pilot for consideration on his fall schedule, returning *The War Room* to life. On this second time around, the project will not be hampered by a thin summer budget (indeed, the budget for the second pilot will check in at $1,166,980, which is about average for a half-hour taped show) or a tight production schedule. Pre- and postproduction will not be rushed, as they were before. There will be time and money to hire the best available creative talent and to scout the most accommodating studio facilities. And, as a traditional, one-shot pilot, there are somewhat shorter odds for the project's long-term success: The list of summer replacement series surviving into their abutting fall seasons is not long, although it was stretched this year by two

CBS shows with which *The War Room* was to have shared the summer schedule, *Top Cops* and *Northern Exposure*.

The second pilot, it is quickly agreed, will be shot on Stage 12 of Columbia's Sunset Gower Studios in Los Angeles, in the shadow of the fabled HOLLYWOOD sign. The producers are initially reluctant to take the show out of New York (where they will have the entire continental United States to cushion them from their partner's hands-on influence) and place it in their partner's backyard (where they will not), but they must weigh their reluctance against the studio's disinclination to proceed again on a project that has already failed once and has already cost it several hundred thousand dollars. The costs of taping at an independent facility, in Los Angeles or New York, are nearly prohibitive, mostly because the money will actually leave studio coffers in bigger bundles. Clearly, it is far easier for Columbia to absorb $129,764 in facilities and labor costs, for example, when it is paying itself for its own facilities (including $18,750 for twenty-five hundred square feet of office space for two months and $19,950 for twenty parking spaces, also for two months) and its own in-place labor.

The producers, with money to spend, hire top-drawer sitcom director Terry Hughes, who created the British comedy series *The Two Ronnies* and who went on to direct one hundred and ten episodes of *The Golden Girls* for Witt-Thomas-Harris Productions. Hughes, one of the handful of sitcom directors with the perceived ability to make or break a new series, departed *The Golden Girls* after the 1989–90 season to direct a feature film for Paramount (*The Butcher's Wife*, starring Demi Moore and Jeff Daniels), but he appears eager to return to the small screen, at least in small doses. He is in great demand this pilot season, and the Paltrow Group persuades him to squeeze *The War Room* onto his already-crowded plate. He is shooting three other sitcom pilots in March and April: *Good and Evil* and *Nurses*, for Witt-Thomas-Harris, and *Ruth Harper*, for MTM.

"It's quite a lot, actually," the director says, in a mannered British accent, when asked about his frantic pilot schedule, "but I enjoy doing them. I like the immediacy of a pilot, starting something off from nothing. It's also a way of saying to the community, Hey, I haven't deserted television, don't count me out. If there's something interesting, I would like to do it. I like the speed of television, and under the right circumstances, I would absolutely do a season of a show, or a part of a season. I would rather go and do good television than go and direct a bad movie." He stops for a moment to see if there are any other reasons why he is putting himself through such a busy ordeal. When he finally finds one, he smiles: "And I suppose the last reason I'm doing all these pilots is because they're quite lucrative. Of course, that's not the main reason, but it is a major one. They do pay quite well."

Quite well, indeed. Hughes is not saying just how much he is being paid for the *War Room* pilot, and neither are the producers, but it is believed to be in the $100,000–$125,000 range, plus a piece of the show's long-term profits if it makes it to series.

Casting is already under way, in New York and Los Angeles, by the time Hughes signs on to the project. The consensus, among the producers, the studio, and the network, is to recruit an entirely new cast, to move the show as far as possible from the tinge of its initial failure. Geoffrey Nauffts is the only original cast member actively considered for this second pass; but the network insists he audition again, to reclaim his old part of Steve Lawson, a prospect that does not fill the young actor with a great deal of good feeling. "I created the role," he says later, "and now they want me to read for it. I guess it would be fair to say it pissed me off. It's like, you know, if they want to see what I can do with the role, just look at the damn pilot. It's all right there." Despite his objections, Nauffts allows himself to be flown out to Los Angeles to read again for the role, but he is ultimately rejected by the network in favor of actor Joshua Rifkind, who is coming off a star turn in the short-lived sitcom *The Marshall Chronicles* (ABC, 1990).

Mary Beth Hurt is passively considered to reprise her role, but the producers do not offer it to her, in a misunderstanding. Or, at least, with regret. It is thought that Hurt would not relocate to Los Angeles for a television series, although later the producers learn the actress would have contemplated such a move. They would have known this if they had asked. "Anyway," Tom Fontana says, "she had done this Jane Curtin sitcom in the meantime [*Working It Out* (CBS, 1990)], and so whatever it was that made it special to have her in our cast the first time was now less special. After *Tattingers'*, it's like, every year she's in a new show. We would have loved to work with her again, and we still would, but it was no longer the same thing."

Heading the cast is *St. Elsewhere* alumnus William Daniels, in the role of B. Laurence Taylor he deserted a year earlier, and his hiring gives the show a shape and dimension it has not yet had. A polished veteran who can dominate the small screen with his voice alone (as he did in the NBC action-adventure series *Knight Rider*, for which he provided the voice of David Hasselhoff's car), Daniels brings a staunch presence to the role and a viewer-friendly persona that his predecessor, William Duff Griffin, could not. He is a known quantity. Just as Hurt's hiring signaled the New York theater community that the Paltrow Group was looking for its best and brightest the first time out, Daniels's signing tells the Hollywood community that the producers have returned to the site of their greatest success and are looking to mine at least some of the same territory.

The rest of the cast is assembled quickly, with some deliberation and a few surprises. To play Bonnie Cole, for example, the producers go to the network with veteran actresses Polly Bergen and Rose Marie and singer Gladys Knight. Knight, who starred opposite Flip Wilson in the *Cosby*-clone sitcom *Charlie and Company* (CBS, 1985–86), has lately mixed concert and recording dates around her nascent acting career. "I act in my music all the time," she explains of her recent career shift. "You know, like in 'Neither One of Us Wants to Be the First to Say Goodbye,' I sing that song and people just know that someone has just broken up with me. That's a kind of acting. And 'Midnight Train to Georgia.' That's performing, in a sense. You use different techniques in acting, you don't have the melody or the imagination, but there's a lot that's the same."

Gladys Knight, who has not sung with the Pips (her brother and two cousins) in more than two years, is the wild card in this group, and, as such, she is most interesting to the producers, and most problematic to the network.

"Rose Marie was hilarious," Fontana tells, "but she came at Bonnie exactly as written. She did exactly what you would think Rose Marie would do with the part. There's nothing wrong with that, but there were no surprises." Polly Bergen, too, brought out the caustic cynicism that the producers wrote into the character. Gladys Knight did not. She tried—in fact, she came back to give a second, "harder" reading at the producers' request—but her warmth and humanity overshadowed her effort.

"With Gladys," Fontana continues, "we all started to realize that we had a few too many cynical characters in this group and that Billy Daniels is such a dominant personality, and so we were drawn to her. The part was originally written like an Eve Arden part, a smart-ass old broad who had been there a million years and seen everything, but it was starting to look like that whole office was just yelling and being cynical. It was all a little too loud, too barbed. Gladys wasn't anything like the part, but we wanted to rewrite it for her, and the network agreed."

But not without one final reading, for the cameras. The entire trial is crazy-making for Gladys Knight, this last hurdle most of all. The only time the network will agree to see her is at four-thirty on the afternoon of a televised *Soul Train* awards show, at which she is scheduled to perform live, at five o'clock, at the Shrine Auditorium across town. This is tight. To save time, Knight arrives for her reading at the network in a formal, calf-length, beaded black dress, which she is supposed to wear for her first *Soul Train* number, a medley with singers Luther Vandross and Patti LaBelle. "So I'm like completely out of character, right?" Knight describes, "and they've got this police escort waiting for me outside of CBS, to take me back to the Shrine, and I just have no idea what's going on. They hurry me up to this room, which is like a little, small theater. And it's dark, except for this one light. And there's this one chair, right? And then there's a bleacherful of people, sitting there. So I walk into this room, and I sit down in this chair, and I'm trying to relax. you know? And then the young lady throws me the first line. And I go totally blank. I mean, I just stared at her. I say, Yeah, uh-huh, uh-huh. I'm just blank. It's the worst reading. I'm, like, tongue-tied.

"Tom Fontana comes over to me after I leave the room, and he tells me he knows the pressure I'm under. They knew about this *Soul Train* thing. Oh, yeah. They knew I was gonna turn up in this gown and everything, all out of character and all. They knew all of this stuff. And he said he wants me to come back and talk to everyone a little bit, read it again. So I'm thinking, you know, that's great, but I'm also thinking, you know, we don't have that much time to get back to do the other show. I'm still not concentrating. But I read it again, and this time I get all the lines right, but I'm still not really capturing the character right. I walk out of there and I'm thinking, you know, I blew it. Let's just move on to the next thing."

Knight is astonished when the part is offered to her. Overjoyed, but astonished. She lets out a shriek when her agent gives her the news over the phone, but when she settles down, she cannot quite figure out why she was hired for the role. She convinces herself that she got the job despite this harried final reading, not because of it. "They must have seen something in one of the previous readings," she figures. "I think I really nailed it the first time, that's the only thing I can think, you know. All those other readings, I didn't feel good about a single one of them."

Rounding out the cast are George Newbern, a young actor from Arkansas with a slight drawl and wholesome good looks, perhaps best known for his recurring role as Dixie Carter's son in the CBS sitcom *Designing Women,* as Jim Smith; Lewis Black, a gravelly-voiced comedian and sometime playwright currently seen on Lifetime's *Days and Nights of Molly Dodd,* as Hammond Egley; Haviland Morris, a starlet-seeming, redheaded New York actress who was featured in the movies *A Shock to the System* and *Gremlins: The New Batch,* as the no-longer-physically-challenged Marsha Katzenberg; and Michele Lamar Richards, a dark-skinned, dark-haired actress who once ran her own theater in Paris and whose episodic television credits include *Gabriel's Fire, The Flash,* and *Hill Street Blues,* as the no-longer-pregnant Sara Scadutto, even though she looks nothing at all like the would-be Italian she has been tabbed to play.

(The names of Marsha Katzenberg and Sara Scadutto are soon changed to Alyson McLeod and Roxanne Robinson, to accommodate the physical types of the actresses hired to play them.)

As before, the actors are made to sign test deals with the studio before the execution of formal contracts. The money for this full-fledged fall-season pilot is somewhat richer than it was for the projected summer series a year earlier. This time out, the lesser-known ensemble cast members are offered $15,000 for the pilot episode and a long-term compensation package that escalates according to the following schedule:

First series year:	$7,500 per episode
Second year:	$9,000 per episode
Third year:	$10,500 per episode
Fourth year:	$11,550 per episode
Fifth year:	$12,705 per episode
Sixth year (if first year starts mid-season):	$13,975 per episode

Furthermore, the actors are guaranteed, on a pay or play basis, the following number of episodes: in the first series year, all shows produced, but not less than seven (including the pilot); in the second series year, all shows produced, but not less than thirteen; in the third and subsequent years, all shows produced, but not less than twenty-two. In other words, the performer effectively earns a salary of $231,000 the moment the series enters its third year of production, using the standard test-deal terms outlined above, whether or not the studio produces the full slate of twenty-two episodes, and whether or not the actor actually appears in each episode. Over the projected, contracted life of the series, assuming first- and second-season runs of seven and thirteen episodes, the entire compensation package totals at least $1,249,082, and potentially more with fuller slates of shows during the first two seasons.

The show's name-brand stars—Daniels, Knight, and, on the strength of his recent *Marshall Chronicles* work, Rifkind—will earn between $30,000 and $50,000 for the pilot episode and begin the first year of the series at between $15,000 and $30,000 per episode, with similar percentage increases for each succeeding year.

Lewis Black says the money is like heroin, borrowing an analogy from one of his actor friends, Joe Grifasi, who appeared in the drama series *WIOU* (CBS, 1990–91), for producer Grant Tinker. "It is like heroin," Black maintains, "when you think about it. First you want to do the pilot, and you're happy just for that. And then you do the pilot and it's, Aaah, if we could just do seven of these things. That's all, just seven more paychecks and I'll be okay. But then you do the seven, and you start to think, Aaaah, if I could just get those next six, that would really help, just give me six more, just six more. And then it's, Why not twenty-two? Just one more season. We've all watched people go through this. You look at the numbers, and it's easy to get seduced by them. It's like an addiction."

The test deal also covers merchandising and commercial tie-in rights (a talking Hammond Egley doll, for example, would bring Lewis Black 5 percent of the studio's standard net proceeds for same, reducible to 2.5 percent), travel and living expenses ($75 per diem during production of the pilot episode, in lieu of reimbursement for all other expenses), billing (separate card, main titles), and exclusivity. (The various terms of this last are too unwieldy to be reduced to a parenthetical comment and will therefore be detailed on the other side of this colon):

"During other than production periods, Artist may perform outside services for others in live or film television subject to the following restrictions:

"Artist may not render such services in a continuing, recurring or host role in another series. A six-hour miniseries does not constitute a continuing or recurring role.

"Artist may not render such services in a program which Artist knows or in the exercise of reasonable prudence should know is scheduled to be broadcast or telecast at the same time as the Pilot/ Series or during the premiere week of the Series.

"Artist may not make more than three guest appearances on television in each thirteen week period provided that, in such appearances, Artist may not portray the same continuing character as that portrayed herein. Artist may make unlimited game, award, panel, and talk show appearances. A miniseries up to six hours shall be deemed one guest appearance. . . ."

"These contracts can be a little intimidating," admits Michele Lamar Richards shortly after she signs on for the project. "But I can't think about it in that way. I think about this as freedom, this series. It is freedom. At least in one way. It's oxymoronic, of course, because it's liberating, but at the same time I'm going to be tied to this one show, for however many years, and there are all these exclusive demands on my time and everything. But it does represent a kind of freedom to me. It does. I'm hoping this show goes on for years and years, until my character is finally honed and has her niche and I can just come in and do this and enjoy this. That's not work, at that point. Then it's like I'm living this other life, where I write speeches for the president of the United States.

"I think they call it 'Golden Time,' after four years. That's when you have enough episodes for syndication and it becomes effortless for the character. That's when you've tossed out your first contract and renegotiated another. And that's when the really good ensembles, like your *Taxis*, or your *Cheers*, or your *Night Courts*, that's when these shows really start to work. That's when the characters finally become just so fluid that they just speak for themselves."

Seventeen

LOT _____

In Hollywood's infancy, and on into its teens, the neighborhood surrounding the intersection of Sunset Boulevard and North Gower Street was known as "Gower Gulch" and was famous for its ramshackle housing and soundstages. Much of the movie industry's early filler was produced here, on the quick and cheap, much of it by Harry Cohn's upstart Columbia Pictures Studios.

Up, and started, the motion picture studio came to dominate these few square blocks like a motor home in a side alley, and it continues to do so. The area still answers to its old name on occasion, although now it is littered with trendy Vietnamese restaurants, thriving prop and costume shops, and premature shopping plazas. In the driveway of one of the since-renovated but still-ramshackle houses on Gower, there is a cherry-red Mazda Miata, mint-seeming, on blocks, with its top down and a FOR SALE sign taped to its rear window. And, at the Gordon Street entrance to the studio, there is a curly blond actress in a fishing hat, patrolling the gate with a sandwich board displaying the pleading message AUDITION ME, along with a name and telephone number. It is not hard to imagine Bruce Paltrow out here in a sandwich board of his own, trying to get his show on the air, the title of one pass crossed out to make room for the next: E.O.B., The War Room, Word of Mouth.

Abby Singer, the veteran television producer who has been hired

165

by his old friend Bruce Paltrow to line-produce the second speech-writers pilot, has roamed the halls of 1438 Gower Street since before the mainstream television industry was ever born. Actually, he has not done much roaming here lately. In fact, he has not set foot on this lot since 1957, but before that his feet were set here all the time. In the early 1940s and through the waning days of the old studio system, he would closet himself in one of the tiny, drab offices along the maze of indoor/outdoor hallways leading from the executive offices to the back lot and pass the time playing cards with the extras and the crew. There was always a game going, he recalls, and it would stay going until Harry Cohn himself poked his head through the door to chew out the repeat offenders.

There is a great deal of history crammed onto the too-small lot of the Sunset Gower Studios, much of it grand, although lately the history-in-the-making has been trimmed to scale. The dozen-plus soundstages are now filled mostly with sitcoms: *Who's the Boss?*, *Married...With Children*, *Babes*, *Married People*, *The Fannelli Boys*.

It is Wednesday morning, March 20, 1991, just a few minutes short of ten, and Bruce Paltrow, Tom Fontana, and John Tinker are once again trying to transform their presidential speechwriters idea into some television history of their own. And if they cannot make television history, they would at least like to make television. There are about fifty people gathered in Rehearsal Hall A on this morn-ing—network and studio executives, Paltrow Group staff, stage and technical crew—for the show's first table reading. The cast members, also assembled, are meeting each other for the first time. In truth, some more assembly is required, because Gladys Knight is not here. Yet. She left her home in Las Vegas at three o'clock this morning for the (normally, for her) four-hour drive to Los Angeles, but she was caught in a storm along the San Bernadino Pass and watched the drive stretch itself to nearly seven hours. Now she is sitting in clogged traffic on the Santa Monica Freeway, waiting for things to unclog and worrying about the first impression that is preceding her at the studio.

The producers are anxious to begin, and everyone is seated at the long, horseshoed banquet table in the center of the room. Tom Fontana, at the curve, kills some time by announcing that *Word of Mouth* T-shirts have been designed and ordered and should be arriving soon. "First the clothes," he says, "then the shows." Underneath the easy laugh is a disturbing truth: The Paltrow Group has produced more T-shirts in the past year than television shows. This is not a good thing.

Fontana has shaved his beard since the New York pass at this show. He still looks like Jerry Garcia, only clean-shaven. He is wearing jeans, and a "Jane's Addiction" T-shirt, underneath a black leather biker jacket.

"Why don't we get started?" suggests Paltrow, in jeans and sneakers, looking no worse, or even different, for the wear of the past year.

Knight arrives just as the reading is about to begin. She makes frantic apologies all around—indeed, she is more sorry than late—but it seems no apologies are necessary. Her reputation has preceded even her first impression; she is an R & B icon to most of the players in this room (most of them under forty, and many not even close); Gladys Knight and the Pips contributed at least a few cuts to the soundtracks of their growings-up, and there is little the singer-turned-actress could do to remove the stars in their eyes.

After the table reading, the cast members receive their dressing-room and parking assignments and break for lunch. George Newbern and Lewis Black go outside to visit their parking spaces, to see their names stenciled on the wide cement bumpers bordering each slot at its nose. It is raining hard, but they do this, anyway. These are a big deal to them, these special parking spaces. It is as though they have never had their names stenciled on a studio parking lot's cement bumper before, and they want to breathe it all in, the whole package. Breathing, and soaking, they move their cars into their designated spaces, even though they are, already parked only a few feet away, one row over. For a moment, Lewis and Newbern discuss going for a drive someplace, for lunch or whatever, particularly considering they will now have these swell parking spaces to return to, but they decide to leave their cars where they are, and seek out something to eat on foot.

Before they leave, they stop to talk. "When Bruce offered me this job," Black recalls after putting his car where it should be, "and he asked me if I was willing to relocate to Los Angeles, I thought to myself, you know, it's such a crapshoot. But I said, you know, sure. Actually, what I said was 'If the price is right, I'd blow an elephant.'

And Bruce laughed and said, 'If you get the job, you're gonna have to blow much worse.' And he's right, there's a greater truth to all of that.

"This is going to be interesting," Black continues, building up a head of steam directed at the industry he is about to embrace. "Whatever happens, it will be interesting. If this were certain other sitcoms, it would scare me. But this is political, so the potential is terrific for me. You know, I've done political stand-up for twenty years, and now all of a sudden someone has given me the opportunity to take it to another level, to play a political character, in a political sitcom. On a weekly basis. Even if it doesn't run, just the opportunity to see how you do it, what the possibilities are, is tremendous. And to do it in the Nazi camp, in a sense, in network television, that's even more gratifying. The concept of risk to these people is like, Oh, geez, the guy's gonna wear a dress! That's risk to them."

Newbern allows that he is also uncertain about the process ahead. "It's always a miracle to me that anything actually gets on the air," waxes the young actor, "and then it's a miracle that anything is ever any good. There are so many cooks, and everybody is throwing stuff into the pot, there are so many opinions, so many chances for something to go wrong. It's like no other business I could ever think of. There are so many mine fields along the way. And especially as an actor, it's a miracle you ever get cast. There are so many other guys out there, and you're beating your head against the wall."

Later, in from out of the rain, Newbern downshifts to philosophical: "So what happens is you try not to invest anything emotionally into a show like this, but a part of you always does, you can't help it, and that's the sucky part about being an actor. You know, it's not like doing a show at the Guthrie Rep or the Goodspeed Opera House, where you know it's two months and that's it. And that's great. But out here, every job you do, a movie or a TV series or whatever, it could conceivably change your life. So you never know, and you kinda always think about that, before every audition, or before you get close to every role, it's like, God, this could conceivably change my life."

Also inside, underneath Stage 12, is actor Joshua Rifkind. He is in his dressing room, with the door closed. He is eating a brown-bagged tuna-fish sandwich and listening to *La Boheme* on a portable cassette player he has brought from home. In between bites, which he breaks off with pinched fingers rather than put his mouth to the extra trouble, he flips at the pages of a book about the Holocaust.

"Everything about this gives me a boner," he says of the din surrounding this start-up production and not of the book he puts down to make room for his reflection. "It's all a great big kick. Today is just like the first day of school. Actually, it's great. And I think it's because I don't feel like I'm carrying the show. The first day of *Marshall Chronicles*, I showed up and sat at the corner of the table, just way out of the way, and the producer picked me up and said, No, you come sit right here in the middle. And that was it. I was, literally, the meal ticket. And there were as many people there for that table reading as there were here today, and I knew that everybody was just watching me. It was nerve-racking.

"Today, though, I don't feel any pressure. I feel confident. I knew that a lot of other people had auditioned for the role and if they didn't want me, I wouldn't be there. You know, you just sit down there at the table with all these people, and you say, Hi, I'm George, Hi, I'm Michele, I'm Joshua, I'm playing Jim, or I'm playing Sara, or whatever, and then you get to hear all these characters come to life for the first time. That's a kick. That's fun.

"This, I would do this for free. If I didn't have to worry about money, yeah. I mean, there are other things I would like to be doing, too, but what you're talking about, here, is paying people a lot of money for doing something they love. It's all most of us want to do. It's all most of us have wanted to do for a long time."

After lunch, Terry Hughes leads his new cast in a second table reading, on the *Word of Mouth* set. They are joined around the table by Paltrow, Fontana, and Tinker, along with associate director Lex Passaris, production associate Robert Spina, and stage manager Tom Carpenter, who have not yet given up their day jobs as same on the Witt-Thomas-Harris *Golden Girls* set.

Property master and co-production coordinator R. J. Visciglia, is also present, but he is not sitting. Well, on occasion, he is, but he is not sitting still. He has got just about a million things to do, and he chips away at his list when he thinks no one is looking. Visciglia, a behind-the-scenes *St. Elsewhere* alumnus who looks like a street-clothed version of the cartoon character Droopalong, has followed a straightforward path to this place. During his growing up, his father worked as a property master over at Paramount, and later for director Sam Peckinpah. In his father's footsteps, Visciglia apprenticed on television shows like *Love, American Style* and *The Magician* and on films like *The Godfather, Part II*. These days, the two Visciglias occasionally compete for jobs, although lately the younger is looking to branch into producing.

"I try to focus on exactly what's in the script," Visciglia, still on the property end, says of his approach to the job, "and then you go from there. If it says that B. Laurence Taylor is supposed to be carrying a briefcase, I start to think, Okay, number one, who is this guy? How old is he? What's his background? You have to go into what I call character analysis. What part of the country is he from? I mean, all this goes into what kind of briefcase he'd be carrying. Now, Taylor shouldn't be carrying some big, shiny Halliburton briefcase. He should be carrying something conservative, something basic, black, not flashy. Maybe even a valise."

Visciglia can put his fingers on almost anything at any time. If it is available for rent, lease, or purchase, he can have it on the stage in twenty-four hours. "It's accumulated knowledge," he allows, "and it's knowing how to go about getting things, where to look. Hey, you know what? The best thing in the world is the Yellow Pages. That and the White Pages. They're still my number-one resources. Still, to this day."

About the only negative aspect to Visciglia's job, as far as he can figure, is how it has changed the way he watches movies and television shows. Hardly a week goes by when he does not come across a prop or two he has used in one production being featured in another. It's a funny thing, he says. Why, just the other night, he was watching the movie *Die Hard 2*, and he recognized the computer equipment from a scene in the airport control tower. He had rented the very same props on two previous occasions—once for a *Columbo* episode and once for a show he can no longer place. "Obviously, there are only so many of those great-looking computer setups available," he explains. "You don't want to go out and make a new one every time you turn around. You know, it's the right stuff, the right look. I don't think anybody notices that it's been used before, except for other prop people."

During this second table reading, the actors start to act, even though they are still sitting down and still reading from their scripts. William Daniels does this most of all. He does a bit with his introductory speech that is quite large. "You know the best thing about being the chief of communications?" his character begins in a bluster after the show's president has referred to the Dalai Lama as "the Dying Llama," on live television. "I have the president's complete trust. In moments of gross incompetence, he leaves it up to me to find the guilty party and either generously bestow forgiveness or kick their can across Pennsylvania Avenue. Today I'm in the mood to punt."

Daniels appears to push his character to extremes and then pull him back to where he is comfortable, accessible. He is alone among the cast in that he did not have to audition, and he seems to be trying on a suit for the first time. Also, he seems to relish his shared history with the producers, and with Visciglia, and he calls it to mind every here and there, as if his easy familiarity is worthwhile currency among the rest of this group. That, or the frequent reminders that he has been here before, in success, helps him to relax and to acclimate.

For example, when Haviland Morris bumps into a stage direction calling for her character to take a lewd bite out of a wet dill pickle, which she claims to be noticing for the first time, she is appalled. It is not the teasing fellatio she is asked to perform that she finds so appalling; nor is she upset by the prospect that her three-month-old daughter, Faith, who is with her on the set, will have to see Mommy earn her living in just this way; rather, and simply, she does not want to have to eat the pickle. "I hate dill pickles," she protests. "There are a lot of things that look like dill pickles that I'll be happy to eat, but I really have an aversion to dill pickles."

"I wouldn't tell these guys something like that," Daniels warns, with his familiarity. "You'll have seven years of dill pickles with these guys."

Meanwhile, as the actors are being put through their first paces by the director, the de Forest Research Company is frantically clearing the *Word of Mouth* script for potential legal problems. They do this with a number of ready resources and a great deal of practice. Mostly, the completed research report will provide the background necessary to obtain clearances for use of the character names and for all of the product and location names peppered throughout the script. For example, a check on the name Steve Lawson reveals one such listing in Washington, D.C., where there is also a Steven Lawson, four Steven Larsons, and two Steven Larsens; one current White House staffer with the surname Lawson is also found. Plumbing the character's background, the report also turns up one Williams

College alumnus and two Yale alumni, including a 1976 Yale graduate who is an agent at International Creative Management, all with the same name (the fictional Steve Lawson is supposed to be a graduate of Williams, with a master's from Yale and a Ph.D. from Brown), as well as one Republican National Committee staff member named Larson. "To avoid a conflict," the report concludes, "a name change would be prudent."

(The altered names of Steve Blumberg and Steve Feldman are also rejected by de Forest before the character is prudently renamed Steve Nadelman, for which no conflicts or potential conflicts are found.)

The check on the full character name James Ross Smith figures to be even more demanding, particularly when it is reduced to the too-common nickname Jim Smith, and the report's findings are so meticulously labored they bear repeating here in full: "In Who's Who, we find numerous listings for the common name James Smith and 10 listings for James Ross. We find one listing for Ross Smith, an ad exec with Gray Advertising in Toronto; James R. Smith, a lawyer in Connecticut. In D.C. we find: 13 James R. Smith, eight Jim Smith, seven Jimmy Smith (two with the middle initial 'R'), three Jimmie Smith, one Jimmye Smith, 12 Ross Smith, more than 15 James Ross. In Council Bluffs (the character's hometown): two James Ross, two Jim Ross, four James Smith, one Jim Smith, no listings for James R. Smith. As White House staff, we find one listing for James Ross. In Congressional and federal staff directories, we find listings for James R. Smith (FAA), and Jim Smith, the communications director for the House Republican Studies Committee. We also find listings for Jim Smith with the Department of the Army and James R. Smith in the Indian Health Service. Research will check an alternate selection if deemed prudent."

All of this, and they are still not sure.

In addition, the report also uncovers any factual errors or inconsistencies in the script. To illustrate: When single mother Alyson McCleod (née Marsh Katzenberg) turns to her eavesdropping colleagues after a phone conversation with her free-spirited son, she says, "I try getting him to play with Tipper Gore's boys, but he says they listen to wimpy music." The de Forest report cautions that the joke is somewhat off target: "The reference in dialogue to 'Tipper Gore's boys' is inaccurate," the researchers find. "In fact, she and

Tennessee Senator Albert Gore Jr., a member of the 102nd Congress, have one boy and three girls."

The line, flagged, is changed to read: "I try getting him to play with Tipper Gore's kids. . . . "

A small catch, this, but it will return subtle dividends if the show reaches the airwaves (and if the Tennessee senator should ever reach, say, the Democratic presidential ticket). One of the last things the producers want is to insult the Tennessee senator, a member of the 102nd Congress, and his wife. One of the other last things they want is for their knowing, inside references to turn up unknowing and outside.

As in New York, the writers revise the script at the end of each day. Sort of. Well, okay, not really. They mean to, though. Ostensibly, they mean to make their revisions in the mornings, hopefully in time for the cast's ten o'clock call. Actually, they get around to finishing the job sometime later, which means that on Thursday, March 21, for starters, when the cast convenes for its first full day of rehearsals, they must begin with yesterday's script, even though some of the material will be discarded or amended.

The new pages are shuttled from the temporary Paltrow Group offices on the second floor of Building 35, at one end of the lot, to Stage 12, at the other, by a hurrying production assistant named Ivan Fonseca. It takes about six or seven minutes for the one-way trip, at a near sprint, and the pages are still warm from the Xerox machine when they are placed, collated, on the actors' table. When they arrive, everyone stops what they are doing and starts over.

Also on Thursday, cast and crew are presented with personalized loose-leaf binders, emblazoned with the presidential seal and the *Word of Mouth* logo, in which to house their ever-changing script. R. J. Visciglia has had these printed for less than a hundred dollars. For somewhat more, he has also made up a dozen personalized, up-high director's chairs, with the actors' names (or the producers', or the director's) scripted on the blue canvas backing opposite the show's derivative seal. Joshua Rifkind's name comes back misspelled (without a *D*), and when the actor points this out to Visciglia, the prop master appears to be genuinely sorry about this. He vows to have a new one made. It is not a big deal, Rifkind says, but underneath this he lets on that perhaps it is. If it was not a big deal, he would not have mentioned it.

In the same way, the chairs are also not a big deal to actor Lee
Tergesen, who has been hired to play the homeless character of
Emperor Norton. Tergesen, in his middle to late twenties, whose
long dirty-blond hair is accented for this particular part by a few-day's
growth of beard (which he plans to cultivate a few days more, until
taping), is not a regular member of the ensemble cast, so he does not
merit a chair of his own, and he professes not to care about this,
although he clearly would like one. After all, he is probably thinking,
his role in this pilot is substantial, and not that much smaller than
some of the other cast members', so he is as regular as anyone else as
far as this pilot is concerned. "Look," he notes, "if this show doesn't
get picked up, we're all guest stars."

Throughout the day, and in the days to come, a bizarre little ritual
emerges around these personalized chairs. Most folks seem to want to
sit in their own, even though each chair is exactly like another, save
for the name. Joshua Rifkind likes to sit in his own chair, as does
William Daniels, and even Terry Hughes, who seems easygoing and
unflappable in all other outward respects. More, they like to have
their chairs empty and available for all of their sudden sitting needs.
They do not say anything when a colleague plops down on their
personalized canvas, as happens throughout the day, but they notice,
and when they do, their eyes keep darting back to the interloping
party, as if they were willing them to rise up and leave: Fie!

Once, when the chairless Tergesen inadvertently rests his weary
bones on Daniels's chair, Daniels flashes the younger actor a look that
could pull rank. "I think I violated protocol," Tergesen says later of his
transgression. (Another proprietary note: Daniels keeps a script
pouch, fetched for him by his friend Visciglia, slung over the arm of
his chair, so Tergesen is not only sitting in Daniels's chair, he is also
sitting dangerously close to Daniels's script.)

The little podiums on wheels that director John Whitesell re-
quested during production in New York are in abundant supply in
Los Angeles, and in abundant demand. Terry Hughes gets the most
out of his, during rehearsals. He sits in his personalized chair, his legs
creased in loose Indian style, and he stretches his hanging-over feet
and knees onto the podium shelf in front of him. He has got the script
angled to where he can follow along against the live action on the
stage, and make notes in his margins, and sip at his short-necked
bottle of Evian water, all with an impressive economy of motion.

When the scene shifts from the War Room set to the adjacent Coolidge Room set (or to the brand-new White House Mess set, which has been built for an added scene in the new! and improved! script), Hughes simply ambles over to his different vantage point, while his chair and podium invariably follow him, with a faithful push from associate director Passaris or production assistant Spina.

There is nothing superior, or lordly, about the way Hughes expects his comfortable working environment to tail him from one set to the next. In fact, he does not seem to expect it at all. It just happens. He even totes his furnishings himself, from time to time, when it occurs to him. At least he tries to. Once, when the director thinks to carry what he thinks is his own chair, he gets where he is going and finds what is actually his own chair already in place. Passaris or Spina has already beaten him to his mark.

"Well, who am I carrying?" Hughes wonders as he spins the lifted chair to inspect the canvas backing.

When it turns up belonging to John Tinker, everyone races for the easy line. Tom Fontana, fleet of wit, gets there first. "I've been carrying John Tinker for years," he says.

Hughes is so absorbed in what he is doing, consumed by it, that he does not stop to consider the mechanics of this maneuver, its doing. In some way, perhaps, the shifting between sets is like switching channels by remote control: reflexive, distracted, easy. His mind is on something else. Sometimes it is even on his other work. He has got these three other pilots in various stages of preproduction and his feature film in postproduction, and he is forever being messaged about some urgent business or other. He collects these message slips and folds them into his podiumed script, for later, but he crinkles his face in consideration of each before he files it away.

Mostly, though, what Terry Hughes's mind is on is some other level. Hughes, whose shock of gray hair contradicts his kind, youthful face, seems to have digested the material to where he is already editing the rough cut in his head. He thinks in small-screen images, sometimes out loud, sometimes punctuated by the crisp fingersnaps of his profession. Days before the camera crew arrives on the set, he snaps his fingers as he walks himself and his assistants through the more than two hundred shots that will make up their twenty-two minutes of finished product. He knows exactly where he wants his actors to be, what he wants them to do when he gets them there, and which cameras will be on them at all times. Unlike Whitesell in New York, he does not lead cast members through an exploration of their characters. If it is not in the script, Hughes does not need to know about it. When, as happens, the actors need to discover something about their characters, the director very graciously helps them to find it, but the impulse never begins with him.

"I respect the written word," Hughes explains of his direct approach during a break in the rehearsals. "Whether I'm here or not, John and Tom and Bruce are the ones who are gonna have to live with this for the next two or three years, or whatever, so I think I have to give credence to their words and help them realize what they have come up with. I guess that makes me a producer's director, right? But I like to think I am also an actor's director. I like to be all those things. I'm not just a technical maven. I know where the actors are coming from. I can help them. I can help them find the extra bit of juice from the script, and I can certainly help them set up and deliver a joke and get the most out of it. I know how to do that. But I have an overview,too. I cannot let a character get locked into something that might be comfortable for them but which might not serve the overall show in the long run. And I'm incapable of staging without thinking through the cameras. I try to let it breathe and find its way, knowing that I would never stage anything that could not be shot. The two go hand in hand.

"So, if you're successful at this, I think you must be all those things, an actor's director, a technical director. You have to serve the producer's needs. It's like choreography, isn't it? That's a lot of what we do. I've also heard television directors described in less flattering terms, as a traffic cop, and there's some truth in that. All direction is about that, really. All directing, whether it's a play, or single-camera film, or three-camera tape, it's all about making entrances and exits and timing, especially in comedy, and making it flow, both to serve the text and to be natural and unforced. And then there are all the little tricks you pick up. On film, for example, you can be on somebody when the other person's talking, and on tape you never are. I don't know why that is. I can never explain it. On TV, tape seems to be cleaner, and it's very seldom that you go from one person to another as they're talking, but on film it seems to be perfectly acceptable. It's just something we all do, and nobody knows why. I wish I could validate it. I'm sure I have tried to invalidate it and seen the error of my ways.

"There are a lot of little things to pay attention to. For instance, I see a lot of shows where the director has somebody make just a totally arbitrary move, it will be absolutely unmotivated, just because maybe the director felt uncomfortable that the character was sitting in the same place for a long time and they thought, Oh, make a move. It looks totally false. I try to avoid that. You can't always avoid that, but it's always the same dilemma. For a director, any director, it's the same dilemma.

"You don't really think beyond the pilot, as a director. You could say you do, but in most cases it wouldn't be true. You just get through the week, and you make things as good as possible, and then after that you see what you can do. For instance, on the *Golden Girls* pilot, which I didn't do, the geography of the house was quite different from what it eventually turned out to be. And, in fact, geographically, that house does not make sense. I don't know the geography of these offices, either, for this show. I haven't even been to Washington. And it doesn't matter, really, to be quite honest about it. It doesn't matter that much. What matters is consistency. As long as you own it."

Haviland Morris goes through much of this morning's rehearsal with her baby Snugglied to her chest. She asks if anyone minds her rehearsing with her infant child in tow, and no one claims to, although the overture smells a lot like asking someone if they mind if you smoke after you have already lit up. The child is colicky and cries fitfully, and Morris must resort to an awkward, hippity-hop bounce to quiet her. It looks as if she has tried everything and somehow, accidentally, settled on this, which seems to pacify the child. She does this in the middle of a scene, trying to read her lines, and eventually this particular piece of parenting seems to disrupt the rhythm of Morris's scenes and the process of trying to find one.

The actress has retained a nanny to care for the baby throughout the day, but mother and child are having trouble staying away from each other, and the nanny is often without anything to do. The pilot is Morris's first acting job since she delivered three months earlier, and these rehearsals mark the first extended periods of time she is separated from her infant daughter.

"Ideally, I didn't think I would be working this soon after the baby was born," reveals Morris, who had auditioned for the Paltrow Group at the front end of her pregnancy the year before, for a part in *High*. (She found the producers "cranky" on that first encounter, but says they have been "perfectly wonderful" on this one.) "But as an actress," she continues, "you can't just decide when to go back to work, because you don't know when you're ever going to get hired. And pilot season is now, and I really wanted to do a series this year. It's nine to five and somewhat steady. I thought it would be perfect, the hours and everything. Right now, though, I'm basically a wreck, because the baby is basically a wreck. She's just having a really horrible time, and it's because of me."

Morris stops, apparently to keep herself from crying. She bites back her upper lip, lets go, breathes deeply and exhales, and then sets her hands out in front of her, palms down, as if to steady herself. "I'm doing it the only way I know how," she finally continues. "I go down to the dressing room as much as I can, and then I wonder if maybe she wouldn't be better if I didn't see her all day. You know, I think of it as just seeing her more, but maybe she thinks of it as me just leaving her more. So I don't know. She's just really having a horrible time of it. She's miserable. I'm miserable. There are sounds coming out of her body that I've never heard before. Just complete terror and everything. Everyone is trying to be really great about this, they really are. Bruce even asked if I wanted to borrow a Port-a-Crib."

At one point, in a *Purple Rose of Cairo/Baby Boom* twist, the actress actually steps from the scene-in-progress and hands her screaming child to Tom Fontana, who is standing nearby, minding his own business, observing everyone else's. "You've just got to take her," a distraught Morris intones, giving the baby over. Fontana, stormed, seems not to know what to do with this unexpected package, and he holds the child gingerly, with arms extended, as if it were a rump roast in need of defrosting. The baby's nanny races to the stage to rescue Fontana and retreats with the child to the audience bleachers facing the stage. Morris returns to her character's desk to resume the scene. She is unable to do this easily, or at first. She is crying and resisting the urge to go back to her baby, who is also crying. Michele Lamar Richards reaches her arm around Morris to see if there is anything she can do to help, but Morris shakes her off. Apparently, this is something she wants to deal with on her own.

The exchange is more compelling than anything that has, or will be, played out on this stage during this production. And it does not go away. The scene repeats itself, in various forms, throughout these first days of rehearsal. This situation is talked about, in the notes session following the first run-through, with some concern. The producers are not unsympathetic to the actress's situation—in fact, they appear genuinely moved by it—but everyone has a job to do here, and Morris, it is sadly agreed, is not doing hers. True, the taping is still nearly a week away, but Morris is doing less with her character than the other actors are doing with theirs. Of course, this last may be because she has not been given too much to work with in his pilot script ("It's just not my episode," she figures), but her heart is with her baby and not with her producers'.

Joshua Rifkind returns from Thursday's lunch break in a jacket and tie, upgraded from the jeans and sweater he was wearing this morning. "On *Marshall Chronicles,* you know, I was basically just playing a kid, and I could dress casually," he justifies when he returns with his more formal duds, "but here I found it was just restraining me to dress that way. It was keeping me from my character." He wants the props of his clothes, even at this point.

Daniels gets into his character by sitting at Taylor's aggressive desk, alone on the Coolidge Room set. He is trying to get comfortable, familiar. While the others are rehearsing on the adjacent War Room set, he sits here and soaks in what he can. He looks around him at some of the mementos property master Visciglia has displayed for his pleasure—a St. Eligius hospital I.D., borrowed from the *St. Elsewhere* archives, for one thing—and tries to imagine another rich history for himself in this new role.

"He's very much down my alley," Daniels says later of the character he is trying to occupy. "He's a no-nonsense guy. It's like the script says, he wants to get the job done, and he doesn't care how many toes he steps on. He has to ride herd on these writers. I'm sure he takes his job seriously. And he's just a tough guy. That's all I know, for now. That's all I've got to go on. You know, in a pilot, there's just so much room there, but if it goes to series, then the character is put in one new situation after another, in each episode, and it grows, and the sides of the character grow, and the complexity of the character grows. And pretty soon, if it happens the way it happens to me, you don't know where you and it begin. And if it's these writers, who I know, they write for you. They see what you do, and the colors that you have, and they're smart enough to go with that and write for it."

Visciglia's props are laced with personal touches, charged by their master's enthusiasm. He has brought his daughter's paintings from home, and pictures of his kids, to decorate Roxanne Robinson's desk. There is also a clay mask that his daughter made for art class, which Visciglia inadvertently drops and smashes when he is trying to reposition the furniture. "Promise," he insists to the room at large as he picks up the pieces and throws them away, "nobody tell my daughter about that."

He has also placed a yellow ribbon around one of the speechwriters' desks, in honor of American troops in the Persian Gulf. Tom Fontana asks him to remove this when he arrives on the set to see how things are going. "By the time this airs," Fontana reasons, "we'll probably be at war with our new friend, Syria."

Visciglia spends a good deal of time injecting sight gags into the script with his props, some of them simply for the benefit of the producers. He graffitis, for example, a mustache and glasses on a picture of Barry Goldwater that hangs on one of the War Room walls.

Or, in a scene where a sucking-up Hammond Egley leaves the War Room to intercept the First Lady on her walk with the First Dog, Visciglia leaves behind a series of pooch toys for actor Lewis Black to take with him on his exit: a rubber ball, a plastic bone, a squeaky toy. Finally, Visciglia stretches the bit to include a setup and payoff not written into the script. For Black's exit, he lays out a plain box of Milk Bone dog biscuits. When the actor returns to the scene a few beats later, Visciglia replaces the first box with another, this one chewed-up and mangled, to underline the punch line: Even the president's dog beats up on Hammond Egley.

The tattered-Milk-Bone-box gag gets a big laugh in Friday's run-through, after which Fontana walks up to Visciglia with his hand extended. "I knew there was a reason we hired you," the producer says, shaking his head.

Visciglia rolls his drooped shoulders in an "aw shucks" shrug, and when Fontana turns away, he allows himself a small smile. He seems to get a special charge out of all of this, and his role within it.

Overheard after Friday's run-through:

Bruce Paltrow, to William Daniels: "I have a good feeling about this, a tremendously good feeling."

William Daniels, back: "Monday nights, ten o'clock. That's what this feels like."

Paltrow: "Anywhere on Monday night. I'll take anything on Monday."

Translated, this means the producer and his name-brand star are hoping to land on the CBS schedule, hammocked between some of the network's most successful shows (*Designing Women, Major Dad, Murphy Brown*), on its most successful night of programming.

"Boom, boom, boom," Paltrow concludes, for sound effect. "That's where I want to be, right there in those boom, boom, booms."

Columbia's Deborah Curtan, in her office on the Sunset Gower lot, does not share Paltrow's enthusiasm for the production or for its prospects. "I still don't see where CBS is going to put this," she worries as she awaits a preproduction meeting for a new Fox series called *Top of the Heap.* "Everybody wants to be on Monday night, but I don't think this show is going to make it. They've got other shows that are funnier, or more relatable, or better cast. Maybe these guys can pull it off, but I don't think so. At this point, I don't think so."

Eighteen

TAPE, AGAIN _____

○ "There is always the danger," Terry Hughes says on Tuesday, March 26, two days before the *Word of Mouth* taping, "that you work on a piece so much it gets stale."

To combat this, the director has sent the actors home early after a light rehearsal. He does not want to push them or to overwork them to where they are bored with the material or too comfortable with it. "In a pilot," he explains in a calm British accent that seems to have nothing to do with the mounting American frenzy surrounding his production, "you have seven or eight days, which is obviously longer than the five days you normally have, and I find you can just hammer it into the ground with all that time. I like it to grow and grow so that the actors are absolutely right there when they have to do it."

By Thursday, then, after a tedious Wednesday of camera blocking and one camera run-through, the actors are absolutely right there where Hughes wants them to be, which is just shy of their peak and far away from the studio. He has them come in late, around noon, for their makeup and hair calls and a final rehearsal to go over any last-minute changes to the script. The "dress show," the first of tonight's two tapings, is scheduled for four o'clock this afternoon, followed by a dinner break, and then the "air show," at seven o'clock.

Gladys Knight, for one, welcomes the late call. She was up until two o'clock the night before, laying tracks for her upcoming solo

182

album. "It's just a crazy time for me right now," she says when she is later asked about her moonlighting. She is sprawled on the couch in her dressing room when she says this, picking at the basket of designer chocolate chip and oatmeal cookies presented to each cast member by Columbia and half-watching a soap opera on television with the sound off. "We had the studio booked, and we're on a tight schedule, so it's not like I have a choice. I just have to do what I have to do."

While the cast sleeps in, the crew is kept busy. First, they are busy with a spread of Oreo cookies and, for some reason, cream cheese, which is being passed off (and eagerly consumed) as breakfast on this final morning of production, but they are soon busied by the set's finishing touches. The "look" of the show is not quite where Hughes and the producers want it to be. The park-bench set, for example, where Jim Smith encounters the homeless Emperor Norton, is not even close to dressed. It was thought to be complete, but it has shown up in the camera run-through as spare and not unlike a high school production of *Sunday in the Park With George*. Two workers are hurriedly stapling ivy to the backdrop walls to help create a fuller, more realistic look. A small tree is placed to the side of the bench, rented this morning for twenty-eight dollars, to contribute to same. And a painter is waiting for the ivy to be stapled so that he can begin painting bird droppings along the park wall and on the bench.

Set designer Tom John stands on the adjacent Mess set and supervises these last details. He is leaning against a spectacular plantation-era window that he has designed onto the rear wall of the White House dining room and which he claims once pulled similar duty at the top of Tara's grand staircase, on the set of *Gone With the Wind*. He says he found the window on the Universal lot, where it was stored unceremoniously, although efforts to corroborate the piece's origins were inconclusive. Still, it is an impressive window, with a potentially exciting history, and John leans himself against it as if it is nothing at all, monitoring this morning's fixings as if they are everything.

While John fixes his eyes directly on these fine-tunings, Bruce Paltrow does the same, from a distance. The producer is sitting in his temporary corner office, back in Building 35, at the far end of the Sunset Gower lot, watching these last design and lighting refinements through his closed-circuit television monitor. The studio is inaugurating a new technology with this production that is intended to make the videotaped end product (shot at thirty frames per second) appear more like film (shot at twenty-four frames per second), and the control room is filled this morning with all manner of technicians and consultants to help accomplish this. Paltrow, who has had a great many thoughtful things to say about the lighting, tone, and texture of his production, is asked to let these experts work their expertise before contributing his opinion (perhaps because he has had too many thoughtful things to say).

For Phil Squyres, one of the Columbia consultants brought in to effect this "film look," the experiment could impact on the long-term health of the television production business and his role within it. "Listen," he figures, "we're already attached at the hip to Sony, so we might as well use their technology to find new ways to produce programming more efficiently. If we don't, we'll end up like Detroit."

For the studio, it is hoped that this new technology will provide a cost-effective bridge between the inexpensive and widely used videotape and the expensive and hardly used high-definition television, or HDTV. For the *Word of Mouth* producers, it is merely hoped that this version of their show will look better than their last.

Paltrow, wanting to stay out of the way, has been watching his monitor all morning long. He wants to see how things are going, how they look, but he does not want to interfere, and he is proud that he has not. Mostly, he likes what he sees, but when he catches a glimpse of the lighting and the dressing for the opening scene, he breaks his silence. It is supposed to be raining outside the War Room windows, and he does not like the way the residual drops of water are clinging to the glass. It doesn't read, he says. It doesn't register. No one's gonna know what's going on. He picks up the phone and calls the set.

"Spina?" he says when production assistant Robert Spina picks up the phone. "Let me ask you a question."

Go ahead, Spina says.

"Has anybody talked about doing a wet-down?"

We've done one, Spina tells, a little while ago.

"With what?"

Water, he guesses.

"Not with water," Paltrow insists. "Not with water. They should use something else?"

What?

"You know what they can use?" Paltrow figures, thinking out loud. "Maybe antifreeze, something with a little more viscosity to it."

Spina, who sold his first *Golden Girls* script last season after more than ten years as a runner and production assistant for Witt-Thomas-Harris, gets on this right away. Afterward, he has some time to sit in Joshua Rifkind's still-misspelled director's chair and reflect on his career, which seems as if it, too, will soon have a little more viscosity to it. "There are some days," says the Ohio-born television buff, who has dressed for today's taping in a button-down shirt and bolo tie, "when I'm feeling real full of myself, when I'm thinking, you know, Gee, I'm in television, or something like that, when I realize that television really has changed for me. It's a business to me now, some of the time. But not most of the time. Most of the time, I can still sit at home and be fooled by it. I mean, I get fooled constantly. And it's great, it's my favorite thing. It's like, remember the movie *Cocoon*, when Don Ameche did the break dancing? And he bounds up and they cut to the close-up and he's smiling? For a split second, I wondered how they ever got Don Ameche to do that. I think you need to always hold on to that, because there are actually people out in the world who think that we do these shows live, and that the actors make up their own lines, and that it takes exactly twenty-two and a half minutes."

Does working on a pilot like this, particularly if it is picked up and spun into a successful series, have any positive, long-term professional impact on a guy like Spina? "Not really, no," he admits. "Not directly, anyway. I mean, I'm only the production assistant here. But I get to work with Terry again, and with Lex [Passaris, the associate director, with whom Spina has pooled his vast library of television literature and formed a lasting friendship], and I get to learn a little bit, and of course we're also on hiatus, so the money is nice, because I'm not working on anything else right now. And I really do love my work. As long as something maintains my interest, and I'm being paid a decent wage, and I'm not repeating myself, you know, for very long, then I figure I'm doing okay. I can't complain.

"It's really such a rush. You know, it's like when I watched my *Golden Girls* episode, the one that I wrote. And it came on the air, and I was sitting with my wife, and we're sitting on the sofa. You have to remember, I've seen my name, and she started out as a runner on *Golden Girls*, and she's seen her name a zillion times at the end of the show. But never at the beginning of the show. Never. And it came on the air, and it was up there for two seconds instead of a third of a second, or whatever, and I'm thinking of all the television books that Lex and I own, you know, how we can look in there to see who wrote the *Mary Tyler Moore* episode where Chuckles the Clown died. Well, gee, that was written by so-and-so. And now I thought, you know, that somebody could look me up, too. It's like I'm a little bit immortal."

Someone can also look up Passaris, Spina's close and like-minded friend, who has directed two *Golden Girls* episodes and who has been hired as the show's principal director for the coming season. As such, he will soon be more than just a little bit immortal, at least in terms of television history. Also as such, the *Word of Mouth* pilot, and the others he will do this spring with Hughes, will potentially mark Passaris's last turns as associate director. At thirty-three, after nine years at Witt-Thomas-Harris (running scripts, and checks, and working every aspect of postproduction) and a lifetime in front of a warm television set (he can still recall the *time slot* of William Daniels's first sitcom!—*Captain Nice* [NBC, 1967], Monday nights, at eight-thirty), he is long ready for the challenge of being a full-time, full-fledged sitcom director.

"I'm not thinking too far past this coming season," admits Passaris, who is wearing a sport coat and bow tie for today's tapings. "I don't want to get ahead of myself. It's kinda like I've taken a train, a long journey on a train somewhere, and I'd like to explore the town, now that I'm there.

"Actually, it's almost a no-lose situation I'm coming into with *Golden Girls*. I won't get the credit if the show continues to do well, and I won't get the blame if the show suddenly dips a bit in the ratings. It's not even a critical year for the show. They've more than gotten their money out of it. They have their syndication package. It's not that people don't care about it and wouldn't like to see it go on. I'm sure they would, and I certainly would, too, but if it didn't, you know, if something happens, it's been more than a good run. So unless I do something completely heinous and kill the show, I'll get a fair shot. I'll do a chunk of shows. It's not like I have three or four and these will make or break my career. I get a very comfortable share of the season. It gives me a chance to really feel something out. It's like, if you've driven a car just once you don't really have a feel for it. I'll get a feel for this. It's not just one show here and there. It's starting off with seven in a row, so I'll have a chance to develop a rhythm and see what's going on."

Second stage director Kent Zbornak, another Witt-Thomas-Harris regular, is corralling the thirty or so extras he has been sent from Central Casting into the audience bleachers for a head count and a look-see. He selects twenty-five—eighteen men and seven women— to appear as background diners in the White House Mess scene. According to the union guidelines governing this production, 30 percent of all extras must be Screen Actors Guild members, so Zbornak makes his selections based not only on appearance and mix but also on membership status.

For this gig, union extras will receive eighty-six dollars, while nonunion performers are paid forty-two dollars. If any one of them is asked to do any "special business"—such as shaking hands with one of the regulars, or passing them a pat of butter, or answering a telephone—they will get a twenty-five dollar bump in their fee. Special business or no, they are not supposed to feed from the catering cart set up toward the rear of the set, even though they will be at the ready from early afternoon until about nine o'clock this evening. Many of the extras have brought along books and magazines and crossword puzzles to help pass the long time between takes and, for sustenance, enough fruit and sandwiches to suggest a picnic.

As the studio audience, procured by an outfit called Audience Unlimited, begins to fill the soundstage, Joshua Rifkind escapes from his makeup chair and seeks out warm-up comedian David Willis, who will introduce the cast before the first scene. He wants to make sure Willis knows how to pronounce his name. (For the record, it is pronounced rif-KIND, accent on the kind, long *i*, although it is often mispronounced RIF-kind, accent shifted, with a short *i* to boot.) It is bad enough R. J. Visciglia got it wrong on the director's chair, and the actor wants to avoid any further indignity.

Rifkind is not the only member of the cast worrying about the warm-up comedian. William Daniels is also concerned, for different reasons. Mostly, Daniels does not see the need for one and fears that the common practice of deploying one somehow diminishes his work as an actor. "I have reservations about bringing in an audience the way they do," he allows while waiting for his turn at makeup. "I'm not a fan of the warm-up comedian, and I'm not a fan of jacking up the audience so that the audience is performing. You're there to win over an audience, but they try to help you out, give you a shortcut. And they get a guy out there, and it depends upon how frenetic he is, he can jump up and down and impress upon the audience that they're really expected to perform, to laugh, and indeed they do, and you never know why you get a laugh. You can come on, and they'll just start laughing. You haven't taken this thing out of town, you haven't found your laughs, and then you can get into trouble, throwing lines into laughs, and it's all because you had to jack them up. The whole thing is suspect."

Haviland Morris is perhaps calmer than any of her colleagues as the first taping nears. Certainly she is more collected than she has been all week. Baby Faith is safely out of earshot, back in her hotel room with the nanny, where she has been these last few days of rehearsal, and the actress has finally allowed herself to concentrate on her performance. Now that she is paying better attention, she would like to have more for her character to do, but all that seems expected of her at this late stage is to remember her lines, hit her marks, and look good. This last is evidently important to the producers, and to the network, who are counting on Morris to be the sight-for-sore-eyes of this production, and the show's hairstylist works hard to ensure the packaging. The actress's hair is up in curlers for most of this afternoon, and when she tumbles out of them, at about four o'clock, the shock of full-bodied red could just about stop traffic. She is shrink-wrapped into a gray-green wool suit, accented by a green suede belt and gray pumps and topped by a hooded black wool cape. She looks like Little Red Riding Hood, grown up and set loose.

Tom Fontana, dressed in his own version of opening-night duds—a flashy gray suit, a black Hard Rock Cafe T-shirt, and a pair of Keds sneakers—breezes into the makeup room to offer his last-minute notes and encouragements, while the somewhat a-jitter Rifkind, Lewis Black, and George Newbern are having the last of their faces put on. The rest of the cast has dispersed, upstairs to the stage, but Fontana has something he wants to say to set these guys at ease. "Listen," he warns, "no matter what happens, remember, it's your careers. I've got a development deal."

Clearly, there is more on the line for Fontana than his laugh lines allow. By five o'clock, when the dress show has finally begun, he is pacing nervously on the stage-left corner of the set. As he paces, his attention is tethered to the large television monitor positioned there and not to the live action unfolding directly in front of him, in person. It is as though he can only absorb these last turns, and deal with them, once removed. As the opening scene makes room for the voice-over speech of the show's fictional president, Fontana is moored to the screen, moving his lips to lines he has long committed to reflex: "My fellow Americans. The White House, America's house, your house, has always rolled out the welcome mat to the world's great spiritual leaders. From as far away as the Vatican, Jerusalem, and Mecca they've come. And so, today, we greet, from Xizang Zizhiqu...The Dolly Lima. The Dying Llama. The Lying Dama...."

Tonight's first taping gets off to a slow start despite Fontana's synched assist. The audience for this early taping is made up mostly of nonindustry types (tourists, mallgoers, television watchers), and many of them do not seem to want to laugh at what the producers have thought is surefire material. The first, most troubling instance comes around at the top of the second scene, when an eager-to-please Jim Smith enters the stodgy White House Mess and notices an empty seat across the table from his new boss, B. Laurence Taylor.

Jim Smith, sitting down: "Mr. Taylor, mind if I join you?"

B. Laurence Taylor, with superiority: "Yes. Every seat in the White House Mess is specifically assigned, based on importance of position. What does that nameplate say?"

Jim Smith, reading the nameplate in front of him: "director of the budget."

B. Laurence Taylor, coolly: "Are you the director of the budget?"

Jim Smith, bailing with a lame joke: "Heck, no. I can't even balance my own checkbook."

The exchange, which has pulled big laughs all week in rehearsals, does not impress this crowd, and the producers cannot understand it. "This is the dumbest audience I've ever heard," Paltrow concludes to the overstuffed control room, where he is watching the taping, also once removed, over the shoulders of his director. "I don't know why we bother writing these fucking jokes. What the fuck is the point?"

Eventually, this first show hits its stride and brings the audience along with it. "They're willing to laugh," observes Hughes, who is distractedly taking the air out of a left-behind sheet of bubble wrap while watching the show on the room's half-dozen monitors, "as long as we hit the jokes right. Let's help them with that."

Even during the taping, Hughes receives messages and packages from his assistant, Diana Leszczynski. As always, he files these away for later, stopping just long enough to process each one as they pile up. Paltrow, noticing these interruptions from over Hughes's shoulder, finally says, "Jesus, Terry, can I borrow fifty thousand dollars?" His tone is loose and good-natured, but underneath his ribbing is a message: Worry about your other projects on your own time; this is my time now, my project.

Between shows, there is a tense and ultimately heated exchange between Paltrow and Steve Warner, the CBS vice president for special projects, who has been involved with this production since New York. It's too dark, Warner says, seeking out the producer after the first taping to offer his notes on the nighttime park-bench scene between Jim Smith and Emperor Norton.

What do you mean, it's too dark? Paltrow says back.

It's too dark, Warner says again. It's got to be lighter.

Paltrow explains how the studio is trying out this new film-tape process and how the look and lighting of the show will be converted in postproduction. The guys in the booth tell me this will convert, Paltrow tells Warner. What you're seeing here is not what the end product will look like.

I don't care, Warner insists. I want you to make it lighter. The CBS executive has a plane to catch—to New York, to spend Passover with his family—and he wants to clear this up before he leaves, before the second show.

"Me, being who I am, I just lost it at this point," Paltrow remembers. "I told him to go fuck himself. I called him an asshole. I knew what I was talking about, and he didn't. That just drives me crazy. I had been talking to all these technical people. I knew what was going on. The scene wasn't too dark. It was just the way it was supposed to be, and I need this guy telling me it's too dark? He didn't know what the hell he was talking about, so I lost my temper. It was like an ego thing between the two of us. And then he leaves because he has to go home for Passover. He was so concerned about the show, and he couldn't even stay to see the second taping. It was so stupid."

(Warner would not respond to telephone queries seeking his interpretation of this exchange.)

The air show begins around eight, after a dinner break (in Rehearsal Hall A) and a final notes session (in a glass-enclosed downstairs conference room). The second audience (network and studio personnel, friends and family of cast and crew), which is filing in upstairs, is expected to be more user-friendly than the first, and the producers are hoping for easier and heartier laughs to help spice their laugh track and charge their actors.

It is a lot to ask of this second audience, and it does not end there. The director is also counting on them to be a tolerant bunch. Hughes is absolutely determined to get things right on this final pass, even at the risk of losing his audience. When the first scene stalls at its midpoint, he decides to shoot it again. The actors are pumped, and Hughes wants to give them every opportunity to nail their performances while their energy is high. Realize, he can always go back and reshoot a scene later, after the audience has been cleared from the studio, but right now he wants to use the spillover energy from the crowd to fuel the cast's performance. This makes sense, on its own, but after the first scene, Hughes stops again at the second. And again. And again. He reshoots the White House Mess scene four times, and with each take, John Tinker does a little spin and stomp in disgust. He is anxious about the director's exacting method and eager to regain some of the momentum of the earlier dress taping, and he vents this anxiety in a contained tantrum.

With each cry of "Cut! Let's try it again," Tinker vows to go back to the control room and persuade the director to loosen the reins a little bit, but he never does. Indeed, as the show moves deeper into its script, the cumulative effect of these stops and starts is unnerving not only to the producers but to the cast and crowd as well. Hughes appears mindful of this, but he does not change his course, and the unnerved producers are reluctant to interfere with someone whose track record and demeanor clearly suggest that he knows what he is doing. There is a creative standoff.

"The ultimate goal is to get everything you can while your audience is still hot," Passaris explains during one of the increasingly long pauses between takes, waiting for the sets and the actors to be redressed and the cameras returned to speed. "Basically, the audience is here to see a play, and it is just like a play, except there are these big stops between each scene, and sometimes they get the same scene a few times before moving on to the next one. The trick is you have to know when you're losing your audience and when you're keeping them. And you have to judge your talent, which actor is going to perform better for an audience, and for which actor it would be immaterial. There are some actors, like Patty Duke, who do not work exceptionally well in front of an audience. She was in the very first show I ever worked on, *It Takes Two* [ABC, 1982–83], and that started as an audience show, but about halfway through the season we switched to a block-and-tape system, and we didn't use an audience, and there was really no difference in the energy or the performance. She's basically a film actor. With *The Golden Girls,* however, there is always a marked difference between an audience take and a pickup take. Bea Arthur especially thrives on the audience. Betty White and Rue McClanahan, too, to some degree. That's where they come from. They need that audience response.

"So, as a director, you need to find the balance. Does the whole scene need to be reshot? Do I need just one or two lines? How long can I keep the audience up? How long can I keep the actors up? What's the best use of our time? It's a constant debate, and there's no right way or wrong way. I think Terry's feeling is that as long as he's doing an audience show, then he should try to at least use the audience as best he can."

During some of these long pauses, the studio audience amuses itself with a makeshift talent competition, encouraged by the warm-up comedian, who is in turn encouraged by the prospect of killing great chunks of the now-considerable time he is expected to fill. A not-quite-teenage boy takes the microphone and tells a riddle. "What's the difference between boogers and broccoli?" he asks, and then answers, "Kids don't eat broccoli." For this, the boy earns a *Word of Mouth* T-shirt.

The largest, most deserved T-shirt goes to an overweight, middle-aged black woman who is here with her church group and who sweetly fills her end of these downtimes with a gospel hymn called "Working on a Building." She is shy about it as she begins, and the studio clamors with the dull hum of restlessness and the bustle of production, but as this lady loses herself in the joyous hymn, the rest of the room falls to quiet. Soon even the cast and crew have turned to face this proud woman as her too-high voice graces the lyric with a plaintive sincerity:

> "I'm working on a building, it's a true foundation,
> I'm holding up the wood beams, pining for my Lord.
> And I never get tired, working on the building,
> I'm going up to heaven, to get my reward."

It is an uncommon moment, reduced by the trappings of network television that surround it and by the complimentary T-shirt. When it passes, it is as if it hasn't happened.

Hughes and company finally reach the last page of the *Word of Mouth* script at about ten-thirty, after which the stage is quickly descended upon by well-wishers and then quickly cleared. Despite the frustratingly fine point the director put on things during this second taping, there are still some necessary pickup shots, a half dozen or so, and the cast goes through the motions of these as if they would rather be someplace else. The well-wishers are made to hush and stand off to the side.

The mood of the room in front of the cameras, where the cast acts its last, is almost somnambulatory and perfunctory, but behind them, where network and studio executives have gathered to await the final wrap, there is boisterous and nearly contagious enthusiasm for the pilot and its prospects. Things went well out here tonight, according to this pulse, and there is little doubt among this group that Paltrow, Fontana, and Tinker have worked their intelligent brand of television magic yet again.

Deborah Curtan, for one, is so charmed by tonight's two tapings (especially the second) that she has now brightened her dire predictions of a few days earlier. "I may have to rescind everything I've said," she about-faces. "They really brought it up to where they needed to be. They really turned it around. I think it's got a shot. I think this could be special."

Understand, most shows wrap amidt a tumult of excitement and great expectations. It is just as difficult to make a bad television pilot as it is to make a good one, and this excess excitement tends to flow from the input more than it does from the outcome. Tonight, though, the spirited response in these early returns seems different, and genuine, and founded. Of course, every response seems different, and genuine, and founded, when you are swept up by it and in its middle, but underneath these surface reads there is also an unflagging sense that this cast, and pieces of this crew, just might convene in the next few months to generate more of the same.

Also of course, and perhaps further underneath, there is the daunting possibility that everyone's best shot may have also been their last.

Nineteen

POST _____

○ According to a memo circulated by CBS Operations and Engineering, the total running time for the finished *Word of Mouth* pilot, including the main title and opening and closing credits, is to be twenty-three minutes and nineteen seconds, give or take a fraction. "If you anticipate the pilot being delivered short, this must be cleared in advance," the producers are instructed. "In no instance, can an episode be delivered long."

The network memo further stipulates that, at the top of the show, during the first six seconds of video, the bottom third of the screen must be in the clear so that the network can superimpose its STEREO SOUND logo; and, similarly, the end credits, which are not to exceed thirty seconds and are subject to network approval, must be clear for a CBS audio promo. Also, all shows containing a "tag"—industry shorthand for the brief, final scene that stands alone as a kind of kicker, or denouement to the first two acts, and which usually runs about a minute or so—must also include a title card leading into the second commercial position. The title card, it is suggested, should feature a member of the cast reading the uninspired voice-over announcement, "Don't go away, we'll be right back." If other copy is used, inspired or otherwise, this, too, must be cleared.

Bruce Paltrow, Tom Fontana, and John Tinker have more on their minds than the rigid CBS operations guidelines in the weeks

195

immediately following the *Word of Mouth* taping. Chief among these is the *Modern Marriage* pilot, a one-camera film comedy, which has been renamed *Home Fires* and is being directed by Paltrow for NBC.

Surrounding the production, the producers take their turns overseeing the editing of *Word of Mouth* at Modern Video, on Sunset, and here they are more worried about the material they have on hand with which to fill their twenty-three minutes and nineteen seconds than they are about these constricting parameters. (To strengthen their hand and goose future trivia buffs, Tinker coerces his father to supply the voice for the off-camera role of president.) Over the past weeks, they have cut, mixed, and sweetened *Word of Mouth* (with assists from Terry Hughes, Lex Passaris, R. J. Visciglia, and editor Richard Russell) to where it is still two minutes too long. Their strategy is to deliver the strongest possible show for series consideration and to worry about its length later, or not at all.

But first they must worry about their suddenly (and strangely) silent partners at Columbia Pictures Television. The final, on-line edit will incorporate the studio's notes, and suggested changes, as soon as the producers are in receipt of the studio's notes, and suggested changes. Trouble is, these are not quickly forthcoming. For a while, they are not forthcoming at all. The producers finish their initial edit on a Wednesday and send it over to Scott Siegler, president of Columbia Pictures Television, the following morning, figuring they will hear back from him within a day or so. After all, they figure, Siegler is well aware that the on-line edit is scheduled for the coming Tuesday, so he will want to give Paltrow and company enough time to digest his substantive comments before then.

And so they wait. And wait. Siegler does not call in with his notes on Friday. He does not call in on Saturday. Sunday, too, passes with no word from the studio. The producers would not be hearing from Siegler on Monday, either, if they were not all attending the same casting meeting at NBC, for *Home Fires*. After the meeting, Paltrow sidles up to Siegler and presses him on the pilot. He hates having to ask like this, but he is tired of waiting for Siegler to get around to it. The on-line edit will not wait forever. The finished pilot has to be delivered to the network by the first week in May. So Paltrow starts in, We should really talk about the pilot. Have you seen it yet?

Not yet, Siegler fumbles. I've been busy. I haven't had the time. I'll watch it tonight.

Fine, Paltrow says. Underneath, he's thinking, This guy's got a million excuses why he hasn't watched the tape. What the hell else does this guy have to do that he can't spare twenty minutes to watch a pilot? I thought this was his job.

Siegler, now pressed, calls Paltrow the next morning with his verdict. He is very disappointed, he explains. There is still a lot of work to do. He has a lot of notes and some general comments. There is too much to go over on the telephone. He thinks they should meet.

Okay, Paltrow agrees, we'll meet. We'll cancel the on-line and we'll meet. What time?

Today is lousy, Siegler squirms. I can't do it today.

We can come to you, Paltrow offers.

Today is still lousy.

What about tomorrow?

Also lousy.

When, then? Paltrow wants to know. He is seething at what he perceives to be the studio's inaccessibility and slow-footedness, but he does not say anything. Better to just get through it, he assesses, and deliver the pilot. Everything else will sort itself out later. Or maybe it won't. Maybe these Columbia guys just go about things a little differently than he's used to, that's all.

Thursday, Siegler finally says. I can fit you in on Thursday morning.

Fine, Paltrow says. Where?

Here, Siegler insists. It'll have to be here. I don't have time to go to you guys.

Here is Columbia Plaza, in Burbank, about a half-hour drive from the Paltrow Group's Sunset Gower office, in light traffic.

Paltrow swallows his anger until the conversation is finished. Then he slams down the phone and relates the exchange to his partners. He is steamed.

What does he mean, he's disappointed? Fontana wonders.

I don't know, Paltrow says, raging still, that's what he said. He's disappointed. He didn't say why, and I didn't ask. At this point, I don't care. And I'll tell you something else. I'm not driving out to fucking Burbank to hear Scott Siegler's notes. You guys go.

On Thursday morning, Fontana, Tinker, and Visciglia drive to Burbank, in separate cars. Paltrow stays behind. Fontana arrives late, on purpose. He is pissed that the studio has kept them waiting on its notes for over a week now, so he vents his frustration by keeping Siegler waiting, even for just a short while. It is Fontana's statement, his protest over the shabby way he and his partners, and their work, are being treated.

Fontana joins Tinker and Visciglia across from Siegler and Steve Mendelson, Columbia's senior vice president for comedy development. None of the relationships work for me, Siegler is saying, when Fontana enters the room.

What do you mean, none of the relationships work for you? Tinker challenges. What does that mean?

Fontana tunes in and cannot stomach what he finds. "That's the kind of generalized note that always makes me fucking crazy," he says later, "because it either means the person has no ability to articulate what their feelings are, or they're just full of bullshit. It's one of those standard lines, like 'It's not funny enough.' 'The relationships don't work.' You could say it about anything."

Scott, Fontana tries diplomatically. How can you say that? What does that mean?

Well, maybe I shouldn't say all of them, Siegler hedges. Maybe some of the relationships work.

Let's go through each relationship, Fontana insists, and you tell me which ones work for you and which ones don't.

One by one, Fontana introduces the various relationships between his *Word of Mouth* characters: Steve and Jim? Hammond and Taylor? Alyson and Roxanne? With each isolated reference, Siegler hedges some more: No, that one's okay; no, I like that one; no, that works.

So what are you talking about? Fontana tries. Which relationships don't work? What he really wants to say is that this partnership, between the Paltrow Group and Columbia Pictures Television, is the relationship that is not working, but he restrains himself.

I guess I was making a generalization, Siegler allows finally. I guess we're okay on the relationships.

As they screen the pilot, Siegler stops the tape to make specific notes—about lighting that seems "off," or a laugh line that fails to deliver, or a prop in the background that rings false—in each specific scene. "They're basically picky little notes," Fontana considers, "you know, but they're his opinion. He has a right to them. He's president of the company."

About halfway through the pilot, Siegler announces he has to leave. He has another meeting.

But Scott, Fontana tries, we have to on-line this. We have to go to the network with it next week. When are we gonna get the rest of your notes?

I don't have any more notes, Siegler says.

You don't have any more notes? Fontana can't believe it. Siegler has had a half-dozen things to say about every scene. His notes have been detailed and thorough. He hasn't let anything slide. It doesn't make sense that, all of a sudden, the balance of the pilot has kicked in to his exacting standards. It's ridiculous.

So, Tinker says, making certain, here on in we're okay, right? We're finished? There's nothing else to talk about?

Not exactly, Siegler says.

What do you mean, not exactly?

I mean, I haven't watched the whole thing.

Fontana, Tinker, and Visciglia do not know what to say. They are incredulous, mostly, their jaws dropped to where you could put someone's feet in them. They look at Siegler and Mendelson, then at each other, then at the floor. then they leave.

"It was a pretty odd moment," Visciglia recalls. "Nobody said anything. We just walked out and went to the elevator and kind of looked at each other, you know, and shook our heads."

Two weeks later, Fontana still cannot get over it. "The president of the fucking company couldn't take twenty-two minutes out of his life to watch the pilot episode that we're about to send over to the network," he says, railing at the memory. "I've never heard of such a thing. I mean, I understand he's a very important guy, he's a very busy guy, but what the hell is he doing? It was the most incredible thing."

(Siegler, too, would not respond to phone calls seeking his version of these events.)

Despite Siegler's inability to sit still long enough to watch a not-quite-half-hour sitcom pilot, the producers ultimately complete their on-line edit, on time. The finished pilot contains three hundred and twenty-two different camera shots (all stitched together at Modern Video) and about three hundred fewer laughs, compressed into just under twenty-three minutes, not counting opening and closing credits.

By May 15, three videocassettes of the *Word of Mouth* pilot—two on half-inch tape and one on three-quarter-inch tape—have been officially delivered to the network, by hand, the fingers of which are now crossed, along with those belonging to almost everybody else who had anything at all to do with it.

Twenty

TAG _____

○ 10:30 P.M. ⬚2⬚   ⬚3⬚   WORD OF MOUTH (CC)
A new Presidential speech writer (George Newbern)
gets a few choice words from his boss (William
Daniels) and a lesson in office politics from his
co-workers. Not on CBS's fall schedule. Bonnie:
Gladys Knight. Hammond: Lewis Black. Steve:
Joshua Rifkind.

—TV Guide listing
Saturday, August 17, 1991

10:30 P.M. ⬚2⬚   ⬚3⬚   ACTING SHERIFF (CC)
Actor becomes lawman

—New York Times listing
Saturday, August 17, 1991

JEFF SAGANSKY (president, CBS Entertainment, in announcing the
network's 1991 fall schedule, which includes only four new half
hours—*The Royal Family,* starring Redd Foxx and Della Reese;
Teech, from producers Norman Steinberg and David Frankel; *Prin-
cesses,* starring Julie Hagerty, Fran Drescher, and Twiggy; and,
Brooklyn Bridge, from producer Gary David Goldberg): "I think we
have the schedule and the pieces to be number one next year, and I'll
be disappointed if we're not. Next year, we're in position to take it
all."

201

BRUCE PALTROW: "The next thing I heard, boom, we're not on the schedule. That's it. Boom. Gone. Finished. I started to hear, you know, Well, we've got a lot of nine-thirty shows, but I never really got a good explanation of why we weren't on the schedule. We just weren't on it. End of story, right? So then I sent the tape to Fox, to see if maybe they were interested, and I sent a copy over to ABC. Remember, this whole thing started at ABC, with a script. So I sent it out, on the theory that if they liked it, they would call. And they never did, so I guess that's the end of it. I never sent it to NBC. I already had *Home Fires* over there [the show was later picked up for a six-episode, midseason replacement run, beginning in June, 1992], and I didn't want to muddy those waters.

"So that was all I heard, that was all I knew. You want to know what I think happened. I'll tell you what I think happened. I think Steve Warner couldn't wait to kill the show, that's what I think. He was in there killing us as quickly as he could. You know, we had these words on the set, in the middle of taping, and he was already bad-mouthing the show before anybody saw the show. He just got to New York and called everybody at CBS and torpedoed the show. He killed it. If you ask me, that's what happened."

LEWIS BLACK (actor, *Word of Mouth*): "I had a real sense of foreboding about this show, based just on reading what NBC was doing with its schedule, and then ABC. They seemed to be going mainstream again, there didn't seem to be much risk. And I also knew that CBS had turned down a pilot that a friend of mine had done for Norman Lear, *Love Child*, and it was also set in Washington. It was also a political show. [The show was later revamped, retitled, and resold to NBC, where it debuted as *The Powers That Be*, in March 1992.] So when I found out CBS turned that one down, part of me thought, Well, you know, if they're not gonna take that one, they're not gonna take us.

"The line that really got to me, though, after I heard the network's reaction, was that the pilot, I'm talking about our pilot now, was that it was too intelligent and not sexy enough. And I heard that, and I said to whoever it was who was telling me this, Well, tell 'em I'll grow tits. The whole system they've got to decide whether or not to order a sitcom is just insane. It's clinically insane. Do you know how they do this? They show it to a giant tortoise, and afterwards, they have on one side of the room a line that says YES and on the other side of the room, a line that says NO. And then they set the tortoise loose and see which way he goes. Actually, I would feel better about the show if that's what happened, because then I could at least understand it."

TOM FONTANA: "The line I heard, which really got to me, was that the network just wasn't passionate about the show. Passionate, that was the word they used. Now, I can certainly respect their decision not to pick up the show. You know, that's their call. They know what they're looking for, and maybe this just wasn't what they were looking for. That's okay. But when they start to bring up passion as a reason for doing a show, you know, I just shudder at the concept. What, they're gonna tell me they're passionate about the Redd Foxx show? Redd Foxx?"

JOSHUA RIFKIND (actor, *Word of Mouth*): "I knew when the networks were announcing their schedules, and I was slightly anxious about it, but I wouldn't say I was preoccupied with it. I really wasn't expecting the pilot to go at that point. I just was not. I had been hearing from a couple of sources, you know, agents, producers, other people in the business, that the network was not that hot on it. These were very reliable inside sources. But I'll tell you what the big tip-off was. The biggest tip-off. I called Barbara Brace, the production coordinator, to see what was happening, and when I got off the phone, that's when I knew.

"I called because I still hadn't seen the pilot, and I thought maybe they'd be having some sort of screening for the cast, or whatever. So I called just to see what was up. She said, Well, it hasn't been finished yet, we're delivering it tomorrow. This is pretty late already, like the second week in May, and she's telling me how the producers were hung up on this other project they were doing, for NBC, and they were just getting around to our show. Anyway, I had her on the phone, and we're talking and I said, Have you seen it? And she said, Un-huh. So I said, Well, you know, how was it? And she said, Fine. Well, that's when I knew. Fine. What more did she have to say. You know, it was fine. Ah. Good. Well, I'm glad it was fine."

LEX PASSARIS (associate director, *Word of Mouth*): "There was no buzz attached to this show. Usually, with the shows that make it, people are talking about it. There's a buzz. The only thing I heard on *Word of*

Mouth was, you know, Washington speechwriters? Who cares? That was the bottom line, I think. I also kept hearing that it just wasn't funny. That was the other thing. To me, it was funny, but it's a different kind of humor. You know, I can watch Bill Daniels all day and night. To me, he's funny. True, it wasn't a front-to-back traditional sitcom, but there were humorous bits in there. You're gonna laugh. I laughed, but then I'm the only guy I know who thought that *Frank's Place* and *Molly Dodd* and *Slap Maxwell* were funny. These weren't laugh-a-minute shows, but I thought they were brilliant. But you're fighting preconceived notions of what a sitcom is, or should be. To make it onto the schedule, you've got to fit that niche. It has to be laugh-a-minute. *Word of Mouth* was funny, but it certainly wasn't laugh-a-minute.

"I'll tell you, there is no sure thing in television. You can't play by any set of logical rules. You have to go on weird hunches. You have to take strange risks. You have to make moves that seem completely illogical. And then you have to just hope your job lasts long enough to prove you right somewhere along the line. Remember, even Brandon Tartikoff, the great mind of television over the last ten years, gave us *Manimal, Supertrain, Mr. Smith,* and *Misfits of Science.*"

TOM FONTANA: "Who knows why this didn't work? No one knows. I'm certainly the wrong person to ask. I thought it worked. It just didn't get picked up. The show is still a good show. It's a much better show than a lot of what's on the schedule. With the first pilot, with *The War Room,* I think I convinced myself that it worked, but at the same time I never really convinced myself that it worked. I wanted it to work more than it did work. But now I have the second one to compare it to, and now I realize, you know, when I saw the first edited version of *The War Room,* I looked at it and went, Holy God! We've got all this work ahead of us! Okay. But then I saw the first edited version of *Word of Mouth,* and I thought, Boy, this is good. You know, maybe a little trimming here, a little fixing here, but rhythmically, it was much more the show we intended to make.

"I realize Columbia didn't want to make this second pilot. I know this was always a show they never particularly liked. I don't know what to make of their involvement on this, I really don't. You know, it's like anyplace. There are some people who are intelligent and some people who are not. And the problem for me has always been

when someone pretends like they have the fucking Ten Commandments. Like they've been to the top of Mt. Sinai to get God's Ten
Comedy Commandments. I think Columbia makes a very specific
kind of television show. And I think what Bruce and John and I do is
completely arrhythmic to their kind of television shows, to *Who's the
Boss?* or anything like that. That's just not what we do."

LEWIS BLACK: "How about that music? That dopey sitcom music
they put on it? But that's just one of those things, you know.
Obviously, the producers are caught knowing they have to sell the
show to CBS, and at the same time CBS has to sell it to advertisers,
or whoever they have to sell it to. That was always the difficulty with
this show. It was always going to be, you know, trying to keep the
sitcom style with a different form of content. Maybe the characters
weren't edgy enough, maybe it needed more pizzazz, in terms of the
character stuff. The biggest thing, though, was that no one was
thinking about it in terms of just this one show. I never really looked
at it as just the pilot. We were playing it over six or seven episodes, is
really what we were doing. This was never the kind of sitcom you
could write in one show. We needed six or seven."

BRUCE PALTROW: "They didn't even run the pilot in the end. First
they tell us it's gonna be on in July, on a Saturday night, so we cut it
down and delivered it to them. You know, we were long, so we cut it
down. Then it was bumped to August. No reason, they just bumped
us to August. This time, they scheduled it. It was on the schedule. I
think it was even listed in *TV Guide*. And then, boom, it's not on. We
open the paper that morning and it's not on the schedule. They put
some other pilot on, I can't even remember. You know, it didn't
matter to me, one way or the other, but if they say they're gonna put
it on, they should put it on.

"So I called Sagansky and I said, you know, What happened? How
come this thing didn't get on? And he said, I have no idea. He didn't.
He absolutely had no idea. He's the president, and he has no idea, so
I have no idea.

"You know, it really doesn't matter, quite frankly, whether they put
this pilot on or not, at this point, whether they burn it off. That's what
they call it, burning it off. What we have is damaged goods. The
network doesn't promote these things. They just stick it on and try to

make back some of their money. You don't get reviews. Nothing. You know, once you've failed, you've failed. That's it. I don't know why we failed. I have no idea anymore. I just don't. I've given up trying to figure it out. To me, it was a wonderful show. I think they should have bought it. I think they should have scheduled it. I think we all would have done very well with it.

"We still have our series commitment with the network. We'll just keep rolling it over until we get it right. Maybe they'll give us the money someday, maybe they won't. That's the miasma of the network television business. It's really crazy. The network can do whatever it wants. They're the buyers. They can promise anything, and then they can do whatever they want, because they're the buyers. It's like, Yeah, yeah, you did spit on me, but that's okay, you're the buyer. Go ahead, spit on me again.

"Look, you always do these shows in a vacuum. Everybody does, finally. You never have real collaboration with the networks. These guys have no clue, therefore I have no clue. So why do I keep doing this? Well, I'm like the guy who sits in a painting studio. And he paints pictures all day. And nobody buys them. Why does he keep painting? It's what he does. This is what I do. I make television shows. I get off on making television shows. I love the process. I love the writing. I love directing. I love the immediacy of the medium. And the ability to try to do things, new things. And I love to work with the guys.

"If I couldn't do this, I don't know, I think I'd like to be a defensive coordinator in the NFL. That's what I'd do. There's always head coaching jobs, every year there are head coaching jobs, but no one is gonna jump to hire me as a head coach. Let's be realistic. But I certainly wouldn't mind working with the defensive line, or I could even work with the linebackers. Either one. Work my way into defensive coordinator. After that, who knows?"